Hollywood Goes to High School

Cinema, Schools, and American Culture

Contemporary Social Issues

George Ritzer, *Series Editor*

Hollywood Goes to High School: Cinema, Schools, and American Culture
Robert Bulman

The Wilding of America: Money, Mayhem, and the New American Dream (third edition)
Charles Derber

Sex Trafficking: The Global Market in Women and Children
Kathryn Farr

The Myth of Self-Esteem: Finding Happiness and Solving Problems in America
John P. Hewitt

UPCOMING VOLUMES

Society of Risk Takers
William Cockerham

Global E-litism: Digital Technology, Social Inequality, and Transnationality
Gili Drori

Speculative Capitalism: Financial Casinos and Their Consequences
Dan Krier

Post-Industrial Peasants: The Illusion of Middle Class Prosperity
Kevin Leicht and Scott Fitzgerald

UPCOMING REVISIONS

Urban Enclaves: Identity and Place in the World (second edition)
Mark Abrahamson

Just Revenge: Costs and Consequences of the Death Penalty (second edition)
Mark Costanzo

Contemporary Social Issues

Series Editor: George Ritzer, *University of Maryland*

Hollywood Goes to High School

Cinema, Schools, and American Culture

Robert C. Bulman
Saint Mary's College of California

Worth Publishers

Chapter 3 is an expanded version of a thesis first put forward by the author in *The Urban Review, 34* (3):251–276, 2002 (Bulman) and is further developed here with kind permission from Kluwer Academic Publishers.

Grateful acknowledgment is extended for permission to use material from Robert N. Bellah et al., *Habits of the Heart: Individualism and Commitment in American Life.* Copyright © 1985, 1986 Regents of the University of California.

Acquisitions Editor: Valerie Raymond
Sponsoring Editor: Erik Gilg
Executive Marketing Manager: John Britch
Associate Managing Editor: Tracey Kuehn
Project Manager: Richard Rothschild/Print Matters, Inc.
Art Director/Cover Designer: Barbara Reingold
Text Designer: Lissi Sigillo
Photo Editor: Patricia Marx
Production Manager: Barbara Anne Seixas
Composition: Matrix Publishing Services
Printing and Binding: R. R. Donnelly and Sons Company

Cover photos: Bill Ross/Corbis (girl in hallway), Creatas (film reel)

ISBN: 0-7167-5541-6 (EAN: 9780716755418)

Worth Publishers
41 Madison Avenue
New York, NY 10010
www.worthpublishers.com

To my grandmother, Frances Fitch Brueckmann.
Her life-long love of learning has always inspired me.

And to my son, Aron Robert Bartz Bulman.
May he grow up to love learning as much as his
great-grandmother.

About the Author

R obert C. Bulman is an associate professor of anthropology and sociology at Saint Mary's College of California. He received his BA in
sociology from the University of California at Santa Cruz in 1989
and his PhD in sociology from the University of California at Berkeley in
1999. He teaches introduction to sociology, the sociology of education,
the sociology of adolescence, social stratification, social movements, race
and ethnicity, and social theory. In addition to his research on films and
American culture, he has published work on educational decision making
and the political dynamics of school choice. This is his first book.

Contents

Foreword   xi

Preface   xiii

Acknowledgments   xv

1 Using the Movies to Make Sense of Society: A Sociological Introduction   1

Going to the Movies as a Research Method   3
A Brief Review of Other High School Film Analyses   5
Films and Culture   6
Outline and Argument of the Book   9
A Final Note   12

2 Middle-Class Individualism and the Adolescent Frontier: What High School Films Reveal About American Culture   16

Hollywood's View of High School:
   The Three Subgenres   17
Individualism and American Culture   24
The American Development of Utilitarian and
   Expressive Individualism: The Protestant Ethic,
   the Capitalist Ethic, and Their Discontents   26
Individualism and Democracy   28
Individualism and the American Frontier   29
The Middle Class and American Culture   30
Teenagers and American Culture   33
A Final Note   38

3 Fighting the Culture of Poverty: The Teacher as the Urban School Cowboy   43

A Cinematic Culture of Poverty   47

Welcome to the Jungle: The Urban School in
Hollywood Films   51

The School Staff: Inept Bureaucrats and
Incompetent Teachers   52

The Outsider as the Teacher-Hero   54

School Success and Hollywood's Misleading Fantasy   56

Learning from the Anomalies   63

The Teacher as a Cowboy Vigilante   66

Neo-Conservative Retreat or Compassionately
Conservative Reform?   69

A Cultural Contradiction   72

Conclusion: The Urban School Frontier   74

4 Expressing Oneself in a Culture of Conformity: Contradictions in Suburban School Cinema   80

Being a White Upper-Middle-Class Suburban
Teenager Sucks   82

The Irrelevance of Academics in the Suburban
School Films   85

The Threat of Academic Achievement   88

Middle-Class Conformity in American Culture   91

We Don't Need No Education: Middle-Class
Teachers as Antagonists   93

The Evil High School Football Coach   95

Adults as Fools   97

Students as Heroes: The Possibilities of Youth   99

Social Class, Symbolic Deviance, and Adolescent
Identity   107

The Paths to Adulthood: Social Class and
Adolescent Strategies to Independence   111

Conclusion: The Cultural Contradiction of
Individualism and Conformity   113

5 **Challenging the Culture of Privilege:**
Class Conflict in the Private School Film   119
"Just Because You Are Accepted, Doesn't
     Mean You Belong"   121
Academic Matters   124
The Burden of Academic Achievement   126
The Moral Bankruptcy of the Rich   128
Revenge of the Middle Class: The Triumph of Well
     Roundedness, Integrity, and Merit   130
The Anomaly of the Catholic School Film   135
Inequality, Education, and American Culture   139

6 **Cinematic Study Abroad: High School**
Films in Comparative Perspective   145
The Cultural Distinctiveness of American Films   148
Characteristics of the Foreign School Films   149
Conclusion: Returning from Study Abroad   158

7 **Film Fantasies as Cultural Myths:**
Applying the Sociological Imagination   162
Who Has Cultural Power?   166

Appendix: High School Film Sample   170

Bibliography   176

Index   183

Foreword

As we move further into the twenty-first century, we confront a seemingly endless array of pressing social issues: urban decay, inequality, ecological threats, rampant consumerism, war, AIDS, inadequate health care, national and personal debt, and many more. Although such problems are regularly dealt with in newspapers, magazines, and trade books and on radio and television, such popular treatment has severe limitations. By examining these issues systematically through the lens of sociology, we can gain greater insight into them and be better able to deal with them.

Each book in the series casts a new and distinctive light on a familiar social issue, while challenging the conventional view, which may obscure as much as it clarifies. Phenomena that seem disparate and unrelated are shown to have many commonalities and to reflect a major, but often unrecognized, trend within the larger society. Or a systematic comparative investigation demonstrates the existence of social causes or consequences that are overlooked by other types of analysis. In uncovering such realities the books in this series are much more than intellectual exercises; they have powerful practical implications for our lives and for the structure of society.

At another level, this series fills a void in book publishing. There is certainly no shortage of academic titles, but those books tend to be introductory texts for undergraduates or advanced monographs for professional scholars. Missing are broadly accessible, issue-oriented books appropriate for all students (and for general readers). The books in this series occupy that niche somewhere between popular trade books and monographs. Like trade books, they deal with important and interesting social issues, are well written, and are as jargon free as possible. However, they are more rigorous than trade books in meeting academic standards for writing and research. Although they are not textbooks, they often explore topics covered in basic textbooks and therefore are easily integrated into the curriculum of sociology and other disciplines.

Each of the books in the "Contemporary Social Issues" series is a new and distinctive piece of work. I believe that students, serious general readers, and academicians will all find the books to be informative, interesting, thought provoking, and exciting. Among the topics to be covered in forthcoming additions to the series are international sex trafficking, the global digital divide, and the declining wealth and increasing indebtedness of the middle class.

—George Ritzer

Preface

When I was an eleven-year-old boy in 1978, my parents took me and my sister to see *Grease* at a local drive-in movie theater in suburban Southern California. Its soundtrack became the first album (actually, an eight-track tape) that I ever bought. I remember as a teen catching glimpses of *Fast Times at Ridgemont High*, *Risky Business*, and *Porky's* on cable television late at night. In the last months of my senior year in high school in 1985 I went to the drive-in again, this time with a friend. As suburban high school students, we were both impressed by the insights of *The Breakfast Club*. In college, as a burgeoning sociologist, I went to see *Stand and Deliver* and *Dead Poet's Society*. I remember debating the merits of each film with my dorm mates. I recall being skeptical that a charismatic teacher like Jaime Escalante in *Stand and Deliver* could be solely responsible for the intellectual awakening of poor inner-city students. I also criticized *Dead Poet's Society* for its overly romantic depiction of the heroic English teacher Mr. Keating. As an adult, I've enjoyed such classic high school films as *Blackboard Jungle*, *Up the Down Staircase*, *Halls of Anger*, and *To Sir, With Love* thanks to the local video rental store.

My interest as a general fan of the high school film genre grew into a serious academic interest as I began to explore ways of teaching the sociology of education using different media. Films such as *Blackboard Jungle* and *Dangerous Minds* nicely offer illustrations of some key concepts in the sociology of education. I further developed this pedagogical method and taught an entire course called "Hollywood Goes to High School" in 2000 at Saint Mary's College of California. The students and I watched and analyzed a dozen or so high school films and compared what was represented on the screen to what we had read in the sociology of education literature and to what we had experienced in our own high schools. As my students worked on their final papers, I began to write up my own observations and analyses of the films. Intrigued by the patterns I began to recognize in the films, I watched as many films about teens and the high school experience as I could get my hands on. This book is the result of that research, a journey that began in a drive-in in 1978.

While most academic analyses of films are left to scholars in the field of film studies, this book is rooted in sociology. My approach to studying film comes from my training as a sociologist in the areas of social theory,

the sociology of education, social stratification, and the sociology of adolescence. Nevertheless, this book will be of interest not only to sociologists, but also to those in the fields of film studies, cultural studies, American studies, communications, anthropology, and education. It will also be of interest to nonacademics who have an interest in schools, teenagers, the movies, or American culture in general.

Finally, since the data for this book come from Hollywood films, it is necessary to tell the story lines, discuss important details, and reveal the endings to many of the movies in the sample. I apologize in advance if in using these films to make arguments about American culture, I spoil your future enjoyment of the films as entertainment. Please consider yourself fairly warned. This potential annoyance, however, can also be seen as an advantage. One of the benefits of doing research with films is that the data are accessible to everyone. Curious or skeptical readers are encouraged to view for themselves these films and others not included in the sample. Readers can easily do their own fieldwork, as it were, in order to confirm or challenge the arguments of this book.

Acknowledgments

Many people read and commented on the manuscript in whole or in part. Thanks to Lynne Bartz, J Schiao, Amy Divine, Carla Koop, Pamela Perry, Jim Elliott, Richard Arum, Bill Domhoff, Joel Devine, Kathy Roper, Valerie Raymond, Paul Stenis, Laura Edwards, and an anonymous reviewer at Worth. Thanks to George Ritzer for his helpful comments and for seeing the potential of this project even before I did. I owe a big thanks to Worth editor Erik Gilg for holding my hand through the process and offering excellent advice. Thanks to all of my students at Saint Mary's College of California. This book truly grew out of the classroom. In particular, thanks to Bryan Edwards, Christina Hu, Malisa Young, and Samantha Hoffman for research assistance. Thanks to all of my colleagues at Saint Mary's College of California. Thanks particularly to Jerry Brunetti for encouraging the research in the project's infancy. While I did not take the advice of all those who read parts of the manuscript, the book is much stronger thanks to all of them. Errors, of course, are mine alone.

Thanks to Ed Biglin, Lisa Manter, Tom Poundstone, and the Saint Mary's January Term Committee for encouraging creativity in the classroom. Special thanks also to the members of the Anthropology and Sociology Department at Saint Mary's for their enthusiastic support (Phylis Martinelli, Paola Sensi-Isolani, John Ely, Margot Winer, Lynn Meisch, Cynthia Van Gilder, Jennifer Heung, and Dana Herrera). Administrative assistant Diane Bianchi has truly been a blessing. And thanks to Frances Sweeney for her support in numerous ways. Thanks to Monica Clyde, Carole Swain, Nancy Clark, the Committee on Teaching and Scholarship, and the Saint Mary's Faculty Development Committee for supporting excellence in both teaching and research—several faculty development grants helped to fund the research for this book. Thanks to Patty Wade and the other reference librarians at Saint Mary's College. Thanks to the folks at Forty-Niner Video and Videos to Go in Davis, California. Thanks also to a man who has probably long forgotten me but to whom I owe my introduction to sociology. It was in Thomas Morrione's introduction to sociology class at the University of California at Santa Cruz in 1986 that I discovered my calling as both a sociologist and a teacher. Thanks to my parents, Bob and Rosemary Bulman, for their continual support and encouragement. Finally, I want to thank my wife, Lynne Bartz, for her unwavering support of me in this project. While she was often incredulous that I called watching movies about high school "research," she nonetheless believed in the merits of this project from the very start. Furthermore, her incisive comments and helpful suggestions made this book much better than it would have been without her.

Using the Movies to Make Sense of Society

A Sociological Introduction

The fact that film has been the most potent vehicle for the American imagination suggests all the more strongly that movies have something to tell us not just about the surfaces but the mysteries of American life.[1]
—Arthur M. Schlesinger Jr.

Sociologists don't often study films. Most sociological research observes people in social interaction, tracks patterns of social inequality, investigates the workings of social institutions, seeks to understand the process of social change, and studies the distribution of power in society. Generally speaking, sociology is the study of social reality, not fantasy. While many people think that movie images accurately represent something about the way the world really is, they are really only presenting an interpretation of reality—an image that resonates with the filmmakers and perhaps the audience, but one that does not necessarily reflect the way things actually are. As bell hooks has written,

> Movies make magic. They change things. They take the real and make it into something else right before your very eyes . . . They give the reimagined, reinvented version of the real. It may look like something familiar, but in actuality it is a different universe from the world of the real. That's what makes movies so compelling.[2]

Hollywood routinely twists and shapes reality to maximize dramatic or comic effect for commercial purposes. Films must also frame complicated social relationships within two hours and on a two-dimensional canvas, thereby simplifying them.

Yet films *do* reveal a certain truth. The truth they reveal, however, is not necessarily what they intend to reveal. While Westerns, mobster films, or high school films (to name just a few genres—clusters of films that share a similar style, form, and content) may not paint a complete picture about life in the Old West, in the Mafia, or in high school, these films, nevertheless, if viewed systematically, tell us truths about the culture that produces and consumes them. In this sense they are very real and meaningful artifacts of our culture.[3]

What types of stories and characters creative people develop, which film projects make their way through the Hollywood system, how a film is edited and framed, and which films resonate with a popular audience tell us much more about the reality of a particular society than the "reality" of a film's subject. The clustering of films into genres helps us to identify which versions of "reality" are particularly salient to the culture that produces and consumes them. As movie critic David Denby has noted, genre films "wouldn't survive if they didn't provide emotional satisfaction to the people who make them and to the audiences who watch them."[4] The goal of this book is to help uncover the cultural significance of one particular film genre—the American high school film.

While I am not a film studies scholar per se, I loosely borrow from film studies the tradition of genre analysis—which, in the words of film studies scholar Timothy Shary, attempts to:

> understand cinema based on group and individual representations in (and/or reactions to) films—for example, how films portray a given population or their conditions—under the tacit assumption that films are both aesthetic and cultural documents produced by an industry whose aim is to appeal to (often larger) populations who will find the films worth seeing.[5]

The success of a film genre over time implies that elements of the genre resonate with a large audience. Diana Crane, a noted sociologist of culture, writes that popular texts (books and films, for instance) can help us to understand the cultural worldviews of the members of a society with whom those texts resonate:

> A text is popular if it resonates with readers [or viewers]. For a text to be popular, its message must fit the discourses used by readers to make sense of their experiences. A popular text reassures the readers that their worldviews (discourses) are meaningful. The satisfaction of consuming popular culture is that of being reassured that one's interpretation of the world is congruent with that of others.[6]

In other words, the enjoyment of popular culture such as movies is a *collective* experience. Part of the pleasure of popular culture is that it is popular—that others are experiencing the same cultural product as we are. This collective process helps to bond members of a society together and to reinforce our collective understanding of the social world we share.

Generally, film studies scholarship is rooted in the humanities, not the social sciences. Film analyses are often based on a small sample of films, and the argument often delves no deeper than the author's interpretation of the "text" of the film. Little effort is made to use the lessons of social science research to help interpret the meaning of a representative sample of films.[7] In this book I attempt to bring a social science sensibility to a film studies tradition and to bring the rich empirical data of films into the realm of social science. Films are deeply a part of our society, and as such they have much to teach us about the social and cultural worlds we live in.[8]

Going to the Movies as a Research Method

To assemble a sample of high school films I surveyed friends, colleagues, students in my sociology classes, the workers at local video stores, and professional movie critics from local newspapers about the high school films with which they were familiar. I collected a list of high school films that have been analyzed by other scholars.[9] I scanned the shelves of many video rental stores and reviewed the weekly television listings of broadcast and cable movies. I ran searches on the Internet Movie Data Base (www.imdb.com) and consulted various video guidebooks. From this list I selected the films that use a high school as their primary setting or films whose plots orbit around the life of a high school or high school students. However, it was not enough that the movie feature (even primarily) high school students. In order to be included in the sample, those students had to be connected to a school or to education in some way in the plot. In addition to the classroom, the connection to high school could be based on high-school-related activities, such as dances, parties, football games, student politics, making college plans, or graduation.[10]

To provide some illustration, *Kids* did not fit the criteria because at no time is a school or school-related issue either depicted or referred to. On the other hand, even though most of the action takes place at home, *Risky Business* was included because the plot revolves around a high school student who is pursuing academic (and extracurricular) activities to get into college. It is not always clear whether a film is a "high school" film or

4

not. Admittedly, the boundary can be fuzzy. Many readers will no doubt remember films they think should have been included in the sample or believe some of the films in the sample should not have been included. This is not meant to be an exhaustive list of all the American films that depict high school and high school students. It is, however, a carefully constructed sample of the most accessible American high school films of the past few decades. Films produced over the past twenty-five years or so are heavily represented in the sample for two reasons. A greater number of high school films have been released since 1980 than before, and earlier high school films are less accessible than more recent ones. Nevertheless, the consistency of the trends and patterns that are revealed in this sample of films (among both older and newer films) suggests strongly that this sample is in fact representative of the universe of American high school films. A full listing of the films in the sample can be found in the appendix.

There are 185 films in the sample—144 in the sample of domestic films and 41 in the sample of foreign films (representing fifteen different countries). Among the domestic sample, eighty-three films feature middle-class students in mostly suburban public schools (the suburban school sample), thirty-two films feature poor or working-class students in mostly urban public schools (the urban school sample), and twenty-nine films feature a mix of rich and upper-middle-class students in private schools (the private school sample). There are a greater number of suburban school films in the sample because there are simply more high school films made about suburban high schools and middle-class students than there are about urban high schools or private high schools.[11]

I viewed each of the films at least once (often several times) and noted the major plot elements, the characterizations, and the explicit and implicit lessons each film teaches. I took note of how the films depict curriculum, pedagogy, the role of the teacher, the role of the administration, peer relations among students, relations between students and adults, student attitudes toward schoolwork, extracurricular activities, the role of the family, the resources of the school, the prevalence of violence, the use of drugs, and the expression of sexuality. It soon became clear that there were significant differences in the ways the students and teachers in the urban public school, suburban public school, and private school films were depicted on screen. There were also many differences between the American school films and the foreign school films. My analysis, therefore, explores the cultural reasons for the differences among the three subgenres of the American high school film and the differences between the foreign and domestic films.

A Brief Review of Other High School Film Analyses

Most studies of the high school film genre neglect to note the significant differences among the films based in urban public schools, suburban public schools, and elite private schools. Few of the existing studies of the high school film place social class differences at the center of their analysis. Most tend to treat the high school film genre monolithically, as if all high school films share similar characteristics. Joseph Reed, for instance, narrowly defines the high school film genre as those films based in high school that are told from the point of view of the students, excluding the many important high school films told from the point of view of the teacher.[12] David Considine, however, notes that there are important differences within the high school genre. Considine analyzes films that feature teachers as the main character and argues that between 1935 and 1977 the image of the teacher in film grew progressively more negative.[13] While Considine argues that this change is a function of history, I suggest that he overlooks the important differences between films based in schools with poor or working-class students and those based in schools with middle- or upper-middle-class students. Contrary to Considine's thesis, there has been a resurgence of films that feature the "teacher-hero" since 1977, and most of these films have been based in urban high schools with a poor or working-class student body rather than in suburban high schools with a mostly middle-class student body.

Picking up where Considine left off, Timothy Shary analyzes variants on the teen film genre, focusing on the many teen films released between 1980 and 2000.[14] Shary offers the most in-depth coverage of the teen film genre to date. His discussion of the high school film subgenre constitutes one portion of his overall analysis of the *youth* film genre in general. He maps out the high school genre according to character types—the nerd, the delinquent, the rebel, the popular girl, and the jock—and how these representations have changed over the years. While his discussion of the delinquent overlaps some with my category of the urban school film, he does not make an analytic distinction among urban, suburban, and private high school films, which I find to be the most important distinction to make in the analysis of the high school film genre.

Paul Farber and Gunilla Holm divide the high school films between those that focus on the student and those that focus on the teacher or principal.[15] I agree with their argument that both the students and the "educator-heroes" act independently of the institution of the school. However, their analysis does not highlight the tendency of educator-centered films to be set in urban high schools with poor students while student-centered films tend to take place in suburban high schools with middle-class students. Therefore, they overlook the important theoretical implications about social class, education, and American culture that I highlight in this book. Similarly, Mary Dalton and David Hill analyze films that focus on teachers.[16] While they recognize differences between films that depict "good teachers" and those that depict "bad teachers," neither of their analyses exploits the tendency of "good teacher" films to be based in schools with poor and working-class students while the "bad teacher" films are most likely to feature middle-class students. As I argue in this book, the socioeconomic status of the students depicted in these films is the most important variable to help us explain the ways in which Hollywood represents high schools and adolescents.

The above authors do not view elite private school films as a subgenre distinct from the urban or suburban school films. In short, most of the existing analyses narrowly focus on the relationship between teacher and student regardless of the school's social context. However, by not analyzing the socioeconomic context in which these movie plots take place, and how the plots and characters differ accordingly, they fail to appreciate the significant lessons about social class and American culture that a sociological analysis reveals.

Furthermore, it is surprising that many academic studies of Hollywood films claim to say something about American culture yet fail to contrast American films to foreign films. Only in contrast to the cinema of other countries can we be certain that Hollywood films truly express something about the American culture that produces and consumes them and not just the medium of film itself. Therefore, this book analyzes a sample of foreign films in order to see if and how their depiction of high school students and adolescents differs from that of the American school films.

Films and Culture

What is the relationship between film and culture? What do films have to teach us about the cultures in which they are produced and consumed? Are films primarily a reflection of culture, or do they in some ways help to independently shape cultural life?[17] I suggest that films both reflect and shape culture. To fully understand the social and cultural significance of films, we need to understand both the production of films and the consumption of films. In other words, we need to understand the social processes that create certain films and film genres, and we need to understand how members of a society interpret and react to those films. Both sides of this equation help us to make sense of the relationship between films and culture.

Genre films, for instance, reflect the culture that produces and consumes them in a variety of ways. First, films reflect the culture to the extent that the creative artists who imagine and make the films are themselves a product of that culture and are attempting to express something about the social world they inhabit. Second, commercial interests (the studios that fund the films) reflect the culture as they strategically select projects, develop them, produce them, advertise them, and market them to the public. Finally, the audience reaction to the films at the box office reflects the cultural milieu by indicating what resonates with the public. The popularity of certain types of films feeds back to the artistic and commercial interests as they develop new projects. Thus, the genre develops in constant interaction among creative artists, commercial interests, and the audience in a "circuit of culture."[18] As film scholar Thomas Schatz has argued:

> Movies are not produced in creative or cultural isolation, nor are they consumed that way . . . [A genre approach] recognizes the cinema's close contact with its *audience*, whose response to individual films has affected the gradual development of story formulas and standard production practices.[19]

At the same time, films have the cultural power to influence how members of a society make sense of social life. The commercial film industry is a socializing institution. Films *teach* us who we are as much as they *reflect* who we are. When we go to the movies, we absorb messages about the social world in which we live. We learn about heroes and villains, about what is possible and impossible, about conflict and resolution, about relationships, and about norms and values. We do not necessarily accept every message we receive without question (nor do we accept everything our parents teach us, for that matter), but we do learn what messages our culture chooses to convey in its entertainment.

In particular, as I argue in later chapters, Hollywood films convey elements of the dominant ideology in the United States. Specifically, Hollywood films tend to convey the sensibilities of the American middle class—individualism, self-sufficiency, free expression, hard work, and fair play. In many ways the ideology of the middle class is culturally hegemonic in the United States. That is, the middle-class experience is considered to be the "normal" experience in American life. The rich and the poor are usually depicted in Hollywood films as outside the mainstream of society. As a result, Hollywood films tend to privilege the middle-class experience by making the protagonists of films representatives of the middle class. Films, therefore, help to communicate the message of middle-class values, sentiments, and assumptions to all members of society.[20]

Ultimately, it is very difficult to specify exactly how films reflect culture and how they affect it. As sociologist Andrew Tudor has noted, it is too simple to say that Hollywood either creates or reflects American culture. The dynamic relationship between society and the stories society tells about itself is far too complicated to attribute causation. Tudor writes,

> . . . the movies participate in a continual and complex social process. They articulate for us the bases of our social lives; they give the underlying regularities our societies' concrete form. They are both reflection and cause; a link in a closed circle. We act, we create, we form, and even change societies. Our popular culture expresses the irreducibles of these operations.[21]

Films are located at the center of a complex cultural process of production and consumption. Their location within this process provides us with a particularly convenient site in which to conduct a cinematic ethnography to understand something about American culture.

One of the reasons that it is difficult to pinpoint the precise role that films play in a culture is that culture is complex and messy. As the sociologist Kai Erikson argues, every culture is filled with potential contradictions.[22] The symbols and shared values of a society are not seamless. Cultural meanings are not given. People must actively work to make sense of their lives and the complicated social world in which they live. They often must struggle with contradictory notions. I suggest that one way in which we collectively manage to cope with the complexity and confusion of social life is to package reality and to represent it as fiction—to tell stories about our social world that make it more comprehensible. In this sense, films can be viewed as modern-day cultural myths and folktales.

Folktales (or fairy tales) are stories that a culture tells to itself about itself. That is, folktales express elements of a culture (values, norms, beliefs, fears, et cetera) in fantastic stories that get told repeatedly in a culture. These tales help individuals to order their social world and to remind members of a society about the common elements of their culture that bind them together. As Jack Zipes, a scholar who studies fairy tales, writes,

> The classical fairy tale makes it appear that we are all part of a universal community with shared values and norms, that we are all striving for the same happiness, that there are certain dreams and wishes which are irrefutable, that a particular type of behavior will produce guaranteed results, like living happily ever after with lots of gold in a marvelous castle . . .[23]

What Zipes points out about fairy tales (particularly as they find expression in the contemporary United States), however, is that they do not necessarily reflect the values and interests of all members of society. Fairy tales (and films, as I argue in this book) are more than just entertainment that helps to create social solidarity. They may appear to be politically neutral, but they often reflect class interests:

> Yet, amusement is not to be taken lightly, for distraction and divertissement have an important ideological function: almost all the major classical fairy tales that have achieved prominence and are to be enjoyed in the United States can be considered as products that reinforce a patriarchal and middle-class social code.[24]

Outline and Argument of the Book

Chapter 2 is a theoretical overview of certain aspects of American culture. Specifically, it outlines the ways that some sociologists have made sense of individualism, the middle class, and adolescence in American society. The theoretical issues raised in this chapter lay the groundwork for the arguments presented in the subsequent chapters that deal more explicitly with the films in the sample.

In chapter 3 I analyze the films that depict the education of poor and working-class students in mostly urban high school environments.[25] The cinematic classroom of the urban high school is filled with socially troubled and low-achieving students who are dramatically transformed by the singular efforts of a new teacher or principal. All of this is accomplished to the consternation of the inept administrative staff and other teachers, who never believed that these students had such potential. This lone "teacher-hero" is almost always a middle-class outsider—one who has a troubled and mysterious past, little teaching experience, a good heart, and an unorthodox approach to teaching.[26] Invariably, the outsider succeeds where veteran professional teachers and administrators have repeatedly failed. The hero is almost always an adult who encourages the students to conform to middle-class values—to be achievement-oriented, rational, and upwardly mobile. The adult heroes in the urban school films are selfless outsiders (urban school cowboys) who offer salvation to the poor and mostly nonwhite students lost in a culture of poverty and despair.

I argue that the urban high school film genre represents the fantasies that suburban middle-class Americans have about life in urban high schools and the ease with which the problems in urban high schools could be rectified—if only the right type of person (a middle-class outsider) would apply the right methods (an unconventional pedagogy with a curriculum of middle-class norms and values based on utilitarian individualism). This teacher-hero represents middle-class hopes that the students in urban schools can be rescued from their troubled lives not through significant social change, but by the individual application of common sense, good behavior, a positive outlook, and better choices.

In chapter 4 I analyze the films that depict the education of mostly middle-class students in suburban public high schools. The suburban high school film is quite different from the urban high school film. In the films based in suburban high schools, academic success is *not* a central focus of the plot. The suburban school films depict schools less as actual places of learning and more as social spaces where middle-class teenagers search for their identities and struggle with each other for the rewards of social status and popularity. In these films schoolwork is secondary to the real drama of teen angst. A very different notion of adolescence is expressed in the suburban school film than in the urban school film. Instead of conformity to middle-class values, the suburban school students must reject the conformity of their peers, the culture of popularity, and the constraints of adults in order to express their true selves. The hero is almost never an adult as in the urban school films, but usually a student who is able to overcome the conformity of teen society or the authoritarianism of adult society.

I argue that the suburban school films represent middle-class frustration with the conformity and status hierarchy of suburban middle-class life and express fantasies of self-expression and individual rebellion against such a system. The middle class longs to escape the emptiness and meaninglessness that a life of conformity and individual competitiveness fosters. These films reflect a middle-class desire that one can find profound meaning and satisfaction in life not through conventional achievement, but by discovering and expressing one's true identity.

In chapter 5 I analyze the American films that depict the education of private school students. In the films based in elite independent private high schools, academics is once again likely to be featured as an element of the story. However, whereas in the urban school films academic achievement was valued as the answer to the culture of poverty plaguing the inner-city students, in the elite private school films the narrow focus on academic achievement is often portrayed as an oppressive burden upon students. The upper-class students in these films must conform to the wishes of their parents and the school in order to protect their social class status. The hero of these films is often a working- or middle-class outsider who challenges the culture of privilege that pervades the upper-class institution. The upper-class students are challenged to risk their taken-for-granted position in the class hierarchy by finding and expressing their true selves independent of the expectations elite culture has of them. Often this involves following the heart, as in the suburban school films. Individual integrity, well roundedness, academic merit, and personal happiness are deemed more important than inherited privilege, material gain, social status, or family tradition. However, for reasons that will be further explored in chapter 5, the films based in private Catholic and Christian schools more closely resemble the themes of the suburban public high school films than they do the themes of the films based in elite independent private schools.

The elite private school films, I suggest, reflect middle-class ambivalence about wealth. On the one hand, pursuit of wealth through hard work is a cherished American value. On the other hand, the middle class knows that there should be much more to life than the pursuit of money and that wealth potentially threatens our moral integrity.[27] These films also represent an abiding belief among the American working and middle classes that in spite of pronounced socioeconomic inequality in the United States, schools are fair and meritocratic institutions that provide equal opportunity for upward social mobility for students from all social classes.

Chapter 6 introduces the reader to a sample of high school films produced in countries other than the United States. Through an analysis of these foreign high school films I demonstrate that the themes of the high school films discussed in chapters 3, 4, and 5 are not universal. The American high school film indeed reveals unique aspects of American culture. The theme of individualism, for instance, is much more pronounced in the American films than in the foreign films. Specifically, individual heroes overcome the oppressive burdens of society in the American films, while individuals in the foreign school films often succumb to external social forces. Also, while the American films have neat and tidy happy endings with an optimistic outlook, the foreign films present images of adolescent life that are much more complicated, confusing, ambiguous, and dark. I argue that the individual heroism and happy endings of the American high school films reflect an American tendency to want to superficially resolve contradictions rather than to confront difficult and sometimes unpleasant realities about social inequality. The foreign school films throw into stark relief the peculiar trends in the American high school film genre—trends that echo American culture in general. Chapter 7 concludes the analysis with some final thoughts about film, education, and the ironies of American culture.

12

A Final Note

It is important to note that this current study is not a reception study of films. That is, I do not conduct research to see how audiences interpret these films, nor how different groups within society might attach different meanings to the same films. While such a study would shed important light on the social and cultural significance of these films, it is beyond the scope of the present analysis. This book offers an analysis from a sociological perspective of a sample of American films about high schools and adolescents and a sample of their foreign counterparts. As a sociologist, I analyze these films as data—as cultural artifacts—to see what patterns and trends they reveal. Using sociological theory, I interpret the possible meaning of the patterns and trends I observe and hypothesize what they indicate about American culture.[28]

In his classic work *The Interpretation of Cultures*, the anthropologist Clifford Geertz offers advice about how the scholar should uncover the meanings of culture. The answers, he argues, are there for the taking. One need only figure out how to extract them:

> Whatever the level at which one operates, and however intricately, the guiding principle is the same: societies, like lives, contain their own interpretations. One has only to learn how to gain access to them.[29]

I intend to gain access to certain aspects of American society through the myths that Americans tell to themselves in the movies. As the sociologist Will Wright asserts in *Sixguns and Society*, "It is through the movies that the myth has become part of the cultural language by which America understands itself."[30] This book explores the myths of the high school film. What do these myths have to teach us about American culture?

Notes

1. Schlesinger, Arthur M., Jr. 1979. "Foreword." In *American History/American Film: Interpreting the Hollywood Image*. John E. O'Connor and Martin A. Jackson, editors. New York: Continuum.
2. hooks, bell. 1996. *Reel to Real: Race, Sex, and Class at the Movies*. New York: Routledge, p. 1.

3. George Lipsitz argues that films are cultural artifacts in that they are "social-history evidence about the times in which they were made." While I do not disagree with Lipsitz, I do not take a historical approach to the study of films in this book. That is, I find that the themes of the high school films over the past fifty years are relatively consistent across time. As such, they tell us more about American culture in general than the culture of any particular time in American history. See Lipsitz, George. 1990. *Time Passages: Collective Memory and American Popular Culture.* Minneapolis: University of Minnesota Press, p. 164.

4. Denby, David. 1999. "High School Confidential: Notes on Teen Movies." *The New Yorker* (May 31): 94–98, p. 94.

5. Shary, Timothy. 2002. *Generation Multiplex: The Image of Youth in Contemporary American Cinema.* Austin: University of Texas Press, p. 14.

6. Diana Crane. 1992. *The Production of Culture: Media and the Urban Arts.* New York: Sage, p. 94.

7. Powers, Rothman, and Rothman have been critical of this approach. They write, "poststructuralist theorists and scholars who claim to be interested in politics and society have in no way turned to the social sciences to study society but remain utterly committed to the language of aesthetic critique in the formalist and structuralist traditions. The likes of Weber, C. Wright Mills, and Daniel Bell rarely, if ever, appear in their bibliographies." Powers, Stephen, David Rothman, and Stanley Rothman. 1996. *Hollywood's America: Social and Political Themes in Motion Pictures.* Denver: Westview, p. 226.

8. I am indebted to several authors for demonstrating that films can be used successfully as data in sociological research: Wright, Will. 1975. *Sixguns and Society: A Structural Study of the Western.* Berkeley: University of California Press; Tudor, Andrew. 1974. *Image and Influence: Studies in the Sociology of Film.* New York: St. Martin's Press; and Vera, Hernan, and Andrew M. Gordon. 2003. *Screen Saviors: Hollywood Fictions of Whiteness.* Lanham, MD: Rowman and Littlefield.

9. Considine, David M. 1985. *The Cinema of Adolescence.* NC: McFarland and Co.; Reed, Joseph W. 1989. *American Scenarios: The Uses of Film Genre.* Middletown, CT: Wesleyan University Press; Farber, Paul, and Gunilla Holm. 1994. "Adolescent Freedom and the Cinematic High School." In *Schooling in the Light of Popular Culture.* Albany: State University of New York Press, and 1994. "A Brotherhood of Heroes: The Charismatic Educator in Recent American Movies." In *Schooling in the Light of Popular Culture.* Albany: State University of New York Press; Dalton, Mary. 1999. *The Hollywood Curriculum: Teachers and Teaching in the Movies.* New York: Peter Lang; Hill, David. 1995. "Tinseltown Teachers." *Teacher Magazine* (March); Trier, James D. 2001. "The Cinematic Repre-

14

sentation of the Personal and Professional Lives of Teachers." *Teacher Education Quarterly* (summer): 127–142; Farhi, Adam. 1999. "Hollywood Goes to School: Recognizing the Superteacher Myth in Film." *The Clearing House* 72, no. 3: 157; and Shary, *Generation Multiplex.*

10. For reasons I explain in chapter 6, the criteria used to select the sample of foreign school films were slightly different. For the foreign school films I relaxed the requirement that the school per se be at the center of the plot, and at times films that feature junior-high-aged students are included in the sample.

11. One reason there are more middle-class suburban high school films than any other is because the notions in the United States about what high school is and what adolescence is are wrapped up in middle-class assumptions. A discussion of this hegemonic middle-class worldview in American culture will be explored in chapter 2.

12. Reed, *American Scenario.*

13. Considine, *The Cinema of Adolescence.*

14. Shary, *Generation Multiplex.*

15. Farber and Holm, "Adolescent Freedom and the Cinematic High School" and "A Brotherhood of Heroes."

16. Dalton, *The Hollywood Curriculum*; and Hill, "Tinseltown Teachers."

17. See Mukerji, Chandra, and Michael Shudson, editors. 1991. *Rethinking Popular Culture: Contemporary Perspectives in Cultural Studies.* Berkeley: University of California Press, for more discussion about the popular culture debate.

18. See Harrington, C. Lee, and Denise D. Bielby. 2001. "Constructing the Popular: Cultural Production and Consumption." In *Popular Culture: Production and Consumption.* C. Lee Harrington and Denise D. Bielby, editors. Malden, MA: Blackwell.

19. Schatz, Thomas. 1981. *Hollywood Genres: Formulas, Filmmaking, and the Studio System.* Boston: McGraw Hill, pp. vii–viii, emphasis in the original.

20. While I do not disagree with those who argue that Hollywood also privileges the perspective of whites, I find in my analysis of the high school films that the middle-class perspective overshadows the perspective of whiteness. See Vera and Wang, *Screen Saviors*, for a perspective on whiteness in American films. Also see my discussion of this issue in chapter 3.

21. Tudor, *Image and Influence*, p. 218.

22. Erikson, Kai T. 1978. *Everything in Its Path: Destruction of Community in the Buffalo Creek Flood.* New York: Simon and Schuster.

23. Zipes, Jack. 1994. *Fairy Tales as Myth: Myth as Fairy Tales.* Lexington: University of Kentucky Press, p. 5.

24. Ibid., p. 141.

25. Portions of an earlier version of chapter 2 appeared in Bulman, Robert C. 2002. "Teachers in the 'Hood': Hollywood's Middle-Class Fantasy." *Urban Review* 34, no. 3 (September): 251–276, with kind permission of Kluwer Academic Publishers.

26. A similar point is also made in Considine, *Cinema of Adolescence*; Farhi, "Hollywood Goes to School"; Grant, Peggy A. 2002. "Using Popular Films to Challenge Preservice Teachers' Beliefs About Teaching in Urban Schools." *Urban Education* 37 (January 2002): 77–95; Heilman, Robert B. 1991. "The Great-Teacher Myth." *American Scholar* 60, no. 3: 417–423; Burbach, Harold J., and Margo A. Figgins. 1993. "A Thematic Profile of the Images of Teachers in Film." *Teacher Education Quarterly* (spring): 65–75; Thomsen, Steven R. 1993. "A Worm in the Apple: Hollywood's Influence on the Public's Perception of Teachers." A paper presented at the Southern States Communication Association and Central States Communication Association joint annual meeting, Lexington, KY, April 15; and Ayers, William. 1996. "A Teacher Ain't Nothin' but a Hero: Teachers and Teaching in Film." In *City Kids, City Teachers: Reports from the Front Row*. William Ayers and Patricia Ford, editors. New York: The New Press.

27. See Ehrenreich, Barbara. 1989. *Fear of Falling: The Inner Life of the Middle Class*. New York: Harper Press.

28. This book can be viewed by sociologists of culture as an exploratory study to be followed by a reception study of these films to see if my hypotheses hold true.

29. Geertz, Clifford. 1973. *The Interpretation of Cultures*. New York: Basic Books, p. 453.

30. Wright, *Sixguns and Society*, p. 12.

Middle-Class Individualism and the Adolescent Frontier

What High School Films Reveal About American Culture

To the casual viewer, a film about high school may be nothing more than simple entertainment. These films, however, are more than just entertainment. They are more than just an expression of the director's vision. The high school film genre reveals patterns that transcend entertainment and art and teaches deeper lessons about American culture. While they are not precise social documents of real high schools and real adolescents, these high school films are cultural artifacts that provide clues to the society that made them and paid to see them. In particular, they offer clues to how Americans make sense of education, youth, and inequality. This chapter begins with an overview of the major differences among the different subgenres of the American high school film: the urban public school film, the suburban public school film, and the private high school film.[1] The chapter then explains in some detail the various elements of American culture that find expression in these films. Specifically, this chapter explains the various expressions of individualism in American culture, the importance of the middle class in American culture, and the ways in which Americans makes sense of adolescence. This discussion about American culture will help the reader to put into theoretical context the arguments made about the high school films in subsequent chapters.

Hollywood's View of High School:
The Three Subgenres

In 2001 the film *Not Another Teen Movie* was released to theaters across the country. It is a satirical movie spoof of the many high school and teen films that have been released in the United States over the past twenty-five years. This movie spoof is evidence that the high school film has been successfully established as its own Hollywood genre. The dominant themes of these films are recognizable enough to a general audience to merit the production of a major Hollywood film that pokes fun at the genre. In effect, Hollywood is poking fun at itself and hoping people will pay to see it. As a satire, however, *Not Another Teen Movie* is unoriginal. The reason is clear enough in the revealing title—*Please, not another teen movie! Aren't there enough already?* Indeed, *Not Another Teen Movie* is a redundant film. While its sole purpose is to spoof preexisting high school films, most of those films are themselves heavily derived from previous high school films, creating a string of unintended satires. For instance, if one has seen *Pretty in Pink*, then the themes of *10 Things I Hate About You*, *She's All That*, and an assortment of other similar films are all too familiar and predictable.

Not Another Teen Movie has a frightfully easy job of satirizing previous teen films. It often borrows the *exact* same dialogue, soundtrack, and sometimes even the same actors from several previous high school films. It is almost more correct to call *Not Another Teen Movie* a remake of *She's All That*, *10 Things I Hate About You*, *Pretty In Pink*, and *Varsity Blues* than a satire of those films. *Not Another Teen Movie* also borrows liberally from *Porky's*, *American Pie*, *Lucas*, *Never Been Kissed*, *Bring It On*, *The Breakfast Club*, *Cruel Intentions*, *Can't Hardly Wait*, *Grease*, and *Fast Times at Ridgemont High*.

Not Another Teen Movie takes place, appropriately enough, at John Hughes High School. (John Hughes is the famous writer and director responsible for such teen classics as *The Breakfast Club*, *Pretty in Pink*, *16 Candles*, *Ferris Bueller's Day Off*, *Weird Science*, and *Some Kind of Wonderful*.) It features such common teen film characters as the popular cool guy, the dumb jock, the bitchy cheerleader, the horny virgin boys, the misunderstood rebel, the mean football coach, the wise janitor, the clueless parents, and the nerdy best friend. As with most of the movies it satirizes, its plot has very little to do with schooling per se. Instead, the story revolves around the struggles over popularity and dating as the characters figure out who they are, what is important to them in life, and how to express themselves free of the constraints of the school, social cliques, and their parents. The moral of the story (and the moral of most of the movies in the suburban school subgenre) is that you should follow your heart, regardless of what your friends, your parents, or your teachers advise.

While *Not Another Teen Movie* presents itself as a satire of the teen film genre, it is, more precisely, a satire of a subgenre of the teen film—the middle-class suburban high school film. The movies that depict poor teens in mostly urban high schools are *not* satirized in this film. There are no satirical references to movies such as *Blackboard Jungle, Dangerous Minds, Lean on Me, Stand and Deliver, The Substitute, The Principal*, or *Teachers*. In fact, those films have already been satirized by Hollywood in the 1996 film *High School High*. The fact that Hollywood has chosen to satirize films that depict poor students in urban high schools separately from the films that depict middle-class students in suburban high schools suggests strongly that the urban high school film constitutes its own subgenre with a unique set of themes, story lines, characters, and messages. Just as *Not Another Teen Movie* captured the major themes of the suburban high school films, *High School High* does so for the urban high school films.

High School High takes place at Marion Barry High School (Marion Barry is the former mayor of Washington, DC, who was caught on videotape smoking crack cocaine). It is a severely worn-down, vandalized, chaotic, and violent school that resembles a prison much more than a high school. As with *Not Another Teen Movie*, *High School High* has an easy time with its satirical poke at Hollywood's high school film genre. The urban high school film genre, too, has already been well established with easily recognizable elements common in most of the films. If one has seen *Blackboard Jungle*, then the plots of *Halls of Anger, Up the Down Staircase, Lean on Me*, and *Dangerous Minds*, for instance, are strikingly familiar.

In an exaggerated fashion *High School High* draws on the plots and characters of the previous urban high school films. In short, a naive new teacher (in this case Mr. Clark) believes he can make a difference in the lives of poor and troubled urban youth. Throughout the film he struggles to "get through" to his students. After several difficult setbacks he ultimately triumphs by getting the students to reject their criminal and apathetic ways and to apply themselves academically. As in most of the urban high school films, the moral of the story is that individual determination and hard work can overcome all obstacles. As Mr. Clark tells the students at the end of *High School High*, "Work as hard as you can. Do a couple hours of homework each night and nothing can stop you." The students, who initially treated the new teacher with skepticism and hostility, ultimately adopt his lessons and learn to love him.

Even as spoofs, *Not Another Teen Movie* and *High School High* reveal important differences about how Hollywood represents poor urban and middle-class suburban high schools in popular films.[2] While there has not yet been a satire of the private school subgenre, Hollywood also has a unique way of representing rich students in private high schools, which will be explored in chapter 5. At the moment, it is important to note that these different representations do not arise because of the actual differences between real urban, suburban, and private high schools. The subgenres differ in significant ways because American culture *makes sense of* poor youth, middle-class youth, and wealthy youth (and urban public schools, suburban public schools, and private schools) in very different ways.

Nevertheless, most of the high school films (suburban, urban, and private) express remarkably consistent themes. The theme that most of these movies have in common is an ethic of individualism. Adolescents in these films are expected to transcend the limitations of their communities, the narrow-mindedness of their families, the expectations of their parents, the conformity of their peers, the ineffectiveness of their schools, their poverty or wealth, and the insidious effects of racism or sexism in order to express themselves as individuals apart from social constraints. The source of their academic success and/or personal fulfillment is to be found within the heart and mind of each individual regardless of social context.

There are dramatic differences, however, in the ways in which the theme of individualism plays itself out in the films based in urban high schools, those based in suburban high schools, and those based in private high schools. I suggest that the different expressions of individualism in these three film genres reveal a tension in American culture that is born out of conflicted feelings about social class in the United States.

In the urban school films the dominant theme is "utilitarian individualism." As sociologist Robert Bellah and his co-authors in the 1985 best seller *Habits of the Heart: Individualism and Commitment in American Life* explain, utilitarian individualism is that strain of American individualism that celebrates hard work, materialism, and individual self-sufficiency.[3] In the urban school films, middle-class teacher-heroes insist that their impoverished students become utilitarian individuals—that they work hard in school, set high goals for themselves, and take full individual responsibility for escaping the culture of poverty.

For instance, in *Dangerous Minds* Ms. Johnson is a new teacher who finds herself teaching some of the most "at risk" poor and minority urban students in her school ("rejects from hell," as she calls them). Her primary message to these students is that they can achieve anything they want as long as they put their minds to it. With only a superficial nod to the challenges they face due to poverty, racism, their violent neighborhoods, and their struggling families, Ms. Johnson declares that their lives are defined by their individual choices, nothing more. As she tells her students, "If you want to pass, all you have to do is try." In order to give them the confidence that they can achieve anything they choose, Ms. Johnson breaks from the traditional curriculum and uses "college level" poetry to teach her students. Her class engages in intellectual debate about the similarities between the poetry of Dylan Thomas and Bob Dylan. The upper-middle-class cultural capital (the knowledge, styles, skills, and assumptions unique to a particular social class experience)[4] she imparts to them is in stark contrast to the poor and working-class family lives they lead. The grandmother of two brothers in her class does not see the point of all this book learning and withdraws the boys from Ms. Johnson's class. As she explains to Ms. Johnson:

> [Teaching] poetry and bullshit is a waste of time. They have more important things to worry about . . . I ain't raisin' no doctors and lawyers here. They got bills to pay. Go find yourself some other boys to save.

Nevertheless, most of her students begin to care about schooling and begin to believe that education, including poetry, can make a positive difference in their lives if only they work hard enough. Ms. Johnson develops a particular interest in one student, Raul. She develops a pact with him: She loans him two hundred dollars to pay for a leather jacket but will only allow him to pay back the money on the day he graduates from high school. Ms. Johnson's love (and the candy bars, the dinners at fancy restaurants, and the trip to an amusement park she uses as bribes) inspires her students to believe in themselves and in the power of an education in spite of the hardships they face in the world outside the school and in spite of the anti-intellectual messages many of them receive at home. By the end of the film the students insist that Ms. Johnson has become their "light" and that they now see the path they need to travel toward academic success and a safe, stable, and conventional middle-class lifestyle.

In the suburban school films, by contrast, the dominant theme is not utilitarian individualism but "expressive individualism." As explained in *Habits of the Heart*, expressive individualism refers to that strain of American individualism that values not material achievements, but the discovery of one's unique identity and the freedom of individual self-expression. In the suburban school sample of films, the middle-class student-heroes are *not* expected to apply themselves academically. The utilitarian success of academic and athletic achievement, popularity, and high social status is criticized. In these films a stable and safe middle-class lifestyle is considered to be an obstacle to individual self-discovery. The student-heroes are expected to find their identity and to express their true selves apart from the expectations of their school, their parents, and their peers.

For instance, in *The New Guy* Dizzy Harris is a senior at Rocky Creek High School who struggles with his nerdy identity and, by the end of the movie, ultimately accepts who he is and gains respect for it. He and his friends are "blips"—barely on the radar screen of the school's social life. He is subjected to complete humiliation at the hands of the popular jocks at the school. Desperate to get expelled and start over at another high school, he breaks as many of the school's rules as he can. He is eventually expelled from school and arrested. In jail he learns from a prisoner how to remake himself in a new environment in order to impress the popular kids. He arrives at East Highland's High School with a reputation as a tough ex-convict, "Gil."

East Highland is a school with a highly stratified system of popularity. At lunch the cool kids hang out at the top tier (literally) of the school grounds while the least popular students occupy the bottom of the hill. On his first day of school Gil makes an impression—he beats up Conner, the most popular jock (and biggest bully) at the school, gaining the fear and respect of most of the students. The popular girls, even Danielle, the head cheerleader and Conner's girlfriend, begin to gravitate toward him. His reputation grows and, to the consternation of the jocks, he is soon the most popular student in school.

Gil, however, begins to feel guilty about abandoning his old nerdy friends. He recalls his previous abuse as a "blip" and doesn't want to become another run-of-the-mill popular kid who humiliates others. Gil begins to stand up for the little guy at the school, literally. After the bully Conner sends the tuba-playing midget Ed down the hill in a trash can, Gil confronts Conner and defends Ed. In doing so Gil makes it cool to accept others, even the unconventional "freaks." The beautiful and popular Danielle is so impressed that she leaves her prestigious place at the top of the hill and goes down to join the nerds at the bottom, embracing her old and socially awkward elementary school friend. Gil inspires both the "blips" and the popular kids to work together as friends. Danielle begins to fall in love with Gil because, as she tells him, "you know exactly who you are." Gil, however, has yet to be completely honest with Danielle.

His charade is revealed at prom when his old nemesis from Rocky Creek shows up and tells the East Highland students that Gil is really the nerdy Dizzy. Dizzy makes a speech to the crowd of students:

> I was trying to become something more than a blip on the radar screen. So I made someone up. Someone I thought you would like. And all because I cared more about what other people thought of me than what I thought of me. But I'm willing to bet I'm not the only person here who's ever let that happen.

As a result of his confession, his old friends accept him back. The popular and beautiful Danielle still loves him in spite of his deception and his "true" identity as a nerd. Danielle and Dizzy ride off into the sunset on the school's mascot, a white horse, happily ever after.

In the private school films the themes of expressive and utilitarian individualism coexist. The working- or middle-class heroes question the conformity of elite society, reveal the moral bankruptcy of the rich, and undermine the authority of the elite private school as they express their true selves. At the same time, the student-hero achieves conventional academic and/or financial success. The working- or middle-class student-heroes use their well roundedness, academic merit, and personal integrity to challenge the upper-class culture of privilege that pervades the private preparatory school. Yet they also benefit materially from their affiliation with the school.

For instance, in *Making the Grade* Palmer Woodrow is a very rich, insufferable, spoiled, lazy, and despicable student who hasn't been able to graduate from any elite preparatory school. He's drunk all day and has no redeeming characteristics. His absent parents pull some strings and get him admitted to Hoover Academy, the prep school of "last resort." They say he must graduate or risk getting cut off financially. In contrast, Eddie Keaton is a working-class, street-smart, and savvy kid who owes a bookie a thirty-seven-hundred-dollar gambling debt. Eddie escapes the loan shark's goons by running into a country club, where he meets Palmer. The two make a deal—Eddie will get paid to attend school in Palmer's place while Palmer is off traveling through Europe.

Eddie does not fit in at prep school. In contrast to the pink, green, and yellow pastel sweaters, Izod shirts, and sport coats of the wealthy prep students, Eddie wears a bright orange suit, an open collar, and gold chains. He is quite the spectacle at the normally staid Hoover Academy, and he gets lots of positive attention for it. His casual and fun-loving approach to school, his down-to-earth attitude, and his personal confidence impress everyone, including the wealthy Tracey Hoover. Tracey is attracted to Eddie's unique style and to how he is a true individual—different from everyone else in her social world: "What's important is that you are what you are. You're genuine. That's what I like about you." In an attempt to impress her, however, Eddie tries to act "preppy" and, ironically, disappoints her. Tracey begins to resent his changes—as he begins to resemble all the other rich and predictable guys she knows.

Bif, the stereotypical rich asshole, is jealous of Eddie's popularity at the school and, in particular, of his relationship with Tracey. He tries to exact his revenge by setting Eddie up for expulsion—"He's just not one of us," he tells the headmaster, "I hate to see Hoover's reputation stained like this." But Bif's plan to humiliate Eddie backfires, and Bif ends up getting expelled from Hoover. Eddie successfully graduates from Hoover Academy and wins the Hoover memorial award (thanks to the fictional donations his "father" had promised to the financially strapped school). During his acceptance speech, however, Eddie confesses his deception. He reveals his true identity:

> I forgot who I was. When I did that I hurt the most important person in my life. I'm Eddie Keaton from Jersey. I was hired to play Palmer Woodrow . . . I'm the kind of guy that most of you wouldn't let into your house.

His confession notwithstanding, Eddie still receives the financial reward and a Porsche from the real Palmer Woodrow. Eddie prepares to leave Hoover in style. At the last minute Tracey decides to join him even though, or perhaps because, he is "not exactly Mr. Alligator shirt." The two of them drive off, leaving the morally bankrupt Bif, Palmer, and Hoover Academy behind forever.

Why do the urban public school films feature adult middle-class heroes, an emphasis on academic achievement, and the theme of utilitarian individualism, while the suburban public school films feature middle-class student-heroes, almost no focus on academics, and a theme of expressive individualism? Why do the private school films extol the integrity and merit of the working- or middle-class heroes in contrast to the moral and emotional bankruptcy of wealthy antagonists? The differences among the three subgenres will be explored in greater detail in chapters 3, 4, and 5. To help make sociological sense of these films and the differences among the urban, suburban, and private school subgenres, however, we must first explore some of the essential characteristics of American culture. Specifically, it is impossible to analyze these high school films as cultural artifacts without understanding the various strains of American individualism, the dominant perspective of the middle class in American culture, and the ways in which American society makes sense of teenagers.

The following pages help to put these elements of American culture into theoretical perspective. The ideas outlined here establish the groundwork for much of the analysis that follows through the remainder of the book. In short, Hollywood's understanding of high schools and adolescents is highly dependent upon the social class of the students being represented in the films. Hollywood conveys different messages about individualism, the importance of an education, and the nature of adolescence in the urban public school films that depict poor students, the suburban public school films that depict middle-class students, and the private school films that depict mostly wealthy students. In each of the three American high school film subgenres, the perspective of the middle class is privileged over that of other social classes.

24

Individualism and American Culture

The problem with individualism is not that it is immoral but that it is incorrect. The universe does not consist of a lot of unrelated particles but is an interconnected whole. Pretending that our fortunes are independent of each other may be perfectly ethical, but it's also perfectly stupid.[5]

—Philip Slater

While individualism has many manifestations, at its core is the idea that the individual has autonomy and independence apart from social groups and institutions. To fully appreciate the cultural importance of individualism in the United States, it is necessary to go back in time. In this section we first explore the early sociological insights about individualism in modern industrial society. Then we explore the ways in which Protestantism, American democracy, and the western frontier helped to shape utilitarian and expressive individualism in American life.

Emile Durkheim, one of the earliest sociologists, wrote of the increasing sentiment of individualism in the modern world in his classic work of 1893, *The Division of Labor*. According to Durkheim, there was very little differentiation among individuals in premodern traditional societies. Traditional societies were based on the *similarities* of members. All individuals in a community shared similar beliefs, had similar skills, and lived similar styles of life. These societies based on similarity were held together by what Durkheim called "mechanical solidarity." In effect, the solidarity of traditional societies was automatic. It was taken for granted and held together by the "collective consciousness" of the group. Individuals recognized their membership in the society due to the qualities they shared in common with all of the other members. Furthermore, such similarity was enforced under the threat of punishment.

As society advanced, however, the population grew, technology developed, urbanization increased, and social life became more complex. Rather than all members sharing similar skills, as in a traditional society, individuals in modern society began to develop specialized skills and unique individualized traits. In other words, individualism was born of modernity:

> As evolution advances, the bonds that attach the individual to his family, to his native heath, to the traditions that the past has bequeathed him, to the collective practices of the group—all become loosened. Being more mobile,

the individual changes his environment more easily, leaves his own people to go and live a more autonomous life elsewhere, works out for himself his ideas and sentiments.[6]

The glue that keeps modern society cohesive is not mechanical solidarity based on similarity as in traditional societies, but "organic solidarity" based on individual *differences*. Due to the specialization of skills, individuals are necessarily interdependent upon each other. While unique and special, the modern individual needs others to perform tasks that she cannot. Modern society is like a biological organism: The heart, liver, and lungs, for instance, each have very specific and individual functions, but they each depend upon the other organs in order for the organism (and all the individual organs) to survive.

Durkheim pointed us toward an important irony that is a characteristic of modern society. At just the historical moment when members of modern society feel the sentiments of individualism the strongest (when individuals are unique with skills and characteristics that distinguish them from the crowd), individuals are the most dependent upon others. Individualism, while a product of social life, can ironically prevent individuals from recognizing their connections to the social world. The power of individualism in modern society makes it difficult to exercise what the famous twentieth-century American sociologist C. Wright Mills called the "sociological imagination"—the capacity to see the connections that we as individuals have to the larger social landscape.[7]

Durkheim believed that it was a moral duty for individuals to be aware of their social bonds and obligations. A proper equilibrium between the needs of the individual and of society is required for the health of both. The recognition of the "dualism of human nature," however, has proven more difficult in modern life than Durkheim imagined, particularly in a country such as the United States where the importance of the individual has grown to impressive heights.[8]

While individualism is not a uniquely American trait, it has found particularly fertile ground in the United States. As Bellah, et al., note, "Individualism lies at the very core of American culture."[9] While Americans may voluntarily come together to form communities from time to time, they believe strongly that each individual is ultimately responsible for his or her self. Americans tend to believe that one's success or failure in life is due almost entirely to the effort, ability, values, and decision making of the individual. There are multiple and complex reasons why individualism is particularly a strong element of American culture. To simplify, however, it can be said that American individualism has its roots in Protestantism, capitalism, democracy, and the history of the western frontier.

The American Development of Utilitarian and Expressive Individualism: The Protestant Ethic, the Capitalist Ethic, and Their Discontents

As a largely Protestant country, the United States has inherited much of the individualistic ideology associated with Protestant theology. The Protestant Reformation was predicated on the idea that it is the individual's relationship with God that determines salvation. Departing from the Catholic Church's emphasis on good works, on participation in a religious community, and on a relationship with God that is mediated through a priest, the Protestant Reformation ushered in a powerful cultural emphasis on the role that the individual plays apart from a community. Rather than seeing faith as something that one naturally inherits from one's state or community, Americans tend to see faith as a deeply personal matter to be decided by each and every individual.[10] While Americans *do* come together in groups to celebrate their faith, the decision to do so is ultimately an individual one.

Protestantism also contributes to American individualism in its relationship to capitalism. As Max Weber, another early sociologist, eloquently argued in *The Protestant Ethic and the Spirit of Capitalism*, certain elements of Protestantism contributed to an ethic that fostered the development of capitalism. Without mediation through a religious community, early Protestants were filled with anxiety about their salvation. If faith alone (and not participation in religious rituals or good works) determined one's salvation, how was one to know for certain if one was saved? The Protestant sect of Calvinism offered a solution to this problem by suggesting that salvation was predestined by God. There was nothing believers could do to win salvation. They could, however, determine if they were among the saved by observing certain signs. If they worked hard in a "calling," if they were rational and methodical in specialized work, if they earned money but spent it only on essentials, if they reinvested profits rather than indulging wants, and if they lived ascetic lives, then they might be among the select few who were saved.

Such a powerful incentive to live a rational and methodical way of life provided important ingredients to capitalism. This ethic of rationality, put into motion by the spiritual needs of the Protestant, quickly became the capitalist ethic. Capitalism, for instance, requires dutiful workers and the reinvestment of capital. The rational way of life of the Protestant soon became the rational way of life for everyone. The Protestant capitalist and the Protestant worker conducted themselves in such a rational and efficient way as to compel even the non-Protestant into methodical and efficient practices in the marketplace and on the job. Otherwise, the non-Protestant would risk losing the economic competition (for profit or for jobs) to the more efficient Protestant.

The new capitalist ethic found its greatest expression in America. Ben Franklin's writing is Weber's favorite example of the capitalist ethic. In his autobiography, Franklin writes about how he managed to succeed in life through hard work, in spite of his humble origins.[11] Franklin's advice for success is indeed a perfect example of the capitalist ethic, with an emphasis on temperance, industry, frugality, sincerity, and moderation. It is not the moral content of the ethic (the formerly Protestant but now capitalist ethic) that is valuable, but the material gain that results:

> According to Franklin, those virtues, like all others, are only in so far virtues as they are actually useful to the individual, and the surrogate of mere appearance is always sufficient when it accomplishes the end in view.[12]

In *Poor Richard's Almanac* Franklin writes many pieces of advice that have since become well-ingrained "truths" known to most Americans— "Early to bed and early to rise, makes a man healthy, wealthy, and wise" and "God helps those that help themselves," among many others.[13] The authors of *Habits of the Heart* cite Franklin's lessons as the clearest example of the "utilitarian individualism" that has remained a central part of American culture:

> In short, Franklin gave classic expression to what many felt in the eighteenth century—and many have felt ever since—to be the most important thing about America: the chance for the individual to get ahead of his own initiative.[14]

Such utilitarian individualism, however, is not the only form of individualism that has taken root in the United States. As Bellah and his colleagues note, expressive individualism has arisen alongside utilitarian individualism and, in many ways, in opposition to it.

Expressive individualism has its roots not in the capitalist ethic, but in the criticism of an American culture dominated by materialistic values. The American philosophers Ralph Waldo Emerson and Henry David Thoreau gave voice to this alternative way of understanding individualism in America. Thoreau, for instance, abandoned the "fool's life" of labor and retreated alone to the wilderness to support himself on the land, to learn about himself, to be conscious of life, and to live as fully as possible. Thoreau was explicitly critical of the work ethic that most Americans accept blindly:

> Most men, even in this comparatively free country, through mere ignorance and mistake, are so occupied with the factitious cares and superfluously coarse labors of life that its finer fruits cannot be plucked by them.[15]

Thoreau condemned the "quiet desperation" suffered by most men and sought out on his own to pluck the finer fruits of life. He recognized the irony that was concealed in the utilitarian individualism of American culture: In effect, to pursue material independence through achievement in mainstream society, one had to conform to certain behaviors and practices of work. In contrast, he valued the *nonconformity* of expressive individualism. He respected the individual who rejected conventional measures of success and social pressures and instead marched to the tune of his or her own drummer:

> Why should we be in such desperate haste to succeed and in such desperate enterprises? If a man does not keep pace with his companions, perhaps it is because he hears a different drummer. Let him step to the music which he hears, however measured or far away.[16]

While Thoreau's expressive individualism is not as dominant in American culture as Franklin's utilitarian individualism, it is, nonetheless, a cultural theme that survives and finds expression in a variety of forms, including, as we shall see, in many Hollywood films.

American individualism grew not only out of the cultural roots of Protestantism and capitalism, but out of its democratic traditions as well. It is to these traditions that we now turn.

Individualism and Democracy

Just as Protestantism broke with Catholicism over the issue of the believer's relationship with God, the United States broke with England over the issue of the citizen's relationship to the state. In both cases the rights of the individual challenged the hierarchy of an aristocratic power. In theory, a democratic government values the opinion of each individual citizen. Each citizen, regardless of social status or wealth, is entitled to certain rights under a democratic constitution. Such a belief in the equality of opportunity (whether it is realized or not) is a central part of the picture Americans paint about themselves. It is also what Alexis de Tocqueville, the nineteenth-century French theorist, found to be particularly remarkable about the American experiment. For Tocqueville, democracy created conditions of equality and a belief in the autonomy of the individual. Under such conditions, however, Tocqueville feared that the individual would lose sight of society and social obligations. In fact, it is in Tocqueville's masterpiece *Democracy in America* (based on his travels in the United States near the middle of the nineteenth century) that the term *individualism* was first coined:

> Individualism is a mature and calm feeling, which disposes each member of the community to sever himself from the mass of his fellows and to draw apart with his family and his friends, so that after he has thus formed a little circle of his own, he willingly leaves society at large to itself.[17]

For Tocqueville, the repudiation of aristocratic rule in favor of democracy diminished the social ties that citizens have to the greater community. Democracy, as he wrote, "breaks the chain" that connects everyone from "the peasant to the king." Anticipating Durkheim's concern, Tocqueville feared that individuals in a democracy would begin to see only themselves in the present moment and not their relationship to groups, institutions, or history:[18]

> Thus not only does democracy make every man forget his ancestors, but it hides his descendants and separates his contemporaries from him; it throws him back forever upon himself alone and threatens in the end to confine him entirely within the solitude of his own heart.[19]

Tocqueville's observations of American culture were filled with both admiration and concern. As we shall see in later chapters, the contradictory elements of American culture that Tocqueville noted—the brilliance of equality and individualism and the denial of community—find expression still in Hollywood films.

In addition to its religious, economic, and democratic origins, individualism in the United States was encouraged by the cultural characteristics that developed in the country's expansion into the western frontier.

Individualism and the American Frontier

American individualism also has roots in the particular history of the growth of the United States into the western portions of the North American continent. The expansion of the Union into the frontier helped to create an American character marked by independence, adventure, and endless possibilities for free men. This "rugged individualism" grew out of a political belief that Americans had God-given domain over the North American continent. This "manifest destiny" was embodied in the pioneers who left their homes, moved west, and, with the help of the U.S. government, conquered the Native peoples who lived in the western territories. Such expansionism, and the pioneers who colonized the West, contributed to a particular type of individual character that has become an important part of American culture: the cowboy. The historian Frederick Jackson Turner made the argument that the independent American character was largely shaped by the experiences of frontier life:

> The result is that to the frontier the American intellect owes its striking characteristics. The coarseness and strength combined with acuteness and inquisitiveness; that practical, inventive turn of mind, quick to find expedients; that masterful grasp of material things, lacking in the artistic but powerful to effect great ends; that restless, nervous energy; that dominant individualism, working for good and for evil, and withal that buoyancy and exuberance which comes with freedom—these are the traits of the frontier.[20]

Turner's thesis about the importance of the frontier to the American character has been challenged by new western historians.[21] Nevertheless, even if the frontier individualism is in historical reality a myth, the truth remains that Americans *believe* the myth. That is, Americans collectively believe that the frontier experience helped to forge the individualism of the American character. This belief, in and of itself, is enough to make frontier individualism a part of the American national culture. As the sociologist W. I. Thomas observed, if an actor defines a situation to be real, it is real in its consequences.[22] And those consequences can still be seen. Americans remain a very mobile people. We are not often committed strongly to a geographic place. If opportunities arise elsewhere, we pull up our roots and plant them elsewhere. The frontier is still alive in the hearts of many Americans.

Individualism is characteristic of most Americans, but it is particularly strong among members of the middle class. In fact, if one wants to understand the nuances of American culture, it is perhaps best to start with an inquiry into the nature of the American middle class.

The Middle Class and American Culture

Americans, generally, are not comfortable talking in terms of social class. The individualistic orientation of most Americans leads them to overlook *group* differences based on education, occupation, income, or social prestige. Such differences, to the average American mind, are best explained by looking at the characteristics of the individual. Not surprisingly, most Americans, when forced to characterize their class position, report that they are in the "middle class." What this means to them, however, is not exactly clear. Most likely, it means that they know people who are wealthier than them and they know people who are poorer than them. Therefore, they are, by definition, in the middle. The term *middle class*, however, does have a more precise meaning. While sociologists disagree about how best to measure the middle class, most are in agreement that there are objective criteria that distinguish the middle class from the upper and lower classes (that is, class is not just a matter of subjective identification, but of objective measurement).

I define the middle class broadly as those members of the American population who have attended at least several years of college (and usually have a BA degree), are dependent primarily upon their educational skills and credentials to earn a living, work as white-collar managers or professionals, earn most of their income from a salary rather than hourly wages or assets, and have a moderate amount of wealth, usually accumulated in the equity of their homes. They are most likely to live in the suburbs. While sociologist Martin Marger estimates that the middle class constitutes as much as 50 percent of the American population, social critic Barbara Ehrenreich suggests that the figure is no more than 20 percent of the population.[23] Part of the difference is due to the fact that Ehrenreich excludes from her count the lower middle class (those who may not have a college degree, who earn a lower salary as a result, and who work in lower and midlevel management positions). Working with my definition, I estimate that the middle class constitutes approximately 30 percent of the American population.

While not a numerical majority, the middle class has become a hegemonic cultural force in American culture. That is, middle-class life has been defined as the social norm, and the middle-class experience is generally understood as *the* American experience. As Barbara Ehrenreich notes in her social analysis of American culture, "the professional, and largely white, middle class is taken as a social norm—a bland and neutral mainstream—from which every other group or class is ultimately a kind of deviation."[24] The central place that the middle class occupies in American culture is due in part to the central place it occupies in the current organization of the American economy.

After World War II, the United States experienced a tremendous period of economic growth, shifting from an industrial-based economy with a strong "blue-collar" (wage laborers) working-class base to a postindustrial, information-based economy with a growing number of "white-collar" (salaried professional) middle-class workers. In the coming decades the computer revolution, together with the increasing export of industrial jobs from the United States to foreign countries (where the cost of labor was cheaper), further increased the prominent position the educated middle class played in the new American economy. These economic transformations were recognized early by such sociologists as David Riesman and C. Wright Mills, who noted that what was developing was a "new" middle class. The independent businessman and the entrepreneur of the "old" middle class were being replaced by the white-collar employee who worked for others in bureaucratic and corporate organizations.[25] Riesman and Mills also noted that the new middle-class worker was emerging not only as an important economic player in the United States, but as an important cultural player as well. If you want to understand what it means to be an American in the postwar period, Mills argued, you have to understand the world of the new middle class:

> By examining white-collar life, it is possible to learn something about what is becoming more typically 'American' than the frontier character probably ever was. What must be grasped is the picture of society as a great salesroom, an enormous file, and incorporated brain, a new universe of management and manipulation. By understanding these diverse white-collar worlds, one can also understand better the shape and meaning of modern society as a whole, as well as the simple hopes and complex anxieties that grip all the people who are sweating it out in the middle of the twentieth century.[26]

The most eloquent and persuasive narrators of the American middle-class cultural story are Robert Bellah and his co-authors of *Habits of the Heart*. Interested in exploring the terrain of American culture, Bellah and his colleagues talked to middle-class Americans about their jobs, families, communities, and religious faith.[27] Their interviews touched on the ways in which members of the middle class understand their individual lives and how they relate to their communities. Bellah and company show how the middle-class values of educational and occupational achievement, calculating rationality, and individualism (rather than a commitment to community, tradition, and cooperation) have defined not just the professional lives of middle-class Americans, but also how they govern their lives generally:

> The middle-class is defined not merely by the desire for material benefit but by a conscious calculating effort to move up the ladder of success . . . for middle class Americans, a calculating attitude toward educational and occupational choice has been essential and has often spilled over into determining criteria for the choice of spouse, friends, and voluntary associations.[28]

While the lower and upper social classes are not as defined by individualism or as dependent upon it as the middle class is, they have been affected by the ethic of individualism nonetheless. In contrast to the middle class, however, these other social classes are oriented more toward community, history, tradition, and ethnicity than individual achievement and calculating rationality. Bellah and co-authors argue that the lower and upper classes find meaning not only in their individualism, but also in their social relationships. These social relationships help to combat the sense of loneliness and emptiness that individualism can otherwise encourage.

Without such ties to a community, history, or tradition, middle-class Americans often feel alienated. In spite of its cultural power, there is a tension and ambiguity that pervades middle-class individualism. The middle class longs for the sense of community and shared meanings that their ethic of individualism denies. The longing is real, but they lack the language to articulate it. As the authors of *Habits of the Heart* put it:

> We deeply feel the emptiness of a life without sustaining social commitments. Yet we are hesitant to articulate our sense that we need one another as much as we need to stand alone, for fear that if we did we would lose our independence altogether.[29]

Hollywood has long represented the middle-class ethic of individualism. As Bellah, et al., note, the Western and the hard-boiled detective film genres have depended upon the heroic efforts of a lone outsider who has few social attachments and constraints.

The high school genre, too, depends upon such lone heroes who stand outside society. As we shall see, there is very little use for history, community, or tradition in these high school films. Instead, messages of utilitarian and expressive individualism predominate. Because these high school films are made by and largely consumed by members of the middle class, and because middle-class culture is the hegemonic culture in the United States, these high school films tend to reflect middle-class worldviews and assumptions.

Understanding how Hollywood uses such middle-class American values to tell stories about high school, however, requires an understanding of what it means to be an adolescent in the United States and how those meanings vary by the social class of the adolescent.

Teenagers and American Culture

As soon as the young American approaches manhood, the ties of filial obedience are relaxed day by day; master of his thoughts, he is soon master of his conduct. In America there is, strictly speaking, no adolescence: at the close of boyhood the man appears and begins to trace out his own path.[30]

—Alexis de Tocqueville

Sociologists tend to see adolescence as socially constructed. That is, even if puberty marks the biological ending of childhood, it is society that determines when one becomes an adult and how the period between childhood and adulthood is socially organized. As Tocqueville observed, the existence of adolescence is culturally variable. While the American child of 1830 may not have experienced much of an adolescence, American youth today experience an extended period of adolescence, often well beyond the teenage years. Does adulthood in the United States today begin at age eighteen, when voting is legally permitted in the United States? Or is it rather at age twenty-one, when drinking alcohol is legally permitted? Perhaps it has nothing to do with age and legal recognition per se, but is marked by the end of formal education and the beginning of full-time work. If that is the case, then adulthood may begin for some people at age seventeen and for others not until the age of thirty or later. The boundaries of adolescence are not always clear. A sociological view suggests that the definition of adolescence and the meanings we attach to it are always shifting, particularly in concert with the shifting of the economic organization of social life.

As a recognized stage of life between childhood and adulthood, adolescence is of relatively recent invention.[31] Before the era of industrialization in Western societies, there was little division of labor among home, work, and school in nonwealthy families. The family was the basic economic unit of production, the site of domestic life, and the place of learning for children. There was little question about the future of the children—they would likely inherit an occupation and social status directly from their parents and live lives similar to those of their parents. There was very little sense of adolescence as a time of preparation for and transition to adulthood because the there was very little uncertainty about what the child would be preparing for or transitioning to.[32]

With the spread of industrialization and urbanization, however, there eventually grew a division of labor between home, work, and school. The futures of middle-class children were not as predetermined as they had been in the past. Adolescence became recognized as a stage of life as youth began to prepare for their new and somewhat uncertain adult roles. G. Stanley Hall's 1904 publication of *Adolesence: Its Psychology and Its Relations to Physiology, Anthropology, Sociology, Sex, Crime, Religion, and Education* became a particularly influential source for the new understanding of adolescence.[33] Hall advocated adult-sponsored institutions to help guide adolescents through this particularly difficult period of life. A relatively new institution, the high school, became an important incubator for the adult futures of these children. Until the 1930s high school was predominantly an institution for children of the middle class, and it was in the high school years that adolescence became solidified as a distinct stage of life. As historians of adolescence John Modell and Madeline Goodman write:

> Adolescence, as it developed conceptually in the late nineteenth and twentieth centuries, was first and foremost a middle-class creation. It was a notion that initially made sense in those institutional contexts for young people that promoted their socialization as adults able to hold their own in the competitive middle class. Initially, young people not of the middle class were often perceived as having no adolescence.[34]

The high school and notions of adolescence, however, were undergoing profound changes in the early part of the twentieth century. Public high schools gradually expanded to serve a more diverse segment of the population. Capitalists began to demand skilled workers, and members of the working class demanded opportunities for upward social mobility.[35] As a result, public schooling expanded to serve more members of the working class. Around the same time, the United States experienced a dramatic increase in the number of new immigrants to its cities. Many people became concerned that the children of these immigrants would not have American values and would not speak English if they were not properly educated.[36] Concerns about juvenile delinquency, too, spurred efforts to educate and socialize young people of all backgrounds in public schools. By the time of the Great Depression, unemployment forced many more youth out of the workforce and into the high school. As a result of these changes, a record high 65 percent of all American teens were enrolled in high school in 1936.[37]

It is not an accident that the emergence of the adolescent as a social and cultural category in the United States coincided with the profound social and economic changes in the first half of the twentieth century. As a distinct phase of life, adolescence is not "natural." Instead, it is the result of social, cultural, economic, and political developments that have created it and imbue it with certain meanings and expectations. Adolescents are responding not only to their biological development, but also to the social demands placed upon them by the organization of society.

Neither is it a coincidence that the emergence of the "new" white-collar middle class occurred at the same time that "teenagers" were *fully* recognized as a distinct social group in the United States with their own cultural characteristics. In fact, it was not until the Second World War that the term *teenager* was commonly used.[38] Historian Grace Palladino shows how the emergence of the teenage culture in the 1940s and 1950s coincided with the development of an economy that exploited the youthful consumer. She argues that the growth of teen culture was due primarily to "a changing economy, a national culture of consumption and individualism, and the age-graded, adolescent world of the high school."[39]

The emergence of the "teenager" as a distinct social, cultural, and economic group in postwar America encouraged the development of the "teen-pic," a genre of films specifically directed to an audience of adolescents. In fact, the film scholar Donald Doherty argues that in the 1950s Hollywood films took a distinct marketing turn to capture the new teen audience, thereby "juvenilizing" most filmmaking.[40] It has been said that James Dean's character in 1955's *Rebel Without a Cause* became the defining image of the American teenager (at least the white middle-class teenager) and helped to define the age group.[41] In fact, a 1975 television documentary about Dean was titled *The First American Teenager*.

The emergence of the new teenage social group, however, caused a great deal of alarm in the United States. Americans tend to have mixed feelings about young people. While adolescence represents a great deal of creative potential to Americans, it also causes a great deal of anxiety.[42] Fears of juvenile delinquency reached a fevered pitch in the 1950s. Films such as *Blackboard Jungle* (released the same year as *Rebel Without a Cause*) spoke directly to this national hysteria. Academic studies, too, sounded the alarm about this new "adolescent society." In 1961 sociologist James Coleman argued that high school students constituted their own culture, with their own value system that was at odds with the values of adult society.[43] Coleman was particularly concerned that students seemed to care more about athletics and popularity than they cared about academics. Concerns about youth continue today, with some arguing that adolescents have become a scapegoat for the ills of the rest of society.[44]

Whether viewed as a promise or a threat, adolescence had arrived as a full-fledged stage of life by the middle of the twentieth century. Furthermore, it was a stage of life that seemed to be expanding. As high school expanded to members of the working class, as the technical requirements for jobs increased, as competition for employment put pressure on youth to pursue more credentials in college and graduate school, and as the average age of marriage increased, the period between sexual maturity and full adult status grew longer and more visible in our culture. Adolescence continues to be the subject of national fascination and anxiety, as the spate of teen movies released in the past few years attests.

If sociologists are correct that adolescence is dependent upon social, cultural, and economic conditions to define its boundaries (rather than biology), then what constitutes the essential features of adolescence in the twentieth and twenty-first centuries in the United States? I would suggest that adolescence today is marked by two distinct social processes. First, the adolescent must search for an identity. Modern American adolescents must make many important decisions about who they are as youth and who they want to be as adults. Nothing is certain in this increasingly postmodern world. Teenagers must decide what their values are, what their interests are, how they should present their "self" to others, what social groups to associate with, what activities to participate in, and what racial, gender, class, and sexual identity to assume. In short, they must come to terms with their expressive individualism. Second, the adolescent must search for independence. They must make plans about their schooling, decide what career to pursue, terminate the dependence on their parents, take responsibility for their individual lives, and figure out how to support themselves materially in a capitalist society. In short, they must in all practical terms exercise their utilitarian individualism.

As will become clear in chapters 3 and 4, however, there are often very different cultural standards applied to American adolescents depending upon their social class position. In short, I argue that American culture expects poor youth to exercise utilitarian individualism to climb out of poverty, while it allows more freedom to middle-class youth to exercise their expressive individualism as they search for a meaningful identity.

Finally, it should be noted that adolescence is also a metaphor in American culture for the possibilities of the future. High school films speak directly to an audience of youth, but they also speak indirectly to a middle-aged audience. The theme of possibility is one that the middle-aged American does not want to abandon. Anything is considered possible in our individualistic culture. If you are unhappy in your job, your family, or the way you express yourself, you can always change. The themes and messages of high school films resonate with Americans of all ages on many different levels. They express the possibility that if you work a little harder you can be successful, the possibility that if you follow your heart you can discover your true self, the possibility that you can find true love, and the possibility that your worth as a person is not measured by your performance in competitive capitalism or bureaucratic organizations. In this sense, too, the frontier is still alive in the United States. It is an adolescent frontier. These films permit the exploration of this frontier by audience members of all ages.[45]

38

A Final Note

The themes of American culture introduced in the previous pages will surface again, sometimes explicitly and sometimes implicitly, in the coming chapters. In particular, the various strains of American individualism, the hegemonic perspective of the American middle class, and the search for independence and identity among Americans of all ages will be explored in the analysis of the high school film genres that follows. As will become clear in the coming chapters, the American urban, suburban, and private school films are dominated by the theme of individualism. Whether utilitarian or expressive individualism predominates depends upon the social class of the students who are featured in the film. Regardless of the theme, the movies in all three subgenres are told from the perspective of the middle class. The patterns of each subgenre reveal a particular image that middle-class Americans tend to have about education, adolescence, and inequality. The patterns of the foreign films analyzed in chapter 6, however, stand in stark contrast to the themes of the American films. In particular, the triumph of the heroic individual over antagonistic forces is not found in the foreign school films. Instead, the foreign school films depict individuals who are defeated by or who attempt to escape oppressive social forces. The themes of these foreign school films are the antithesis of the individualism so prominently on display in the American high school films.

Films do indeed reflect something real about the cultures that produce and consume them. In the cinematic images of high schools and adolescents, Hollywood reveals some of the characteristics and contradictions of American life. It is my hope that the analysis of the films in the coming pages can help the reader to shed light on some of the mysteries of American culture. Motion pictures provide an entertaining and enlightening laboratory in which to examine culture. However, it must be said that this exploration takes place within the very culture it seeks to understand. My analysis and the reader's interpretation, therefore, may be colored by our own social location and our unique lived experiences. Therefore, an analysis of these films, these curious cultural artifacts, can not only help us to understand something about American culture, but, if done attentively, also help us to understand something about our selves and our relationships to American culture. Hollywood may not have much of C. Wright Mills's "sociological imagination," but that does not prevent us from exercising our own.

Notes

1. As will be explained in chapter 5, there is a difference between the Catholic school films and the elite private school films. When I refer to the "private school films" in this chapter, I am referring primarily to the nonreligious elite private school films.

2. There is an urban teen genre of films that is not represented in this sample of high school films. Films such as *Straight Out of Brooklyn* (1991), *Boyz 'N the Hood* (1991), *Menace II Society* (1993), *South Central* (1992), and *Juice* (1992) are African American urban teen dramas that do not use education or the high school as a central feature of their story. Following Timothy Shary's (2002) genre categorization, I have excluded these films from the high school genre. Furthermore, Hollywood endorses this separate categorization as well—the urban teen genre has its own spoof film, *Don't be a Menace to South Central When Drinking Your Juice in the Hood* (1996). For the same reasons, I have excluded teen horror and slasher films from this study. Once again, Shary categorizes the genre separately from the school genre—as does Hollywood, which has produced the teen horror spoofs of *Scream* (1996) and its sequels and the *Scary Movie* (2000) series, which is itself a spoof of the *Scream* films.

3. Bellah, Robert N., Richard Madsen, William M. Sullivan, Ann Swidler, and Steven M.Tipton. 1985. *Habits of the Heart: Individualism and Commitment in American Life.* New York: Harper and Row.

4. *Cultural capital* refers to the stock of cultural knowledge, styles, and skills acquired through school and family upbringing. Cultural capital is also used as a marker to distinguish one's place in relation to others within the social world. The more privileged one's position is in society, the more cultural capital there is readily at one's disposal, the more valuable it is, and the easier it is to acquire more. See Bourdieu, Pierre. 1977. "Cultural Reproduction and Social Reproduction." In *Power and Ideology in Education.* Jerome Karabel and A. H. Halsey, editors. New York: Oxford University Press.

5. Slater, Philip. 1976. *The Pursuit of Loneliness: American Culture at the Breaking Point.* Boston: Beacon Press, p. 15.

6. Durkheim, Emile. 1984. *The Division of Labor in Society.* Translated by W. D. Halls. New York: Free Press, p. 333.

7. Mills, C. Wright. 1959. *The Sociological Imagination.* New York: Oxford University Press.

40

8. For more on these issues, see Bellah, Robert N. 1973. "Introduction." In Durkheim, Emile. 1973. "Individualism and the Intellectuals" and "The Dualism of Human Nature and Its Social Conditions." In *Emile Durkheim on Morality and Society*. Chicago: University of Chicago Press; and Durkheim, Emile. 1973. *Moral Education: A Study in the Theory and Application of the Sociology of Education*. New York: Free Press.

9. Bellah, et al., *Habits of the Heart*, p. 142.

10. See Varenne, Herve. 1977. *Americans Together: Structured Diversity in a Midwestern Town*. New York: Teachers College Press.

11. Franklin, Benjamin. 1964. *The Autobiography of Benjamin Franklin*. Edited by Leonard W. Labaree. New Haven, CT: Yale University Press.

12. Weber, Max. 1985. *The Protestant Ethic and the Spirit of Capitalism*. Translated by Talcott Parsons. London: Counterpoint, p. 52.

13. Cited in Bellah, et al., *Habits of the Heart*, p. 32.

14. Bellah, et al., *Habits of the Heart*, p. 33.

15. Thoreau, Henry David. 1960. *Walden*. New York: Signet, p. 9.

16. Ibid., p. 216.

17. Tocqueville, Alexis de. 1945. *Democracy in America*. Translated by Henry Reeve. New York: Vintage Books, p. 104.

18. There is, however, an antidote to rampant individualism, and that, too, is found in the democratic institutions of America. Tocqueville saw in political freedom and the voluntary associations that constitute civil society opportunities for Americans to exercise their individualism in the direction of the common good. Tocqueville's prescription of participation in voluntary associations is similar to Durkheim's hope that individuals would be integrated in and regulated by social groups. Whether or not Americans avail themselves of this opportunity and contribute to the social good through participation in civil society, however, is still hotly debated today, as illustrated by the wide attention received by Robert Putnam's 2000 national best-selling book *Bowling Alone: The Collapse and Revival of American Community*. New York: Touchstone. While there is great nostalgia in the United States for the values of community, where strong ties of "social capital" help individuals to feel that they are always "at home," the reality is that even when they join groups, Americans remain deeply individualistic.

19. Tocqueville, *Democracy in America*, p. 106.

20. Turner, Frederick Jackson. 1985. *The Frontier in American History*. Malabar, FL: Robert E. Krieger Publishing, p. 37.

21. See, for instance, Hine, Robert V., and John Mack Faragher. 2000. *The American West: A New Interpretive History*. New Haven, CT: Yale University Press.

22. Thomas, W. I. 1928. *The Child in America: Behavior Problems and Programs*. New York: Knopf.

23. Marger, Martin M. 2002. *Social Inequality: Pattern and Processes*. Second Edition. Boston: McGraw Hill; and Ehrenreich, Barbara. 1990. *Fear of Falling: The Inner Life of the Middle Class*. New York: Harper Press.

24. Ehrenreich, *Fear of Falling*, p. 3.

25. Riesman, David, with Nathan Glazer and Reuel Denney. 1961. *The Lonely Crowd: A Study of the Changing American Character*. New Haven, CT: Yale University Press.

26. Mills, C. Wright. 1956. *White Collar: The American Middle Classes*. New York: Oxford University Press, p. xv.

27. See also Gans, Herbert J. 1988. *Middle American Individualism: The Future of Liberal Democracy*. New York: Free Press.

28. Bellah, et al., *Habits of the Heart*, p. 148.

29. Ibid., p. 151.

30. Tocqueville, *Democracy in America*, p. 202.

31. See Palladino, Grace. 1996. *Teenagers: An American History*. New York: Basic Books; Hine, Thomas. 1999. *The Rise and Fall of the American Teenager*. New York: Perennial; Kett, Joseph F. 1977. *Rites of Passage: Adolescence in America, 1790 to the Present*. New York: Basic Books; and Modell, John, and Madeline Goodman. 1990. "Historical Perspectives." In *At the Threshold: The Developing Adolescent*. S. Shirley Feldman and Glen R. Elliott, editors. Cambridge, MA: Harvard University Press.

32. See Modell and Goodman, "Historical Perspectives."

33. Hall, Granville Stanley. 1904. *Adolescence: Its Psychology and Its Relations to Physiology, Anthropology, Sociology, Sex, Crime, Religion, and Education*. New York: D. Appleton and Company.

34. Modell and Goodman, "Historical Perspectives," p. 102.

35. See Katznelson, Ira, and Margaret Weir. 1985. *Schooling for All: Class, Race, and the Decline of the Democratic Ideal*. Berkeley: University of California Press.

36. See Katz, Michael B. 1987. *Reconstructing American Education*. Cambridge, MA: Harvard University Press.

37. Palladino, *Teenagers*, p. 5.

38. Palladino, *Teenagers*.

39. Ibid., p. xxii.

40. Doherty, Thomas. 2002. *Teenagers and Teenpics: The Juvenilization of American Movies in the 1950s*. Philadelphia: Temple University Press.

41. See Lewis, Jon. 1992. *The Road to Romance and Ruin: Teen Films and Youth Culture*. New York: Routledge.

42. See Modell and Goodman, "Historical Perspectives."

43. Coleman, James S. 1961. *The Adolescent Society*. New York: Free Press.

44. Males, Mike A. 1999. *Framing Youth: 10 Myths About the Next Generation*. Monroe, ME: Common Courage Press.

45. According to data from the Motion Picture Association of America (the "2003 U.S. Movie Attendance Study"), 27 percent of all moviegoers in 2003 were between the age of twelve and twenty, 21 percent were between the ages of twenty-one and twenty-nine, 19 percent were between the ages of thirty and thirty-nine, 14 percent were between the ages of forty and forty-nine, 11 percent were between the ages of fifty and fifty-nine, and 8 percent were over the age of sixty. While twelve-to twenty-four-year-olds are overrepresented among moviegoers compared with their numbers in the population, it is noteworthy that 61 percent of all moviegoers are twenty-five years of age or older. In spite of the "juvenilization of American movies" that film scholar Thomas Doherty, *Teenagers and Teenpics*, writes about, the movies still offer a powerful appeal to moviegoers of all ages.

3

Fighting the Culture of Poverty

The Teacher as the Urban School Cowboy

What is it you want? With your brains you can have it. Knowledge will get it for you.

— Mr. Mason in *Cooley High*

The mind is like a muscle. If you want it to be really powerful you have to work it out. Each new fact gives you another choice.

— Ms. Johnson in *Dangerous Minds*

Almost without exception, the American urban public school films celebrate utilitarian individualism. A middle-class teacher-hero (an urban school cowboy, if you will) rides into the classroom and rescues low-income inner-city students who are wallowing in a culture of poverty. In order to be rescued from academic failure, these students must adopt the middle-class values of hard work, materialism, and individual achievement. These films suggest that if only these "at-risk" students were to adopt a solid work ethic, they could attend college and secure reliable middle-class jobs. While not entirely without merit, the messages of these movies tend to ignore the structural obstacles to academic and occupational success (such as unequal school funding, lack of employment in the inner city, lack of affordable housing, lack of affordable health and child care, poor public transportation, culturally biased curricula, class- and race-based discrimination in the classroom, and so forth). As sociological research has shown, it takes much more than individual effort to succeed. Also, while the potential of utilitarian individualism is celebrated in the urban school films, they neglect to depict the expressive individualism of these low-income students. That is, the students in the urban school films are not depicted as whole human beings—they are not allowed to fully express themselves as free individuals. Hollywood only gives license to the middle-class students in the suburban school films analyzed in chapter 4 to express such individuality. This contrast between the urban and suburban public school films has been in evidence for at least fifty years.

The now classic 1955 film *Blackboard Jungle* is the granddaddy of urban public school films. It opens with this serious message about juvenile delinquency and American education:

> Today we are concerned with juvenile delinquency—its causes and its effects. We are especially concerned when this delinquency boils over into our schools. The scenes and incidents depicted here are fictional. However, we believe that public awareness is a first step towards a remedy for any problem. It is in this spirit and with this faith that *Blackboard Jungle* was produced.

The film, the first set to a rock-and-roll soundtrack, graphically portrays poor and working-class urban youth assaulting teachers, stealing automobiles, disrespecting authority, and dismissing the importance of an education. It does not exactly represent the peaceful schools and studious youth that Americans now believe to have characterized public education in the 1950s. It is surprising to audiences today, and it was shocking to audiences in 1955. This film is not intended to be mere entertainment. This is a film with a social message. It takes itself very seriously as a social document about real social problems in the nation's real schools. The theatrical trailer advertises the film as "fiction torn from big city modern savagery . . . where teenage savages turn big city schools into jungles." Its negative representation of American schools was of such concern to government authorities that they asked MGM to withdraw the film from the 1955 Venice Film Festival.[1] In the midst of the Cold War, *Blackboard Jungle* did not paint a picture that Americans wanted broadcast to an international audience. It was seen by some as a film that could be used as communist propaganda. Darryl F. Zanuck, the chief of rival film studio Fox, appreciated the quality of the film, but did not think it was politically appropriate to release it:

> I felt when I originally saw the picture that in spite of its quality, it could only give an erroneous impression of the American school system to European audiences. I also felt that it would be welcomed with open arms by the Communists.[2]

For many reasons, the film clearly struck a chord with Americans. It also seems to have struck a chord with generations of screenwriters, directors, and producers. *Blackboard Jungle* is the film that establishes the urban high school film genre, and the one from which all of the other urban school films lift their major plot elements and characters. Nearly all of the urban school films discussed in this chapter owe a great debt to *Blackboard Jungle*.

The basic plot of the film is quite simple, and likely familiar even to contemporary film audiences who have never seen the film. Richard

Dadier, a World War II navy veteran with a newly minted teaching credential, applies for a job teaching English at a rough-and-tumble New York City public high school that serves an impoverished and racially mixed student population. Mr. Dadier is frustrated with the ineffective school administration, the cynical teachers, and the hostile students. He struggles throughout the film to "get through" to his students. His job is made particularly difficult by a gang of students that disrupts his class, attacks him, and harasses his pregnant wife. In spite of these obstacles he is determined to reach these students. He uses unorthodox methods to get the attention of his students, to convince them to care about their education, and to raise their academic expectations. He also establishes a personal relationship with one particularly promising but troubled student. In spite of some modest success, however, he nearly quits his job in anger and frustration at his apparent inability to reform these "savage" students. Yet he soon changes his mind after he realizes that he is actually getting through to them and that they truly appreciate his efforts to help them. MGM/UA Home Video describes the film this way:

> Newcomer Richard Dadier can understand why his fellow teachers have given up on their students at North Manual High. Raised in a big city slum, these kids aren't just mischievous teens, but vicious young hoodlums well on their way to careers of crime and violence. Determined to reach them, Dadier stages an uphill battle, defying their threats and brutal beatings until he's forced into a final, winner-take-all confrontation . . . where all he has left to lose is life itself.[3]

By 1995 the Cold War was over, but there was still a tremendous concern about the "crisis" in public education.[4] While the United States, including its public schools, had changed significantly in the forty years since *Blackboard Jungle* was released, Hollywood's representation of urban high schools had not changed at all. *Dangerous Minds* premiered in 1995 and was, in many ways, the same movie as *Blackboard Jungle*. Coolio's "Gangster's Paradise," rather than Bill Haley's "Rock Around the Clock," plays in the background during the opening credits. In nearly all other respects, however, the passage of forty years had not had much of an effect on how Hollywood understood urban education. Hollywood Picture Home Video describes *Dangerous Minds* as follows:

> Former U.S. Marine LouAnne Johnson [is] a first-time high school teacher, assigned to a class of tough-but-smart inner city students. When conventional methods fail to reach them, the feisty Ms. Johnson tries the unconventional—defying the rules and creating her own curriculum! In the process, she instills a new self-confidence in her students—motivating them towards their greatest potential.[5]

Sound familiar? Both Ms. Johnson and Mr. Dadier are military veterans and first-time teachers. They each teach English to a classroom of low-income, racially mixed inner-city students. They are each surprised and frustrated by the hostility they initially encounter in the classroom. Yet neither of them surrenders to cynicism as many of their fellow teachers do. They are each driven to succeed against the odds. Neither of them finds the out-of-touch administrators or the traditional curriculum to be particularly helpful. Therefore, they each use their own unique and unconventional methods to get through to these low-income urban school students. They each try to convince their students that school is valuable and that they have the ability to achieve academic success provided they put their minds to the task. In the climax of each film Ms. Johnson and Mr. Dadier momentarily lose faith in their students and in their ability to reach them effectively. Both Mr Dadier and Ms. Johnson, however, survive the crisis and decide to continue teaching after their students show academic progress and a sincere appreciation for the efforts of their teacher.[6]

Nearly all of the urban school films resemble the basic plot of *Blackboard Jungle* and *Dangerous Minds*. In spite of the seriousness with which these urban school films take themselves as documents of real social problems, these films teach us much more about American culture (specifically, how Americans make sense of education and inequality) than they do about the actual condition of public schools and the attitude of urban youth.

In his critique of *Dangerous Minds*, the educational theorist Henry Giroux argues that the movie represents "whiteness" as the "archetype of rationality, authority, and cultural standards."[7] While I agree generally with Giroux's critique of *Dangerous Minds* (and, by extension, a critique of many of the other urban school films as well), I believe that these urban school films as a whole are more likely to represent *middle-class* values, not necessarily whiteness, as the archetype of rationality, authority, and cultural standards.

While the students in these urban school films are very often African American and Latino, and race is certainly a relevant factor in the story, the social class differences between the students and their teacher-heroes are more significant than the racial differences between them. The middle-class protagonists of *Halls of Anger, Lean on Me, 187, Cooley High, Detention* (1998), and *Stand and Deliver*, for instance, are all African American or Latino. Also, there are white working-class students in need of salvation from a middle-class hero in *Blackboard Jungle, Class of 1984, Teachers, The Beat, Summer School, Wildcats,* and *Cheaters*.

Americans generally lack the cultural language to articulate an understanding of social class. To the extent that they recognize social inequality, they often name it in racial terms. Racial differences in these films, for instance, are very often conflated with and often a stand-in for underlying social class differences. I agree with the social critic Barbara Ehrenreich when she notes in her review of *The Wild One*, *Rebel Without a Cause*, and *Blackboard Jungle* that these films deliver "impeccable middle-class messages: Crime doesn't pay; authority figures are usually right; you can get ahead by studying."[8]

I argue in this chapter that the urban school films represent a middle-class American fantasy about the dynamics of social inequality and education. With the dramatic backdrop of troubled urban public schools, Hollywood reinforces cultural myths about the causes of and prescriptions for poverty. Specifically, these Hollywood films about urban public schools suggest that low-income inner-city students need to believe in themselves, believe in the American dream, believe in the power of an education, work hard, and make better choices in their lives in order to escape their culture of poverty. The academic failure of students in poverty, according to American cultural beliefs and the fantasies of Hollywood, is due entirely to the attitude and behavior of the individual and not to any obstacles in the social structure.

Remarkably, as we will see in chapter 4, Hollywood completely ignores academic achievement in the suburban school films. In these films middle-class students are *not* expected to work hard and excel in school. Instead, they are expected to find their true selves and to fully realize their expressive individualism. In contrast, Hollywood expects impoverished urban school students to become utilitarian individuals. If only urban school students would act according to the pragmatic advice of Benjamin Franklin, they would become responsible and self-sufficient.

A Cinematic Culture of Poverty

Lose no time; be always employ'd in something useful; cut off all unnecessary actions.[9]

—Benjamin Franklin

In *Blackboard Jungle*, *Dangerous Minds*, and most of the other urban high school films, the plot revolves almost exclusively around the activities of one particular classroom of rowdy students and their heroic teacher in a troubled and violent school. The students in this class are depicted homogeneously—they all share similar social class characteristics and similar problems. The audience is rarely offered a glimpse into the complexities of their individual characters, their histories, their identities, or their families (these student complexities are given more flesh in the suburban high school films discussed in the next chapter). The urban high school students, for the most part, are from lower- and working-class homes, are often nonwhite (but not exclusively so), come from broken families who do not understand or do not care much about their child's education, have low educational aspirations and expectations, behave poorly in the classroom, and express a great deal of frustration with the formal structure of the school.

The students in these films represent the working- and lower-class populations as they are stereotypically imagined by suburban middle-class Americans. These students represent what middle-class people fear most about low-income urban youth: that they have no family values or work ethic; that they are out of control, loud, disobedient, violent, lazy, and addicted to drugs; and that they reject dominant social institutions. The rejection of the school is particularly offensive to members of the middle class since they are largely dependent upon educational credentials for occupational attainment and because historically schools have served their interests quite well.[10]

Cameron McCarthy and co-authors have argued that such stereotypical notions are the result of psychological projections—that middle-class suburbanites project these images onto the residents of inner cities so as to relieve the burden of carrying such negative characteristics of themselves. In other words, the self-identity of the middle-class suburban resident is formed in opposition to the inner-city resident, who is imagined to be impoverished both economically and morally. The growing social distance between suburban and urban America is reflected in the exaggerated representations of inner-city residents in the popular media:

> As tax-based revenues, resources, and services followed America's fleeing middle classes out of the city, a great gulf opened up between the suburban dweller and America's inner-city resident. Into this void contemporary television, film, and popular culture entered creating the most poignantly sordid fantasies of inner-city degeneracy and moral decrepitude. These representations of urban life would serve as markers of the distance the suburban dweller had traveled away from perdition.[11]

In response to the anxiety they feel about life as they imagine it in the inner city, McCarthy, et al., argue that the suburban middle class seeks to impose their particular values and strategies for success upon the residents of the inner city. What prevents inner-city residents from achieving educational and occupational attainment is believed by many not to be a political or economic problem, but an individual problem and a moral problem. Hollywood reinforces these middle-class fantasies about how best to address the problems of the inner city.

Hollywood's depiction of urban life and urban schools generally reflects the "culture of poverty" thesis. This view holds that residents of inner-city neighborhoods are poor not because they face racial and/or class discrimination or because they lack access to stable employment opportunities. Rather, it is argued that the urban poor are impoverished because they have the wrong values and the wrong attitudes about school, work, and family. It is assumed that inner-city residents share a culture of poverty that, as sociologist Christopher Hurn describes it, is

> Characterized by a widespread belief that individuals cannot control their environment, a related belief in fate or luck as determinants of a person's life, a low degree of control over aggressive impulses, a present rather than a future orientation, and low levels of aspiration for educational and occupational achievement.[12]

In contrast to what is considered the "normative" cultural values of the middle class (material goals, rational calculation, and a belief in the efficacy of individual effort), the culture of poverty thesis posits a culture that is lacking in the requisite values to achieve individual success. Edward Banfield has argued that the urban poor (particularly poor African Americans) remain poor due to their failure to adopt middle-class values and to fully integrate into the dominant culture of the United States. While the urban poor may in fact confront significant hardships, Banfield suggests that the adoption of middle-class values and lifestyles by the poor would help them to escape their poverty.[13]

Much social science research, however, has since discredited the idea that cultural values are responsible for either success or failure in life.[14] This research has shown that while cultural values and attitudes do vary, they do so primarily as they adapt to larger historical, social, political, and economic conditions. As sociologists have studied the inner city, they have found that many of the social problems there are less the result of cultural values and more the result of low levels of public investment in infrastructure, poor public housing, inadequate health care, poor schools, and, most importantly, a disappearing employment base.[15] William Julius Wilson has written extensively on the problems of the urban poor. His meticulous research convincingly shows that while many inner-city neighborhoods do exhibit signs of social "pathology" (crime, teen pregnancy, high school dropouts, and so on), these behaviors are not the result of cultural values or individual attitudes. Rather, they emerge out of particular conditions in the social structure—the lack of jobs in particular. He writes:

> If ghetto underclass minorities have limited aspirations, a hedonistic orientation toward life, or lack of plans for the future, such outlooks ultimately are the result of restricted opportunities and feelings of resignation originating from bitter personal experiences and a bleak future.[16]

The social problems in the inner city, then, cannot be solved through the application of individual-level solutions. Wilson's research has helped to demonstrate that since these problems are inherently structural, they require a structural solution.

Nevertheless, the culture of poverty framework has found its way into the popular imagination, and it is difficult to dislodge. Rather than focusing on the social, political, and economic sources of the problems in the inner city, Americans prefer to place the blame upon the individual moral failings and bad decision making of the residents of the inner city. American culture, rooted in Protestantism and capitalism, suggests that individual failure is often the result of an insufficient work ethic. A recent national survey found that a majority of white Americans believe that a lack of personal motivation is the primary reason African Americans, on average, have a lower socioeconomic status than white Americans.[17] Also, in his 1998 study of middle-class Americans, Alan Wolfe found that 65 percent of his respondents believed that "the problems of America's inner cities are largely due to people's lack of personal responsibility for their own problems."[18] Wolfe concludes that "the ideal of personal responsibility is very deeply ingrained in the middle-class mind."[19] In another national survey in 2003, 72 percent of respondents agreed or "somewhat agreed" with the statement, "most people who want to get ahead can make it if they are willing to work hard." Only 25 percent of the sample thought that hard work was not a guarantee of success.[20]

Americans generally assume that a solution to the problems in the inner city must be applied individually rather than structurally. As President George W. Bush remarked early in his presidency, "Much of today's poverty has more to do with troubled lives than a troubled economy. And often when a life is broken, it can only be restored by another caring, concerned human being."[21] Explaining poverty as the result of individual failure helps to relieve the suburban middle class (and upper class) of its share of responsibility for having politically and economically neglected the inner city. The frame that Hollywood uses to make sense of problems in urban high schools vividly reinforces the culture of poverty thesis and assists the middle and upper classes in their displacement of responsibility from troubled social structures to troubled lives.[22]

There are a handful of urban public school films that reflect a more sociological view of urban education—films that take social forces seriously. These films, however (which I explore in more detail later in the chapter), are in short supply and are not very popular with movie audiences. The most common and most popular urban school films depict a culture of poverty out of which utilitarian individuals are expected to pull themselves up by their bootstraps. The following section outlines the basic structure of the films in the urban school genre.

Welcome to the Jungle: The Urban School in Hollywood Films

Most of the urban public school films portray the individual attitude of the students as the *primary* obstacle to their academic achievement. These students don't have the right manners, the right behavior, or the right values to succeed in school. They have low aspirations, have a poor self-image, and believe the odds are stacked against them in school and in the wider society. The schools, therefore, are unable to effectively educate these students, and the reproduction of their disadvantage seems inevitable.

In the classic *Blackboard Jungle*, the 1955 film that was discussed at the beginning of this chapter, a class of working-class New York boys are depicted at first as nothing but a street gang who spend their days causing havoc in their vocational high school: A female teacher is nearly raped, a baseball is heaved at a teacher's head, a teacher's wife is harassed, and a newspaper truck is stolen. The metaphor in the film's title is all too literal—these students are seen as working-class animals.[23] These are "beasts" that even music won't soothe—in one scene the students destroy a teacher's priceless collection of jazz records. In *The Principal*, one teacher compares the students to animals, only to have another teacher claim that she would prefer to teach animals because at least animals do not carry knives. In *Teachers* the song "In the Jungle" plays while police search student lockers for drugs. In *Lean on Me* the high school is depicted explicitly as an untamed jungle. In the opening moments we see students selling drugs, assaulting teachers, harassing women, and generally running amok. All of this takes place as the movie soundtrack plays Guns N' Roses' angry anthem "Welcome to the Jungle" in the background.

The jungle metaphor conveniently summarizes the imagined difference between middle-class suburban Americans and the low-income urban students portrayed in these films. These are not students as middle-class Americans expect students to act. Their depiction as "animals" suggests that the problems in these schools are rooted in student behavior and, furthermore, that their behavior is rooted in an inferior culture. These "animals" have not been domesticated. The school is nothing but a zoo meant to contain them.

In the opening scenes of *Teachers* one student is stabbed, another student bites a teacher, the school psychologist has a nervous breakdown, and we see a teacher pack a gun in her briefcase. The assistant principal of the school casually explains that these events are typical problems for a Monday. In *The Principal* Rick Latimer single-handedly breaks up a gang fight on his first day on the job as the principal of an inner-city school. In *The Substitute* a gang has such firm control over an urban public high school that members attack a teacher with impunity. In *The Beat* a street gang fights rivals, gets stoned, listens to heavy-metal music, and ignores schoolwork. In *Dangerous Minds* the middle-class and somewhat naive Ms. Johnson walks into her class for the first time only to walk right back out after encountering nothing but abusive and hostile students who first ignore and then ridicule her. These are the same students who, by the end of the movie, Ms. Johnson (and we the audience) will embrace warmly.

Or is it that by the end of the movie "they" (the at-risk, poor, and inner-city students) will have learned to embrace "us" (the educated, middle-class, and suburban audience, as represented by Ms. Johnson)? This distinction is an important one. Will the audience learn that these students are not animals after all? Have the students simply been misunderstood? Will the audience be the ones who learn a lesson? Or will the students radically change their behavior as they come under the civilizing influence of the middle-class teacher who will socialize them in the culture of middle-class life? With the exception of two urban high school films that will be discussed at the end of this chapter, my viewing of this genre supports the latter interpretation. The films suggest that the students, and sometimes their parents, are to blame for their animal-like behavior and poor academic performance. If there is to be a happy ending (and there almost always is), it is the *students* who must learn and change, and not the members of the movie audience. But what about the educators? What role do the teachers and principals play in the transformation of the students in these urban school films?

The School Staff: Inept Bureaucrats and Incompetent Teachers

If the students are portrayed in a negative light, the school administrators and teaching staff are not depicted much more generously. The teachers and staff are generally shown as uncaring, cynical, incompetent, and ineffective educators. In short, the administrative and teaching staffs in these movies represent the worst fears that suburban residents have of urban public school administrators and teachers. These characters represent what many Americans believe is at the heart of the urban public school "crisis"—a selfish, inept, wasteful, and uncaring bureaucracy. These are schools with no soul—just troubled students, failed educational methods, burned-out personnel, too many arcane rules, and too much paperwork. If the harshest critics of public education were to make a movie about the public schools, their fictional schools would look much like the schools in these films.[24]

In *Blackboard Jungle* the stern principal is offended by the suggestion that there are discipline problems in his school. He seems unaware of the obvious problems all around him. In *Dangerous Minds* the soft-spoken principal is so narrowly focused on teaching the students to follow the most minor of rules that he is blind to their real life-and-death problems. Similarly, the administrators in *Up the Down Staircase* are more concerned that teachers follow the strict rules, obey the proper procedures, and fill out the right forms than they are with the welfare and education of their students. The principal in *Teachers* is blissfully ignorant of all the chaotic events in his school. Most of the administrative energy in the school is spent fighting a lawsuit filed by the family of a student who graduated without knowing how to read. The school authorities in *Stand and Deliver* have little faith in their students and do not believe that they could possibly do well in an advanced math class. The school psychologist in *The Beat* doesn't understand the first thing about the problems of alienated, low-income urban youth. In *Lean on Me* the dramatic deterioration of the high school over the years is blamed on the actions of the selfish teachers' union and the corrupt politicians in city hall. In *The Principal* the teachers complain bitterly when the principal insists that the "thugs" of the school actually attend their classes. In *The Substitute* the principal is actually one of the thugs! He has established an alliance with the dominant gang in the school to distribute drugs throughout the school district.

The vast majority of the teachers in these films have cynical attitudes about their jobs and seem to believe that most of the students are well beyond the point of hope. As one teacher from *Up the Down Staircase* summarizes her pedagogical philosophy, "You keep them off the streets and you give them a bit of fun and you've earned your keep." A cynical teacher in *The Substitute 2* offers this advice to a new teacher: "Punch in, punch out, and just try to stay alive." These veteran teachers are burned out and have nothing left to give but pessimistic appraisals of the potential for each year's class of students. They have failed to do what was assumed to be their professional obligation—to reform these urban school students into respectable, educated, and well-behaved citizens with middle-class aspirations and values.

With representations such as these, is it any wonder that a majority of Americans believe the national public schools are failing miserably? In the fall of 2004 only 26 percent of a random national sample of Americans awarded the nation's public schools a grade of A or B. When asked to grade the public schools in their local district, however, 47 percent of the sample awarded a grade of A or a B. Even more dramatically, of the parents in the sample who have children enrolled in the public schools, 70 percent awarded an A or B to the public school that their oldest child attends.[25] It would seem that the closer one is to the public schools and, presumably, the more information one has about them, the more likely one is to evaluate the public schools favorably. Without such firsthand knowledge about particular schools, however, the American public's estimation of the public schools in general may be based upon what they hear in the media, including Hollywood's unflattering representations. Nevertheless, there is one character in these urban school films who makes a difference. An outsider, a representative of the middle-class work ethic, comes to the school to "save" the students by teaching them how to be utilitarian individuals.

The Outsider as the Teacher-Hero

While all of the students, all of the administrators, and most of the teachers are depicted as impediments to education, there is one bright light of hope in these films: the teacher-hero (or in the case of *Lean on Me* and *The Principal*, the principal-hero). This lone figure is able to ignore the cynicism of veteran teachers, escape the red tape of the school bureaucracy, and speak directly to the hearts and minds of these troubled youth who are, by the end of the film, transformed from apathetic working-class and poor students into studious and sincere students with bright middle-class futures.

The heroes of these films do not need teacher training, smaller class sizes, a supportive staff, strong administrative leadership, parental participation, technological tools, corporate partnership, school restructuring, a higher salary, a longer school day, charter schools, tuition vouchers, or more financial resources. All they need to bring to the classroom is discipline, tough love, high expectations, and a little good old-fashioned middle-class common sense about individual achievement and personal responsibility.

In each of these movies the hero is someone new to the school, and often new to teaching entirely. The teacher-hero is a mysterious figure who literally becomes the savior of these students.[26] All hope would be lost if not for the intervention of this unconventional new teacher to break the well-established but failed methods of the school and to effectively reach the students with his or her own unique approach. I suggest that the teacher-hero in the urban school films represents a likely fantasy of the suburban middle-class audience—a character they can identify with goes into a troubled urban high school and single-handedly rectifies its problems. The teacher- or principal-hero can clearly see through the confusion that has bewildered many educators and policy makers for years. He or she can clearly identify the faults in these students and the problems in these schools and knows just what it takes to correct them. The teacher-heroes teach the students to escape the depressing and limiting world of their parents, to appreciate art and poetry, to develop manners and cultural skills, to acquire new study habits, to set high goals for themselves, to have an optimistic attitude, and to believe that hard work pays off. In short, the teacher shows the students how to overcome their culture of poverty. It is through this figure of the heroic outsider that the audience feels some sense of control over an otherwise chaotic and hopeless situation.

We already know Mr. Dadier from *Blackboard Jungle*. He is a white man with plenty of upper-middle-class cultural capital (he recites Shakespeare in his job interview with the principal) who enters the "garbage can of the educational system" (as one cynical teacher puts it). After several thuggish students assault him and a fellow teacher after work one day, Mr. Dadier is tempted to transfer to a middle-class high school where well-dressed and well-behaved students study earnestly and patriotically sing the national anthem. Mr. Dadier, however, is determined to reach the students in his "jungle." He wants them to care about an education, to learn "to think for themselves," and to make something positive of their lives. He takes a special interest in Gregory Miller, an African American student and the charismatic leader of the class, and tells him that he should not settle for being an auto mechanic—that in 1955 racial discrimination and poverty are no longer excuses for blacks not to make something of their lives in the United States. The following exchange between Gregory Miller and Mr. Dadier summarizes Mr. Dadier's (and, by extension, *Blackboard Jungle*'s) educational philosophy:

Gregory Miller: I don't need no more schooling. What's wrong with being a mechanic?
Mr. Dadier: You don't want to be, do you?

> *Gregory Miller: There ain't much choice, is there? Same reason I live in this neighborhood. A Colored neighborhood . . . What's the use? Nobody gives a hoot. Not the other fellahs, not the teachers, not my folks even.*
>
> *Mr. Dadier: So you quit trying. That's the easy way out, Miller . . .*
>
> *Gregory Miller: We talking from different sides of the fence. You're not black.*
>
> *Mr. Dadier: That's not a good enough excuse nowadays and you know it, Miller!*

Through his persistence and dedication, Mr. Dadier is, in the end, able to convince Miller to stay in school. They create a pact—Mr. Dadier will not quit his job if Miller doesn't drop out. In addition to Miller, Mr. Dadier eventually wins the respect and admiration of most of the other inhabitants of his classroom "jungle."

In *Stand and Deliver* Mr. Escalante leaves a lucrative engineering job in order to teach high school math to Latino students in Garfield High, an East Los Angeles high school. Mr. Escalante insists on teaching calculus to students who normally would take regular or remedial math. His unconventional methods and his high expectations succeed. He is able to get his students to believe in themselves in spite of the doubts that their parents and the school authorities continue to have about them. His students pass the advanced placement exam in calculus, and he inspires many of them to aspire to college. They begin to believe, as he tells one student who is covered in grease from working on his car, that it is better to design automobiles than to fix them. The only thing preventing them from designing cars, apparently, is a belief in themselves and the application of their abilities.

While Hollywood's pedagogy seems to have effective results on film, how much agreement is there between Hollywood's worldview and the view of social scientists who study inequality, education, and the characteristics of effective schools? In this case the fantasy and the reality do not agree.

School Success and Hollywood's Misleading Fantasy

Designing cars is certainly a worthy aspiration for any student. However, the assumption (in these movies and too often in actual schools) that aspiring to fix cars or to work on an assembly line is a sign of personal failure serves to condemn those students who, for whatever reason, do not have college in their future. Furthermore, it is disingenuous to assume that the *only* obstacle standing in the way of middle-class occupational attainment for these students is their individual attitude and their failure to exercise their brains. It is not that the middle-class values espoused by the teacher-heroes are without educational merit. However, the implication in these films that the failure or success of these students is reducible to their values and their individual effort, rather than taking into consideration the deep social structural processes also at work, is a pedagogical fallacy. The attitude and behavior of poor and minority students in urban public high schools can have many explanations that these films implicitly (and sometimes explicitly) dismiss. Social science research offers several explanations for the negative attitudes and orientations that poor and minority students sometimes exhibit toward schooling. These social science explanations find the source of such attitudes within structures such as the employment base in urban areas, past and current racial discrimination, and unequal public school funding.

The attitude and performance of lower-class students in school is not necessarily a reflection of their culture or values, but may be a reflection of the opportunities that await them in the labor market. In *Blackboard Jungle*, for instance, Miller knows through experience that auto mechanics is a career he can likely attain and succeed in reasonably well. His initial dismissal of the platitudes about the importance of an education is not due to an inferior culture or an irrational choice, but to knowledge about the bitter realities of the life chances for most low-income, urban African Americans in 1955. The relatively low aspirations that students living in poverty often express in school (which Hollywood interprets as a sign of their flawed values or poor choices) may in fact be a reasonable reaction to the objective expectations that they see waiting for them outside the walls of the school.

Jay MacLeod, author of the modern sociological classic *Ain't No Makin' It: Aspirations and Attainment in a Low-Income Neighborhood*, studied two groups of high school boys from poor and working-class families in a housing project outside Boston. He found that the group of white boys, the "Hallway Hangers," had come to the conclusion that the American achievement ideology was a lie. They were witness over the years to the failure of their friends and family members in school and the job market. They concluded that for people like themselves, hard work does not pay off. As a result, they lowered their aspirations in life so as not to be disappointed with themselves should they fail to become upwardly mobile. Indeed, the Hallway Hangers failed to achieve much educational or occupational success. They reproduced the impoverished and troubled lives of their parents. But how much of their "failure" was due to their own actions and how much was beyond their control?

The brilliance of MacLeod's research is that he contrasts the experiences of the Hallway Hangers with those of "the Brothers," a group of African American boys from the same housing project facing the same set of educational and occupational opportunities as the Hallway Hangers. In contrast to the Hallway Hangers, the Brothers believed in the achievement ideology, worked hard in school, and had high aspirations. Hollywood and American culture would expect the Brothers to experience success as a result of their utilitarian individualism. Unfortunately, they did not. MacLeod concludes that both groups of boys faced limited opportunities in school and the workplace due to their social class position and the structure of the American economy. The negative attitude of the Hallway Hangers was not the primary cause of their failure. Rather, their negative attitude was the internalization of grim objective conditions for them in the job market.[27]

Additionally, John Ogbu's research has shown that different minority groups have drastically different orientations toward schooling as a result of the historical legacy of their racial or ethnic group's incorporation into the dominant society. As "involuntary minorities," African American students, for instance, often resist cooperation with the white middle-class standards of the school because the bitter experiences of previous generations and the hardships of the current generation have left them distrustful of the dominant institutions of society. Success in school, seen as "acting white" for many African American students, threatens their identity, which was partly formed in opposition to dominant social institutions.[28] Furthermore, as the social psychologist Claude Steele's research has shown, even the minority students who *do* identify and cooperate with the school often perform poorly in school not because they come from a culture of poverty, but because they fear that their performance will confirm the worst stereotypes that others have of their racial or ethnic group. Such "stereotype threat" can insidiously become a self-fulfilling prophecy.[29]

Oppositional identities and stereotype threat need not be unique to racial minorities, however. Any disadvantaged group can develop oppositional identities that affect performance in school. As Jay MacLeod has shown in his detailed ethnography described above, working-class white students also face stereotypes in the wider society and often reject dominant social institutions such as schools due to the low probabilities for success that await them in the middle-class occupational world.[30]

Jonathan Kozol's impassioned work over the years has demonstrated that the severe funding inequities between urban and suburban public schools have an insidious effect on the educational experience of students. While much social science research, starting with the Coleman Report in 1966, has suggested that differential levels of school funding are not *primarily* responsible for differential levels of student academic performance, Kozol's work shows how school funding is nonetheless a factor that contributes to the overall well-being and self-image of students.[31] In his 1991 book *Savage Inequalities: Children in America's Schools*, the inequities Kozol observes between urban and suburban public schools mirror the inequities of Hollywood's urban and suburban high schools. The following description of the urban schools Kozol visited could refer to almost any of the urban schools depicted in Hollywood films:

> . . . these public schools were, by and large, extraordinarily unhappy places. With few exceptions, they reminded me of 'garrisons' or 'outposts' in a foreign nation. Housing projects, bleak and tall, surrounded by perimeter walls lined with barbed wire, often stood adjacent to the schools I visited . . . Their doors were guarded. Police sometimes patrolled the halls. The windows of the schools were sometimes covered with steel grates.[32]

Whereas Hollywood expects students in underfunded public high schools to rise above their depressing circumstances, Kozol sees how such conditions gradually wear a student down and can lead to a fatalistic attitude about school:

> . . . most adolescents in the poorest of neighborhoods learn very soon that they are getting less than children in the wealthier school districts. They see suburban schools on television and they see them when they travel for athletic competitions . . . About injustice, most poor children in America cannot be fooled. Children, of course, don't understand at first that they are being cheated. They come to school with a degree of faith and optimism, and they often seem to thrive during the first few years. It is sometimes not until third grade that their teachers start to see the warning signs of failure.[33]

If, as I have suggested, these films present themselves not just as entertainment, but as serious social documents about real social problems, then we must treat seriously what they offer as potential solutions to such problems. Hollywood suggests that all students (with the help of the right teacher) have the power to do whatever they choose to do in life. The only limitation facing students is the limitation within themselves. Unfortunately, the dramatized solutions, while perhaps satisfying as entertainment, fall well short as answers to the social problems they purport to address and leave audiences with misleading impressions about educational inequality.

The students portrayed in these urban school films come from low-income families with few material resources, their parents have low levels of educational attainment, they live in impoverished neighborhoods with few promising economic opportunities, they are faced with racial and/or class-based discrimination in school and in the labor market, their schools have inadequate resources, and many of their peers are involved with gangs and drugs. The teacher-hero, however, tells them that their academic progress is impeded because they are not working hard enough. By not addressing the structural conditions in which these urban students live, however, these films present a dishonest explanation of the negative attitudes and poor academic performance of many students living in poverty.

Teachers *can* make a difference in the lives of poor students. Particularly gifted, motivated, and charismatic teachers may be able to inspire some low-income, inner-city students to raise their aspirations and to reorient their attitudes toward school. Establishing personal relationships with students, having high expectations of them, and encouraging them to apply themselves in spite of their own self-doubt are indeed positive and potentially effective pedagogical methods. However, as an answer to the problems of past and current racial discrimination, lack of economic opportunities in the labor market, and the inequities in funding between urban and suburban public schools, a few highly charismatic teachers can have only a limited impact. Without a depiction of the social, political, and economic context in which these stories take place, the educational lessons of these urban school films are incomplete.

To be convinced to apply themselves in school, students must know that the schoolwork they are asked to do has some relevance to their future lives and that their efforts will likely be rewarded in school and in the wider social structure.[34] The personal attitudes and academic efforts of poor inner-city students will likely change not simply because a middle-class teacher whips them into academic shape, but because the educational, economic, and social opportunities made available to them change.

Short of widespread social and economic changes, however, there are some educational reforms at the level of the school that research has shown to increase student performance.[35] The educational reforms that have shown promise in the real world, however, are not reflected in Hollywood's fantasy about how to improve the academic performance of students in urban schools. What is noteworthy about this research is that it places the responsibility not simply upon the individual student, but upon the coordinated efforts of a community of teachers, students, staff, administrators, and parents. A collective effort is required to succeed in the face of structural inequalities.

It has long been known that students are more likely to achieve academic goals when significant others in their lives expect and encourage them to do so.[36] To be fair, the educator-heroes of *Blackboard Jungle, Lean on Me, Stand and Deliver,* and *Dangerous Minds* succeed in part because they have high expectations of their students. The expectations that Hollywood's teachers have of their students, however, are usually vague, shallow, and devoid of social context. The teacher-heroes present their students with a simple choice. They can *choose* success or *choose* failure. The educational hero *expects* them to choose success. As we saw in *Blackboard Jungle,* Mr. Dadier expects Miller to choose to stay in school as if the fear of racial discrimination and the lure of a stable auto mechanic's job should not be real considerations in the decision. Ms. Johnson tells the impoverished students in her class that they alone are responsible for their success or failure in school and in life: "You have a choice. It may not be a choice you like, but it's a choice . . . there are no victims in this classroom." Louis Stevens, the teacher-hero in *Only the Strong,* tells a low-income, inner-city student, "this world can be about as big as you want it to be, or as small as your tiny little 'hood. I'm showing you some choices. You decide."

To be convinced that they have the power that their teachers tell them they have, however, social science research suggests that the students must have relationships with significant others in the school and in the wider community that support their goals in the face of structural inequalities. While these films do emphasize the importance of the student–teacher relationship, they do not represent educational achievement as the result of a cooperative effort between students, teachers, administrators, parents, and other members of the community (such as employers). If anything, these films view other students, teachers, administrators, and parents as *obstacles* to the individual success of each student. The viewer is left to assume that the students *alone* are responsible for their success or failure, and that there is little that schools can do to increase student performance.

There are many ways in which Hollywood's pedagogy is at odds with what educators know about effective schools. For instance,

- While the teachers in these urban school films transform their students in spite of bad principals, scholarship on effective schools shows that strong school leadership with clearly defined goals is an important element of school success.[37]

- While the teachers in these films transform students in spite of the apathy of their parents, effective schools' literature suggests that school success requires the cooperation and involvement of parents.[38]

- While the teachers in these films transform their students in spite of a cynical and uncooperative staff of teachers, the school effectiveness literature suggests that schools with a supportive and cooperative staff can increase student performance.[39]

◆ While the teachers in these films transform their students by encouraging students to be individually competitive, recent scholarship suggests that collaborative learning can yield high academic results.[40]

◆ While teachers in these films do not attempt to incorporate pedagogies or curricula that reflect the unique social world and culture of the students in their classes, recent scholarship has shown that attention to cultural differences in the classroom can increase student engagement and performance.[41]

◆ And, as we will see in the next section, while some of the teacher- or educator-heroes in these films succeed by excluding the most "at risk" students from their classes, the school effectiveness literature suggests that mixed-ability classes rather than rigidly tracked and exclusive classrooms can raise the achievement level of all students.[42]

The movie *Dangerous Minds* provides a particularly revealing opportunity to analyze Hollywood's lesson plan and to compare it to reality. *Dangerous Minds* was based on the nonfiction book *My Posse Don't Do Homework*, by the real-life teacher LouAnne Johnson.[43] There are, however, some interesting differences between Johnson's book and Hollywood's "true story" version of it. In spite of the cinematic Ms. Johnson's speech about personal responsibility, the real Ms. Johnson writes, "I can't help feeling that it's me as a teacher and the school system as a social institution that are, in reality, failing our children and their future."[44] The movie suggests that Ms. Johnson's success was achieved over the course of one semester, but Ms. Johnson's real-life success took several years. Finally, and most revealing of Hollywood's bias, the film overlooked many pedagogically important details of Ms. Johnson's "Academy" class. Designed as a program of last resort for troubled but promising students, the real Academy received additional funding from the federal government to lower class sizes and to purchase computers. The students were assigned mentors from the local business community. And the students received personal attention from a team of teachers, not just Ms. Johnson.[45]

Ironically, one of Ms. Johnson's real-life students expresses wisdom that Hollywood actively chose to ignore. After reading Shakespeare's *Taming of the Shrew* and then watching the movie version of the play, the student writes disapprovingly in a classroom journal:

> The movie was all right, but it didn't have as much action as the book and there was some seens [sic] in the movie that wasn't in the book and that ain't right. If somebody tells a story and you make a movie out of it, you shouldn't make up your own stuff and put it in the movie because then it isn't the other guy's story anymore.[46]

As noted earlier, there are a few urban school films that do not conform to the major themes discussed thus far. While small in number, their exceptionalism reveals all the more strongly Hollywood's tendency to interpret urban education from the perspective of middle-class individualism.

Learning from the Anomalies

Cheaters and *Light It Up* are noteworthy as anomalies in this sample of urban high school films because they are dramas with a form similar to that of the other urban high school films, but their content directly challenges the central features of the genre. In their departure from the genre formula, they highlight the predictability of the messages conveyed in most of the other urban high school films.[47]

Cheaters is based on a true story of working-class students in an underfunded and gritty Chicago public high school who cheat in order to win the Illinois State Academic Decathlon contest. What is remarkable about this film is that while it initially appears to follow in the footsteps of all the urban school films (a classroom of poor and troubled urban students is poised to be "saved" by a middle-class teacher-hero), its moral message is radically different. Rather than inspiring the students to work hard and achieve their full potential honestly, the teacher-"hero" actually encourages the students to cheat, facilitates their cheating, and helps them to conceal their cheating from the authorities.

The teacher-"hero," Mr. Plecki, recruits the brightest students at the school to be part of the Academic Decathlon team. He has a hard time finding enough students to participate. The students are not willing to put in the time it would take to be successful. Nor are the working-class students impressed by a promotional video that boasts that the Academic Decathlon is "building skills that work in corporate America." After all, what future do *they* have in corporate America? Nevertheless, he is able to organize a team, and they begin to compete against other schools. They do moderately well at first, exceeding expectations by placing fifth in the citywide competition. As a result, they narrowly qualify for the state championship. Knowing that they stand little chance of success at the state level, however, few students are interested in continuing to compete. As one student remarks, "I love the dream you gave to us, but at a certain point you have to realize it's just a fucking dream." With an assortment of work and family obligations, the time to prepare for the competition at the state level is simply too consuming for the students. Their attitude soon changes, however, after one of the students finds the test book for the state competition. They all agree, with Mr. Plecki's support, to cheat.

Mr. Plecki rationalizes the cheating as an act of civil disobedience—a collective effort to strip away the built-in advantages of social class and social connections enjoyed by the upper-middle-class students at a very prestigious and well-funded public magnet school across town, Whitney Young. Whitney Young has abundant resources and has dominated the State Academic Decathlon championships for years. Mr. Plecki and his students believe there is a suspiciously cozy relationship between Whitney Young and the Academic Decathlon authorities. The administrative offices of the national Academic Decathlon are even located on the grounds of Whitney Young High School.

Mr. Plecki wishes to level the playing field for his working-class students not for learning's sake, but for the sake of winning. Mr. Plecki cannot in good conscience spout platitudes to his students about playing by the rules and working hard. He knows through bitter personal experience that the achievement ideology and meritocracy are myths. His working-class immigrant father played by the rules and worked hard his entire life only to be cruelly laid off by his lifelong employer when he contracted cancer late in his career. Mr. Plecki has learned that in the United States it is winning that ultimately counts, not integrity. He feels unrewarded as a dedicated and talented schoolteacher while many of his less worthy peers have prospered. Mr. Plecki encourages his students to work cooperatively in order to challenge the system—to rebel against a structure that further benefits the advantaged and impedes the upward mobility of the disadvantaged.

One of the things that make this film remarkable is that the teacher, the students, and the film do not apologize for the blatant breaking of the rules. The students are eventually caught and Mr. Plecki loses his job. Yet there are no regrets. As Jolie, a bright student who actively participated in the scheme and serves as the narrator of the story, remarks at the end of the film, "I learned more about the way the world really works from my nine months on the Decathlon team than most people will learn in a lifetime." By consciously not conforming to the common formula of the urban school film genre, *Cheaters* is almost refreshing in its cynicism. One need not condone the cheating to respect the film for its unidealized portrayal of an urban school and for its attempt to portray the elements of the wider social structure within which the students must act.

Light It Up is also an exceptional film in the urban high school genre. The heroes of this film are the students themselves, not middle-class adults.

The students in Mr. Knowles's class are mostly good-intentioned and motivated kids who show a lot of promise. However, they are poor, they have troubled home lives, and there are few opportunities for them at school. There is no heat in their classroom, the ceiling leaks, and the windows are broken. Fed up with these inferior conditions, Mr. Knowles takes his class to a local restaurant during school hours. As a result of breaking school policy, the principal suspends Mr. Knowles.

Angry that their favorite teacher was suspended, several of the students stage an impromptu protest in the principal's office. A police officer is called to break up the protest and the principal suspends several students, including Ziggy, a troubled but sensitive student and talented artist who is often beaten by his father. Desperate to avoid more trouble at home, Ziggy tries to run. In a struggle with the police officer, Ziggy grabs the officer's gun and accidentally shoots the officer. Lester, a football player with a solid grade point average whose dad was shot and killed by the police three months earlier, picks up the gun and threatens the officer and the principal. Lester, Ziggy, Rodney (a gang member), Stephanie (an honor student with a bright future), Lynn (a good-natured but troubled white student who just learned she is pregnant), and Rivers (a slick con artist with a good heart) take the police officer hostage, barricade themselves in the school, and create a list of demands. They demand that the school rehire Mr. Knowles, buy more textbooks, fix the broken windows and leaks in the school, establish a career day, and routinely test all the teachers in the school.

This film does not present student attitudes, middle-class values, or individual achievement as the solution to the problems in inner-city schools. Rather, it tackles head-on the structural and social problems that these students are faced with on a daily basis. These students consciously struggle against racism, poverty, an underfunded school, and the stereotype that they are violent thugs who don't care about (and therefore don't deserve) an education. These students have been victimized by the system and misunderstood by society (including, as this film explicitly portrays, by the media). Ultimately, the story ends in tragedy as Ziggy is shot to death by the police.

While Mr. Knowles is a favorite teacher who cares about the students, he does *not* become anyone's savior in this film. Mr. Knowles is merely a secondary character. The help that these students need is beyond that which a single teacher can provide. Rather than looking exclusively toward the help of Mr. Knowles, the students look to themselves for answers, and they take action (as flawed as it may be). They do not eventually adopt new values and attitudes. Instead, the audience begins to learn more about who these students are as individuals and sympathetically understands

66

why they took such drastic actions. Even the wounded police officer testifies on behalf of the students at the criminal trial.

Cheaters and *Light It Up* are both relatively recent movies, and it is too soon to know if they represent a new trend in the genre. It is doubtful, however, that these two films represent a major change in the cultural understanding of urban high schools. Tellingly, these films are also unique in that they are among the least commercially successful films in the sample. *Light It Up* played in 1,252 theaters and it grossed only $5.8 million.[48] By comparison, *Dangerous Minds* played in 1,783 theaters and grossed nearly $85 million. *Cheaters* was produced by and shown only on HBO. These two films clearly break the mold of the urban high school film genre and offer the viewer something new to consider about urban high schools. Nevertheless, they do not seem to resonate with a wider audience as the other films in the sample do. Their uniqueness only serves to reinforce the dominant theme of most urban school films—that utilitarian individualism can help the students to escape their culture of poverty.

Not all of Hollywood's urban school students, however, are capable of salvation. Some students are simply beyond even the reach of the teacher- and principal-heroes. These students, Hollywood suggests, must be run out of town by the good guys.

The Teacher as a Cowboy Vigilante

In some of the urban school films the teacher- or principal-hero must not only save the students with middle-class values, but also punish and exclude the most dangerous and unredeemable elements of the student population. In *Lean on Me*, for instance, Principal Clark's first order of business as the new baseball-bat-wielding principal of a run-down urban high school is to expel 10 percent of the student body. He asks the teachers to compile a list of the students they believe to be involved with gangs and drugs. He gathers these students on stage at a school assembly and announces their immediate expulsion from school. After these most undesirable students are expelled, Principal Clark concentrates on rescuing the remaining students from their troubled, yet redeemable, lives. Principal Clark's relatively peaceful purge, however, is contrasted with the similar, but more violent, methods of exclusion used by the teacher- and principal-heroes in several of the other urban school films. Violence as pedagogy is used centrally as a method of saving the students in *The Principal*,

The Substitute, The Substitute 2, Class of 1984, Only the Strong, 187 and *Detention* (2003).

While the educational goals of the teacher- and principal-heroes in these seven films are the same as those in the less violent films (to encourage the students to adopt middle-class values and to achieve high academic goals), their methods are clearly unconventional and often illegal. What these more violent films suggest is that not all "at risk" students in impoverished urban public schools are worth saving. Some students are so far beyond the norms of middle-class life that they must be removed from society before their flawed values and deviant lifestyles corrupt other students. While their methods are extreme, these violent educators ultimately send the same message to viewers as the other teacher- and principal-heroes— the problems in urban public schools are primarily caused by the urban public school students themselves, not larger social structural factors. The solutions, therefore, are located within the individual students (either in their moral conversion to the middle class or in their violent exclusion from civilized society).

In *The Principal* Rick Latimer is a high school teacher who is arrested after lashing out violently against his ex-wife's boyfriend. Rather than firing him, the school board punishes him by making him principal of the most troubled school in the city. As the studio represents the film,

> Burglary, drugs. Assault. Rape. The students at Brandel High are more than the new principal Rick Latimer bargained for. Gangs fight to control the school using knives—even guns when they have to. When Latimer and the head of security try to clean up the school and stop the narcotics trade, they run up against a teenage mafia. A violent confrontation on the campus leads to a deadly showdown with the drug dealer's gang, and one last chance for Latimer to save his career . . . and his life.[49]

Rick Latimer is a man with a troubled past and no administrative experience. He is a loner, an alcoholic, and a violent man. He rules the school with an iron fist and emphatically declares that he will no longer tolerate drugs or gang activity in his school. He directly challenges the gang leader for control of the school. "No more" becomes his mantra, and he frequently enforces his rules with his fists. In spite of his unorthodox methods and violent temper, he is able to sensitively reach several "at risk" students and to get them to reverse their negative attitudes toward school.

Even more dramatically, in *The Substitute,* an out-of-work mercenary soldier becomes a substitute teacher at an urban high school in Miami. Using an alias, "Mr. Smith" learns that the principal and the dominant gang, the "Kings of Destruction," run a major drug operation out of the basement of the school. When he is not defending himself against attempts on his life by gang members, the substitute teacher connects emotionally with many of the students in his class and encourages them to reject gangs and drugs. For the first time the students actually begin to pay attention in class. This teacher-hero, however, has far more ambitious goals for the school. In a bloody ending the substitute teacher defeats the "Kings of Destruction" and the thuggish principal. In doing so he nearly destroys the school building, but he makes the school safe for learning and returns it to the students—"at least it's their school again," he says. With his job complete, he and his partner mosey on out of town.[50]

In the *Class of 1984* (based "partially" on real events, as the preface tells us), Andy Norris is a first-time teacher at a violent inner-city high school. A drug-dealing gang, led by the promising but misguided student Pete Stegman, has taken over Mr. Norris's music class. Mr. Norris expels the gang members from his class, but they continue to harass him at school and at home. After a "good" kid dies from the effect of the gang's tainted drugs, Mr. Norris becomes determined to bring the gang to justice. He is frustrated, however, that neither the school administration nor the police take any action against the gang.

Meanwhile, Mr. Norris has been able to "get through" to his music class. Without the distraction of the gang members, he is able to teach the students and to convince them to care about their education. On the night of his class's first school concert, however, Stegman's gang molests the pregnant Mrs. Norris and holds her hostage. Using her as bait, the gang lures Mr. Norris through the empty hallways of the school and into the shop classrooms, where they wait to kill him. In self-defense, Mr. Norris kills one student with a buzz saw in wood shop, burns another to death with gasoline and a blowtorch in auto shop, and kills a third with a wrench. (Note how the working-class tools favored by these violent and rebellious students are used against them as the middle-class outsider, Mr. Norris, enacts his revenge.) Mr. Norris and Stegman face off on the roof of the school for the climactic fight scene. In the midst of their violent altercation Stegman falls through a glass sunroof, gets tangled in the stage ropes, and hangs to death above Mr. Norris's orchestra, in the middle of their brilliant concert performance.

Mr. Norris is the ultimate teacher-hero. He academically inspires his class of troubled youth (as much as Ms. Johnson in *Dangerous Minds*), and he also takes the law into his own hands as he ruthlessly rids the school permanently of its most threatening students. What Principal Joe Clark accomplished in *Lean on Me* by summarily expelling the most troublesome 10 percent of the student population, Mr. Norris accomplishes with righteous violence.

These cowboys of the classroom bring order to the chaos of the urban public schools. As newcomers to their schools, they are asked to deal with problems that are not of their making. Frustrated by lawlessness and the ineffectiveness of the traditional methods available to them, they take matters into their own hands. They use violence to impose righteousness and to clear a path for other students (troubled, yet morally redeemable students) to achieve their full academic potential. As we will see in the following chapter, the tables are dramatically turned on the teachers in the suburban school films. In these films it is the students who sometimes turn violent in order to punish their corrupt teachers.

Neo-Conservative Retreat or Compassionately Conservative Reform?

What political messages do the urban high school movies send to audiences about urban education? Do these films implicitly endorse any particular policy solutions to the problems in urban schools? In each of these movies the answer to the students' problems is revealed to be primarily an individual one—to reform the individual student, not the educational system or the wider society. In a few of these films the implied solution to the crisis in urban education is to first rid the school of gangs and drugs. Second, and more importantly, the teacher-hero in all of these films must teach students the right values and manners, convince them they have the power to improve their lives, insist they make better choices and take responsibility for those choices. As Principal Joe Clark in *Lean on Me* tells the students in his high school, "If you fail I want you to blame yourself. The responsibility is yours."

While there is certainly nothing wrong with encouraging personal responsibility among students, these movies, as I have argued, dramatize only a portion of the story when they portray a lack of individual effort as the *only* reason the future of poor students is often limited. The serious business of school reform or revitalization of the inner-city economy takes a distant backseat to the individual reformation of these poor and working-class students. As Ms. Johnson and Principal Clark make perfectly clear, there are no victims among their students. Success is a *choice* that each individual student must make. In the absence of a portrayal of the social, political, or economic context in which these individual choices are made, however, I argue that there is an implicit (and sometimes explicit) conservative political message conveyed in each of these films.

Near the end of each movie the teacher- or principal-hero faces a crisis that almost causes him or her to give up their mission. In each case, however, the crisis is heroically dealt with and the teacher or principal stays in the job, having found a true calling in life. I argue that the dilemma facing the hero in the climax of each of these movies tells a significant political story about urban policy choices in late-twentieth- and early-twenty-first-century America. Should the state play an active role in the structural reform of urban schools and urban economies? Should the state retreat and let market forces work the magic of the invisible hand? Or is there a "compassionately conservative" third way in which public policy addresses inequality, but only at the level of the individual?

In *Stand and Deliver* Mr. Escalante's students are accused by the testing authorities of having cheated on their advanced placement calculus exams. Mr. Escalante begins to doubt himself and wonders if he placed excessively high expectations on his students. In the end, however, the students retake the test, and they all pass. The students are redeemed. Even more importantly, however, Mr. Escalante is redeemed. In the face of bureaucratic resistance he, as a newcomer to the profession of teaching, was able to apply new pedagogical methods and his students were able to succeed beyond any level the school had experienced before.

Several crises face Ms. Johnson in *Dangerous Minds*. One of her students, the charismatic leader of the class, is shot and killed by a crack addict. Another gets pregnant and is pressured by the school administration to attend an alternative school. Still other students drop out of school altogether. Ms. Johnson begins to lose hope and announces she will not return to teach the following year. Her students, however, protest vigorously. They literally *need* her. They have grown to rely on her. As several of her students complain:

> "If you love us so much and are so interested in our graduating, why are you leaving?"
> "We've been working hard and we stayed in school. What about us?"
> "Ain't no other teacher going to give me no A."

Callie, the promising student who was encouraged by the administration to leave the school when she became pregnant, returns to school on Ms. Johnson's last day and pleads with her to stay in her job. In reference to one of the poems they had read in class, Callie uses some rather heavy-handed symbolism to make her point:

> I thought you'd always be here for me . . . I decided, we decided, we aren't going to let you leave like that . . . you have to rage against the dying of the light . . . we see you as being our light. You are our teacher. You got what we need.

They feel angry and, ironically, victimized by Ms. Johnson's apparent betrayal. Their emotional appeal works. Moved by her students' testimonies, Ms. Johnson decides to continue teaching at the school. How can she abandon them now?

In *Up the Down Staircase* Sylvia Barrett, a new teacher in a rough New York City high school, decides to resign after less than one semester on the job. Frustrated and angry with the school bureaucracy, saddened by a student's attempted suicide, and disheartened that several of her students plan to drop out of school, Ms. Barrett decides she is not up to the challenge of teaching at a "problem-area school." "A teacher should be able to get through to her students, even here," she complains. Near the end of the term Jose, a quiet, shy, and apparently depressed student, comes out of his shell and presides as the judge in a mock trial Ms. Barrett had organized for her English class. "I'm sorry you are leaving us," says Jose, "English was the greatest course I ever took." Thrilled that she had "gotten through" to Jose, Ms. Barrett changes her mind about quitting. Being responsible for the academic awakening of a troubled student makes the struggle of walking "up the down staircase" of the school's bureaucracy worth it.

In *Blackboard Jungle* Mr. Dadier also faces doubts and threatens to quit his teaching job. After he is assaulted and his wife is harassed, Mr. Dadier loses the hope he had for these students and nearly takes a teaching job at an elite high school. In a fit of frustration toward the end of the film Mr. Dadier asks, "What's the point of teaching if kids don't care about an education? And make no mistake about it. They don't!" However, Mr. Dadier soon regains faith in his apathetic students when they team up to defeat the most incorrigible troublemakers in class after they threaten Mr. Dadier with a knife. In *Lean on Me* the corrupt fire chief and the politically vulnerable mayor arrest Principal Clark for putting chains on the high school doors (in order to keep the drug dealers out). The students, however, rally to his defense. They surround the jail and demand his release with testaments to how much he has helped them. The news that 75 percent of the students received a passing grade on the state's minimum skills test redeems him. He is released from jail and victoriously returns to lead his flock.[51] In *Teachers* Mr. Jerrell is pressured to resign after helping a student to obtain an abortion (she was impregnated by another teacher). His class of formerly apathetic students rally to his defense. They successfully convince him to continue teaching and to fight the corrupt and narrow-minded administration of the high school.

In each of these moments of crisis, teachers are at the end of their rope. They are disappointed that they have failed as teachers, angry that the students have not responded to their lessons, and frustrated that the administration has tied their hands. This moment epitomizes the anxiety and frustration with urban schools expressed by politicians and many middle-class suburbanites. I understand this pivotal moment to be a representation of the neo-conservative impulse to retreat from state efforts to solve social problems. It is as if the teacher-hero says, "Well, I've done my best to help these people but it failed. Let's cut school funding, eliminate affirmative action, cut back on welfare, and insist upon personal accountability. Their failure is no longer my responsibility."

Hollywood, however, does not let the story end with such a laissez-faire message. In Hollywood, the well-intentioned middle-class reformer ultimately succeeds just when failure seems imminent. Success, however, is measured not by any institutional or social changes, but by the adoration of the students for the teacher-hero.[52] With such admiration from the students, the "compassionately conservative" teacher-hero continues to work with the students. This is the moment of truth in these movies—proof to the teacher-hero that the students have been successfully reformed. They have progressed from lower-class animals to respectable middle-class students who finally understand and appreciate the efforts of their middle-class teacher- or principal-hero. Their troubled lives have been compassionately transformed by a caring and concerned human being.

A Cultural Contradiction

In spite of an emphasis on the value of individual transformation and self-reliance (utilitarian individualism), the students in these films continue to express a need for a relationship with their teacher. This is a need that the teacher-hero, in all good conscience, can't ignore. Without their work, who else will save these students? In *Blackboard Jungle* Miller agrees to stay in school provided that Mr. Dadier does not quit. In *Dangerous Minds* Raul agrees to graduate only if Ms. Johnson does not leave the school. In *Up the Down Staircase* Jose's transformation as a student is due entirely to the efforts of Ms. Barrett (who decides not to quit because of Jose's transformation). In *Teachers* Palickian's decision to care about school is implicitly predicated on Mr. Jerrell's decision to care about teaching. In *Lean on Me* the crowd of students who gather to demand that Principal Clark be released from jail proclaim, "We don't want a good principal. We want Mr. Clark!"

There is an implicit assumption in most of these movies that if the teacher- or principal-hero does not agree to stay on at the school, the students would quickly jettison the lessons they have learned and return to their apathetic underperformance and violent behavior. There is no other teacher (and certainly no school reform) that can reach these students. There is a *dependence* upon the middle-class teacher by these lower-class students, which points to an inherent contradiction in these movies—a contradiction that stems from the ambiguities of American individualism itself.

The teachers encourage their students to transcend their dysfunctional families, their rotten peers, their lousy schools, and their culture of poverty. The teachers encourage their students to use their power as individuals to compete successfully and to attain a higher social status. Yet to reach this goal, the students are necessarily placed in a position of dependence upon the teacher- or principal-hero. For all of the rhetoric about independence and individual achievement, we never see the students in these urban high school films fully express their autonomy. Rather, their individualism is embedded in their relationship with the teacher-hero. The authors of *Habits of the Heart* make exactly this point when they discuss one of the ironies of American individualism. In short, they argue, the individual needs attachment with society in order to be fulfilled. Individualism requires community for it to have meaning:

> This ambivalence shows up particularly clearly at the level of myth in our literature and our popular culture. There we find the fear that society may overwhelm the individual and destroy any chance of autonomy unless he stands against it, but also recognition that it is only in relation to society that the individual can fulfill himself and that if the break with society is too radical, life has no meaning at all.[53]

Similarly, the lessons that these urban school films teach about autonomy, competition, and individual achievement ironically require a relationship of interdependence, cooperation, and shared goals. The utilitarian individualism of independence and achievement is heralded explicitly, while the lessons about interdependence, cooperation, and shared goals are left implicit. This may reflect American culture's lack of a language to articulate (or an unwillingness to acknowledge) our reliance on community. Nonetheless, these films seem to hint that such social connections may ironically be an important ingredient in the recipe of American individualism. As the anthropologist Claude Levi-Strauss has argued, folktales and myths can help to resolve cultural contradictions.[54] They help to ease cultural tension and make coherent sense out of the world.

Perhaps these urban school folktales provide American audiences with an opportunity to reconcile some apparent cultural contradictions.

Conclusion: The Urban School Frontier

With the exception of *Cheaters* and *Light It Up*, these urban high school films are a celebration of the middle-class values of rational calculation and individual achievement. The low-income students in urban public schools must become autonomous utilitarian individuals if they are to achieve any measure of mainstream success. There is no suggestion that a longer-term solution to the problems in urban public high schools must address employment in the inner city, equitable school funding, sensitivity to racial and class differences, or the restructuring of urban schools. In true Hollywood fashion, the middle-class teachers and principals have saved the day as solitary heroes. These educators—mysterious, well intentioned, alone, selfless, and heroic—are the cowboys of the dangerous and untamed urban high school frontier. They represent the essence of American rugged individualism—they stand outside society in order to save it.[55] The students, meanwhile, are explicitly grateful for their salvation. However, the salvation the teacher-heroes offer is inevitably tangled up with the contradictions of American individualism—the independence they demand of students requires a relationship of dependence to achieve.

Certainly, a high score on a test, an emotional tribute to a beloved teacher, and happy and optimistic students make for a good dramatic conclusion. But what do these endings imply for the public's image of urban schools? The audience is left feeling triumphant and optimistic about the potential for improvement in urban public schools. By simplifying the many problems of urban public education and turning inner-city students and public school teachers into caricatures of their respective social classes, however, Hollywood is doing nothing but reflecting middle-class anxiety about the problems of inner-city schools and the naive hope that such problems need not a sustained political commitment from all members of society, but merely the individual moral conversion of poor students.

When Hollywood turns the lens on middle-class students in suburban public schools, however, the stories change dramatically. The next chapter outlines the ways in which Hollywood and American culture make very different sense of middle-class suburban adolescents than they do of poor adolescents in urban areas.

Notes

1. See Considine, *The Cinema of Adolescence.*
2. Ibid., p. 122.
3. Quoted from the back of the 1996 MGM/UA Home Entertainment and Turner Entertainment Company Vintage Classics VHS packaging.
4. See Berliner, David C., and Bruce J. Biddle. 1995. *The Manufactured Crisis*. Reading, MA: Addison Wesley, for a good discussion of the perceived crisis in American public education.
5. Quoted from the back of the 1995 Hollywood Pictures Home Video VHS packaging.
6. For an elementary school version of *Dangerous Minds* and *Blackboard Jungle*, see 1999's *Music of the Heart*. As the promotional material for the video says, "A single mother with little more than talent and the determination to make a difference, Roberta Guaspari overcame the skepticism of everyone who didn't think she should be teaching violin to students in a tough inner-city neighborhood."
7. Giroux, Henry. 1996. "Race, Pedagogy and Whiteness in 'Dangerous Minds.'" *Cineaste* 22, no. 4: 46–50.
8. Ehrenreich, *Fear of Falling*, p. 94.
9. Franklin, Benjamin. 1941. *The Autobiography of Benjamin Franklin*. New York: Walter J. Black, p. 130.
10. See Eckert, Penelope. 1989. *Jocks and Burnouts: Social Categories and Identity in High School*. New York: Teachers College Press.
11. McCarthy, Cameron, et al. 1996. "Race, Suburban Resentment, and the Representation of the Inner City in Contemporary Film and Television." In *Off White*. Michelle Fine, et al., editors. New York: Routledge, p. 230.
12. Hurn, Christopher. 1993. *The Limits and Possibilities of Schooling*. Boston: Allyn and Bacon, p. 151.
13. Banfield, Edward. 1968. *The Unheavenly City*. Boston: Little, Brown.
14. See, for instance, Wilson, William Julius. 1996. *When Work Disappears*. New York: Knopf; Bourdieu, "Cultural Reproduction and Social Reproduction"; Swidler, Ann. 1986. "Culture in Action: Symbols and Strategies." *American Sociological Review* 51: 273–286; Lareau, Annette. 1987. "Social Class Differences in Family–School Relationships: The Importance of Cultural Capital." *Sociology of Education* 60: 73–85; Willis, Paul. 1981. *Learning to Labor*. New York: Columbia University Press; Gibson, Margaret A., and John U. Ogbu, editors. 1991. *Minority Status and Schooling: A Comparative Study of Immigrants and Involuntary*

76

Minorities. New York: Garland; and MacLeod, Jay. 1995. *Ain't No Makin' It: Aspirations and Attainment in a Low-Income Neighborhood*. Boulder, CO: Westview Press.

15. Wilson, *When Work Disappears*.
16. Wilson, William J. 1987. *The Truly Disadvantaged: The Inner City, the Underclass, and Public Policy*. Chicago: University of Chicago Press, pp. 158–159.
17. Schuman, Howard, Charlotte Steeh, Lawrence Bobo, and Maria Krysan. 1998. *Racial Attitudes in America: Trends and Interpretations*. Cambridge, MA: Harvard University Press.
18. Wolfe, Alan. 1998. *One Nation, After All*. New York: Viking, p. 205.
19. Ibid., p. 204.
20. Roper Poll. January 2003. "Child Tax Credit Survey."
21. Hutcheson, Ron. 2001. "Bush Calls for Faith-Based 'Assault on Poverty.'" *Sacramento Bee* (May 21): A15.
22. Todd Gitlin, too, notes in his study of television that Hollywood prefers to depict individual-level solutions to social problems rather than collective ones. See Gitlin, Todd. 1983. *Inside Prime Time*. New York: Pantheon.
23. While the word *jungle* in the title might suggest a racist overtone regarding which students are truly wild, it is important to note that *Blackboard Jungle* depicts a racially mixed classroom of working-class students. In fact, the African American student turns out to be the most amenable to Mr. Dadier's lessons, while an Irish American student is the most incorrigible.
24. For critics of public education, see Lieberman, Myron. 1993. *Public Education: An Autopsy*. Cambridge, MA: Harvard University Press; and Chubb, John E., and Terry M. Moe. 1990. *Politics, Markets, and America's Schools*. Washington, DC: Brookings Institution Press.
25. Gallup Organization. 2004. "36th Annual Phi Delta Kappan/Gallup Poll" (September).
26. For a good discussion of the teacher as savior, see Ayers, "A Teacher Ain't Nothin' but a Hero."
27. MacLeod, *Ain't No Makin' It*; see also Bourdieu, "Cultural Reproduction and Social Reproduction"; and Wilson, *When Work Disappears* and *The Truly Disadvantaged*.
28. For a good overview of Ogbu's research and similar research by others, see Gibson and Ogbu, *Minority Status and Schooling*.
29. Steele, Claude M. 1997. "A Threat in the Air: How Stereotypes Shape the Intellectual Identities and Performance of Women and African Americans." *American Psychologist* 52: 613–629.

30. MacLeod, *Ain't No Makin' It*; see also Willis, Paul. 1981. *Learning to Labor*. New York: Columbia University Press.
31. Coleman, James, et al. 1966. *Equality of Educational Opportunity*. Washington, DC: U.S. Government.
32. Kozol, Jonathan. 1991. *Savage Inequalities: Children in America's Schools*. New York: Crown Publishers, p. 5.
33. Ibid., p. 57.
34. See Natriello, G., Aaron M. Pallas, and E. L. McDill. 1986. *Community Resources for Responding to the Dropout Problem*. New Brunswick, NJ: Rutgers University Press; and Fine, Michelle. 1991. *Framing Dropouts: Notes on the Politics of an Urban High School*. Albany: State University of New York Press.
35. See Bryk, Anthony S., and Valerie E. Lee. 1993. *Catholic Schools and the Common Good*. Cambridge, MA: Harvard University Press; Natriello, Gary, Edward L. McDill, and Aaron M. Pallas. 1990. *Schooling the Disadvantaged: Racing Against Catastrophe*. New York: Teachers College Press; Darling-Hammond, Linda. 1997. *The Right to Learn: A Blueprint for Creating Schools That Work*. San Francisco: Jossey-Bass; Corbett, Dick, Bruce Wilson, and Belinda Williams. 2002. *Effort and Excellence in Urban Classrooms: Expecting and Getting Success with All Students*. New York: Teachers College Press; and Lee, Valerie E. 2001. *Restructuring High Schools for Equity and Excellence: What Works*. New York: Teachers College Press.
36. See Rosenthal, Robert, and Lenore Jacobson. 1968. *Pygmalion in the Classroom*. New York: Holt, Rinehart, and Winston; and Sewell, William H., Robert M. Hauser, and David L. Featherman, editors. 1976. *Schooling and Achievement in American Society*. New York: Academic Press.
37. Purkey, Stewart C., and Marshall S. Smith. 1983. "Effective Schools: A Review." *Elementary School Journal* 83: 427–452.
38. Epstein, Joyce L. 1987. "Parent Involvement: What Research Says to Administrators." *Education and Urban Society* 19, no. 2: 119–136; and Epstein, Joyce L. 1996. "Perspectives and Previews on Research and Policy for School, Family, and Community Partnerships." In *Family–School Links: How Do They Affect Educational Outcomes?* A. Booth and J. Dunn, editors. Mahwah, NJ: Lawrence Erlbaum Associates.
39. Lee, *Restructuring High Schools*.
40. Darling-Hammond, *The Right to Learn*.
41. Deschenes, S., David Tyack, and Larry Cuban. 2001. "Mismatch: Historical Perspectives on Schools and Students Who Don't Fit Them." *Teachers College Record* 103, no.4: 525–547.

42. Oakes, Jeannine. 1985. *Keeping Track: How Schools Structure Inequality*. New Haven, CT: Yale University Press.

43. Johnson, LouAnne. 1992. *Dangerous Minds*. New York: St. Martin's Paperback.

44. Ibid., p. 117.

45. Furthermore, there were other telling modifications of reality in the Hollywood version. For instance, Ms. Johnson's most academically successful student, Callie, was actually in an advanced class, not the remedial class depicted in the film. Ms. Johnson received much more help from her teacher friend Hal in real life than the movie depicts. Instead of using the folk lyrics of Bob Dylan (poetry more popular with the middle-aged white middle class than nonwhite inner-city kids in the 1990s), the real Ms. Johnson used rap lyrics as poetic examples. Finally, half of the actual Academy class was composed of white middle-class students.

46. Johnson, *Dangerous Minds*, p. 189.

47. While nearly 75 percent of the urban school films in this sample have remarkably similar plots and messages, there are a few exceptions in addition to *Cheaters* and *Light It Up*. Ten of the urban school films do not have an adult teacher or principal hero as the central character. Among them, *Cooley High*, *Class Act*, and *Love Don't Cost a Thing* are also unique as three of the six comedies in the urban school sample. *Fame*, as much a musical as it is a drama, is primarily a series of vignettes about students at a selective performing arts high school. While *Zebrahead* and *Save the Last Dance* take place in urban high school settings, their stories more closely resemble the themes of the suburban school films analyzed in the next chapter. This is perhaps the case because their central characters are white middle-class students who fall in love with poor African American students. *Love Don't Cost a Thing* is a remake of the 1987 suburban school film *Can't Buy Me Love*. The 2003 remake is set in a mixed-race and mixed-class Long Beach, California, public high school. Its theme is the same as that in the suburban school original: The division between the popular and unpopular students is artificial and ultimately destructive—it's best just to be yourself (*then* you will be popular!).

48. *187*, it should be noted, grossed about the same amount as *Light It Up*. Figures are from www.imbd.com and www.boxofficeguru.com.

49. Quoted from the back of the 1988 RCA/Columbia Pictures Home Video VHS packaging.

50. In a strikingly similar sequel, the violent teacher-hero of *The Substitute 2* achieves the same sort of victory. High school members of the carjacking gang "The Brotherhood" kill a popular teacher. The slain

teacher's brother, a mercenary soldier, is hired as a substitute teacher in Lenthrop High, a violent New York City high school. Under the alias "Mr. Perakowski," he discovers (no surprise here) that the ringleader of the gang is a well-respected teacher at the high school. With the help of a former mercenary colleague and the school janitor (a shell-shocked veteran of the Vietnam War), the substitute kills the evil teacher, defeats "The Brotherhood," and rescues the school from the grips of a criminal conspiracy.

51. Before *Lean on Me* was filmed, the real-life principal Joe Clark was praised publicly by President George Bush and his conservative secretary of education, William Bennett, for his no-nonsense approach to expelling the "bad" students and holding the other students responsible for their educational achievement. Principal Clark received a great deal of media attention, including a cover story in *Time* magazine as well as the major motion picture based on his experiences at East Side High. It is noteworthy that Principal Clark's methods were publicized by both the Bush administration as well as by Hollywood. It is not enough to analyze *how* Hollywood depicts stories about schooling. We must also ask how Hollywood *chooses* which school stories to tell. As a principal of an inner-city high school not far from East Side High told Jonathan Kozol, "There is a notion out there that the fate of all these children is determined from their birth. If they fail, it's something in themselves. That, I believe, is why Joe Clark got so much praise from the white media." Kozol, *Savage Inequalities*, p. 142.

52. For more on this point, see Grant, "Using Popular Films to Challenge Preservice Teachers' Beliefs."

53. Bellah, et al., *Habits of the Heart*, p. 144.

54. Levi-Strauss, Claude. 1978. *Myth and Meaning: Cracking the Code of Culture*. Toronto: University of Toronto Press.

55. A point made by Wright, *Sixguns and Society*.

Expressing Oneself in a Culture of Conformity

Contradictions in Suburban School Cinema

Whoso would be a man, must be a nonconformist . . . Nothing is at last sacred but the integrity of your own mind.[1]

—Ralph Waldo Emerson

How could youths better learn to live than by at once trying the experiment of living? Methinks this would exercise their minds as much as mathematics.[2]

—Henry David Thoreau

I don't go to school. I got kicked out . . . for thinking for myself.

—Legs in *Foxfire*

People like you and me, we don't have to play by the rules. We make our own.

—Deric in *Better Luck Tomorrow*

Not all high school films are created equal. The suburban high school film differs significantly from the urban high school film. While this might not be terribly surprising, it is important to note that the differences between these two subgenres are not primarily a reflection of the real-life differences between urban and suburban high schools. The dramatization and sensationalism of Hollywood films make them poor documents of social reality. However, it is Hollywood's predictable tendency to dramatize and sensationalize particular elements of urban and suburban high schools that makes these high school films relevant for critical social analysis. The urban and suburban high school films are consistently told from different points of view, have different moods, have different heroes and villains, tell different stories, and teach different lessons. The American cultural value of individualism is at the heart of both subgenres, but it is expressed in very different ways in each. While the urban high school films highlight the hard work and self-sufficiency of utilitarian individualism, the suburban high school films emphasize the identity formation and freedom of expressive individualism. The differences between these two subgenres are due to the ways in which American culture makes sense of adolescents from different social classes. When poor students are represented on screen, Hollywood portrays utilitarian individualism as their key out of the culture of poverty. When middle-class students are represented, Hollywood portrays expressive individualism as their key out of the culture of popularity and conformity.

This chapter will show that while adults are nearly always the heroes in the urban school films, students are the heroes of the suburban school films. While the urban school films are told from the point of view of a middle-class adult, the suburban school films are told from the point of view of a middle-class teenager. In dramatic contrast to the urban school films, the suburban school films are only tangentially related to the school *as a school*. That is, in the suburban school films the high schools are not recognized primarily as places of learning. In fact, academic content plays almost no role in the suburban school films, while it is the central feature of nearly all the urban school films.[3] In its place, the major concerns facing the students in these suburban school films are popularity, conformity, dating and sex, individual self-expression, and "finding" oneself. While the students in the urban school films must conform to middle-class values and adult authority in order to transcend the culture of poverty, I argue in this chapter that the students in the suburban school films must reject peer conformity and the authority of adults (teachers and parents) in order to realize and freely express their true individual identities.

This pattern has been true for at least fifty years. In the same year that *Blackboard Jungle* was released, *Rebel Without a Cause* made its debut. In contrast to *Blackboard Jungle*'s focus on the activities of the urban school classroom and the heroic actions of the middle-class teacher, *Rebel Without a Cause* focuses on the angst of a middle-class suburban adolescent hero who struggles against adult authority in order to find some meaning to life. This adolescent struggle has become very familiar terrain in the suburban school film over the years. *Pump Up the Volume*, for instance, is the 1990s version of *Rebel Without a Cause*.

82

Being a White Upper-Middle-Class Suburban Teenager Sucks

Consider the life of a teenager. You have parents and teachers telling you what to do. You have movies, magazines and TV telling you what to do. But you know what you have to do. Your job, your purpose, is to get accepted, get a girlfriend and think up something great to do for the rest of your life.

—"Hard Harry" in *Pump Up the Volume*

Oh, the life of a middle-class suburban teenager! As Hard Harry notes, American teens are oppressed by their high school, by their families, by the popular culture, by pressures to conform, and by career expectations. The middle-class suburban teenager in the United States has no freedom and no voice. Hard Harry (meek high school student Mark Hunter by day and raunchy pirate radio DJ by night) is not concerned about developing positive study habits, earning good grades, achieving high SAT scores, or making college plans. Instead, he devotes his energies to saving the soul of the American teenager from the stultifying effects of adult society. He, like J. D. Salinger's adolescent hero Holden Caulfield, desperately wants to be the "catcher in the rye"—to help prevent adolescents from growing up, selling out, and becoming phonies. Hard Harry epitomizes the independent hero of the suburban high school film.

In his radio broadcasts to the students of Hubert Humphrey High School, an orderly, bland, and mostly white suburban high school with a good academic reputation and the highest SAT scores in Arizona, Hard Harry rages against the generation of his parents (the baby boomers), against suburbia, against the teachers and guidance counselors at the school, and against the middle-class conformity he sees as the oppression his generation must overcome. His parents are ex-hippies from the 1960s, and his father is now a school commissioner in the local district. Having moved from town to town as his father moved up the professional ranks, Harry is bitter that his parents sold out in pursuit of conventionally defined success. His parents, however, are unaware of his rage. Mark Hunter is a quiet, shy, and studious boy who gets good grades and lacks much of a social life. His parents are worried that he is not making friends at his new school, but he brushes aside their attempts to help: "The deal is I get decent grades and you guys leave me alone."

In spite of Mark Hunter's quiet and obedient demeanor, Hard Harry is an angry and loquacious spokesperson for all the disaffected youth at his school. He encourages his adolescent listeners to throw off the shackles of their repression at home and school, to stand up to authority, to rebel, to deviate from the norm, to find their true identity, and to turn their anger, boredom, frustration, and depression into creative self-expression. Unfortunately, one of his listeners, a depressed, lonely, and nerdy teenage boy, commits suicide shortly after calling in to Harry's radio show. The school authorities, in particular the rigid principal, Miss Cresswood, blame the suicide on Harry's illegal broadcasts. The Federal Communications Commission begins an investigation to find him and shut down his pirate radio broadcasts. The angry and scared parents in the community meet with school officials to discuss the threat that Harry poses to their children. Meanwhile, the students increasingly look to Harry as their hero and role model.

While Harry speaks directly to the social outcasts at the school—the assortment of nerds, social misfits, low achievers, and punks that occupies the margins of many schools—he also finds a receptive audience in the students at the center of the school—the popular and high-achieving students. Paige Woodward is one of the beautiful, popular, and high-achieving girls at Hubert Humphrey High School. She, too, however, suffers under the oppression of conformity enforced by the pressure of parents, peers, and the school. While popular and successful, she is never truly happy. Yet she suffers in silence until Harry's broadcasts inspire her to reject the expectations everyone has of her and to just be herself. In the community meeting to address the parental concerns about Harry's broadcasts, Paige defends Harry: "He's trying to tell you there is something wrong with this school. We are all really scared to be who we really are. I'm not perfect . . . inside I'm screaming!"

The authorities eventually catch up to Harry. As the FCC zeroes in to shut down Harry's broadcast, he urges his listeners to not let the authorities win. He pleads with the youth of his generation not to give up, not to commit suicide: "High school is the bottom. Being a teenager sucks. But that's the point. Surviving it is the whole point. Quitting is not going to make you stronger. Living will!" As Hard Harry's career as a pirate DJ nears its end, he urges others to pick up his mantle and to exercise freedom of speech. He urges students to "find your voice and use it!"

Harry is the hero of the movie, but he is no martyr. Upon his arrest it is learned that Principal Cresswood was illegally expelling the "losers and troublemakers" in order to maintain the school's high scores on the Scholastic Aptitude Test. Harry's crusade reveals that the narrow middle-class focus on academic achievement is soulless and corrupt. Even Harry's school commissioner father is disgusted and promises to have the principal fired. And Harry (now simply Mark Hunter) finally, and ironically, ends up with a girlfriend.

Some have suggested that *Pump Up the Volume* and similar films represent an underlying student resistance to school and other oppressive social structures.[4] In her study of high school films, Mary Dalton writes:

> There are . . . a few films that depict the school as an overt terrain of struggle where students form a collective group of opposition and begin resistance activities against the educational hierarchy and, by implication, the larger societal institutions of control represented by their school and school personnel.[5]

While *Pump Up the Volume* is perhaps the most explicitly political of all the suburban school films in the sample, and the closest one gets to a film that offers a critical analysis of the schooling of middle-class American youth, I am somewhat skeptical of Dalton's interpretation. While Hard Harry makes some insightful remarks about the emotional emptiness of a high school education, his critique rarely rises above the level of routine teen angst. Ultimately, *Pump Up the Volume* is an anti-teen-suicide film. Admittedly, many of the teens in these suburban school films *are* genuinely dissatisfied with school and with their lives in general. In contrast to the problems of the students in the urban school films, however—underfunded schools, drug dealing, violence, academic failure, dropping out, racism, poverty, unemployment, homelessness, prison, death, and so on—the teen angst of the suburban school students appears to be nothing but the cries of spoiled children who live comfortable lives, have bright futures, but chafe under the vaguely defined "oppression" of their parents and teachers. They are rebels without much of a cause.

Furthermore, in the few cases when the heroes of the suburban school films *do* have a cause (beyond gaining the attention of a love interest), the enemy is almost always depicted as an *individual* and not the wider political, economic, or educational system that a truly critical social analysis would target. Even in the overtly political *Pump Up the Volume*, victory is achieved when the evil Principal Cresswood is revealed as a corrupt administrator responsible for most of the problems in the school. Hollywood does not provide much material with which to craft a critical pedagogy. American culture (and Hollywood) prefers individual transformation to structural transformation.

I am certainly in favor of developing a critical pedagogy that takes student voices seriously (urban as well as suburban school students). And, as Dalton suggests, a critical viewing of these films may provide an opportunity for some students to analyze their own educational experiences in a meaningful way. However, we must recognize that the challenges facing urban school students are very different from the alienation facing middle-class suburban school students. Rather than over-reading the suburban school films as texts that directly challenge the pedagogies oppressing all youth in postmodern society, the suburban school films are better understood when they are viewed in relief against the cinematic backdrop of the urban school films. The same American culture produces and supports both the urban and suburban school films. Hollywood's starkly contrasting images of urban and suburban youth tell us much more about American culture, educational inequality, and the dynamics of adolescent angst than do the images of youth in either the suburban or urban school films alone.

Compared with the urban high school films discussed in the previous chapter, *Pump Up the Volume* is a very different sort of high school film. But it is not an anomaly. It conveniently summarizes the major themes of most of the films based in middle-class suburban high schools. The heroes are independent and freethinking students. The antagonists are narrow-minded achievement-oriented adults (and often narrow-minded popular students). Obedience to authority and conformity to peer pressure are criticized. Mild disobedience and creative self-expression are rewarded. Individualism is celebrated—but it is not an independence from poverty that defines it, as in the urban school films. Rather, it is an independence from peer pressure and the constraints of adult authority that allows students to express their true identities. It is an example of expressive individualism rather than the utilitarian strain of American individualism found in the urban school films. As the next section demonstrates, the expressive individualism of the middle-class suburban school films rejects (or at least ignores) the utilitarian measure of success that was the exalted goal of the urban school films—academic achievement.

The Irrelevance of Academics in the Suburban School Films

While academic achievement is offered as a solution to the problems facing the students in the urban school films, academic achievement is ignored, criticized, or even depicted as dangerous to the students in the suburban school films. For most of the suburban school films the school is central to the plot, but primarily as a social space within which the drama of teen angst is played out. The dramatic questions in the suburban school films are not about passing or failing, graduating or not graduating, going to college or not going to college.[6] The students in the suburban high school films may do well in school or they may do poorly in school, but it matters very little to the story. In either case, the students don't seem to care about learning or academic achievement. While disinterest in school was enough to drive the adult characters of the urban school films into heroic action, it raises very little notice in the suburban school films.

Whether it is Ferris Bueller's wildly successful efforts to avoid class during a "day off" from his suburban Chicago high school, the conspicuous absence of the classroom in *The Breakfast Club*, Cher's shameless bargaining with her gullible teachers for higher grades in *Clueless*, Hard Harry's disgust with the hypocrisy of the school in *Pump Up the Volume*, Jeffrey Spicolli's amused contempt for Mr. Hand's history class in *Fast Times at Ridgemont High*, or the angry and bitter resentment of school by nearly all of the students in *Rock and Roll High School*, academic matters are consistently downplayed in these films.

Unlike the students in the urban school films, the middle-class students in the suburban school films tend to take their education for granted. These students attend schools with plenty of resources, have parents who have been to college, and have peers who are headed to college as well. These characters know they will likely graduate from high school, attend college, and at least reproduce their parents' middle-class status. The rough social trajectory of their lives has essentially been predetermined, independent of their effort in school. They merely need to go through the motions. Therefore, the education of the suburban school students is not a central feature of the plot in these films. What matters most in these films is not academic achievement, but the achievement of one's independent identity.

For instance, in *She's All That*, Zach is the student body president, a star athlete, and the most popular guy in school. He is apparently a gifted student as well (he has the fourth highest grade point average in his class), although that part of his life is never depicted on screen. He has been accepted to Yale, Harvard, and Dartmouth colleges. But Zach has problems. His dad, a wealthy Dartmouth alumnus, is putting pressure on him to choose Dartmouth: "[My dad says] pick a college, Zach. Pick a future. But what he's really saying is pick *my* college. Pick *my* future." Zach, however, wants to finally make his own decisions in life, to be independent. While most of the film tells the familiar story of the rich and beautiful popular student falling unexpectedly in love with the lower-middle-class or working-class oddball (see also *Pretty in Pink*, *The Breakfast Club*, *Say Anything*, *Can't Buy Me Love*, *Some Kind of Wonderful*, *Cry Baby*, *10 Things I Hate About You*, *Crazy/Beautiful*, and *A Cinderella Story*), Zach is tortured throughout the film by the decision of which elite private college to attend. Only in this context can his final decision to choose Yale over Dartmouth be seen as an act of independence and rebellion.

Zach's acceptance to Yale University is never legitimated for the audience. Any schoolwork or learning that justifies acceptance at such competitive colleges takes place backstage, out of the audience's view. Even though schoolwork plays no role in the plot, the last scene of the movie takes place at graduation. While mere participation in graduation was an achievement in and of itself for the students in the urban school films, for Zach participation takes on an entirely different meaning. Expressing his newly discovered individuality (and making good on a bet), he accepts his diploma in the nude—his individuality and self-confidence on view for all.

Similarly, in *10 Things I Hate About You*, Kat is an intelligent, beautiful, and angry young woman who desperately tries not to live up to others' expectations of her. She charts her own path, even if that means the loss of popularity at school. She does not date boys and she does not participate in the quest for popularity that her peers (including her sister) are heavily invested in. The focus of the film is on Kat's efforts to find her true self and to assert her independence. She does so in the pursuit of a love interest and in her choice of colleges. She must choose between two high-status colleges—Sarah Lawrence (her first choice) and the University of Washington (her medical doctor dad's alma mater and preferred choice). As in *She's All That*, the battle between her and her father about which school she will attend becomes symbolic of her developing adult identity. The academic path she traveled to be in a position to choose between such elite colleges, however, is never revealed to the audience. Apparently, Kat's upper-middle-class home life and her experiences in a high-quality Seattle public high school are enough for the audience to believe that she will follow in the successful professional footsteps of her father. In an act of adolescent rebellion and identity formation, however, she will do so at Sarah Lawrence and not at the University of Washington. Kat finds and expresses her adult identity by forging her own path, independent of her family, friends, and school.

If there is any action directly related to academic achievement in the suburban school films, it is usually heroic action by students *against* the achievement ideology and against the authorities of the school. In a stunning reversal of the messages conveyed in the urban school films, Hollywood can be quite critical of academic achievement when the plot takes place in a middle-class suburban high school. For instance, in *Disturbing Behavior*, conformity to the expectations of the school (academic achievement, obedience to adult authority, and joining the "right" crowd) is depicted as a serious threat to individuality and adolescent freedom. The adult authorities of the school and the "successful" mainstream students are defeated by the heroic actions of an unlikely collection of disobedient students who reject the authority of the school and resist the pressure to conform to the expectations of their teachers, parents, or peers.

The Threat of Academic Achievement

In *Disturbing Behavior* something is very wrong at Cradle Bay High School. It is a typical suburban high school in an upper-middle-class community in Washington State. It is populated by a typical grouping of student cliques—the "geeks," the "freaks," the "burnouts," and a special group called the Blue Ribbons. The Blue Ribbons are the jocks and the academic achievers of the school. They have high self-esteem, they identify with the school, they work hard, they are polite to others, they are respectful of adults, they are accomplished athletes and students, they are civic minded, and they are involved in school activities. They hang out innocently at the yogurt shop, dress modestly, and stay out of trouble.

While few teachers are featured in the film, the school psychologist is a prominent character. He is the supervisor of this elite club. The teachers and administrators *love* the Blue Ribbons. Parents, too, love the Blue Ribbons, and many try to get their children to join the club. The obedience, conformity, and high achievement that the club seems to foster are seen by most parents and school personnel as key to overcoming adolescent rebellion, drug use, and poor academic performance. Imagine how the urban school films would celebrate such a club!

And yet there is something not quite right about the Blue Ribbons. While they seem to be the ideal students, they are like robots. They dress alike, act alike, and, oddly, they explode in bursts of rage and violence from time to time. Their targets, however, are usually the burnouts of the school. These occasional transgressions are generally dismissed by school authorities. What is even more odd, however, is that many of the burnouts of the school become mysteriously converted to the Blue Ribbons—they suddenly become model students. Soon most of the school is filled with obedient high achievers. Rather than being celebrated, however, this sudden transformation from adolescent miscreant to honor student is a cause for grave concern. What is at stake is the individuality of the students. As the promotional material for the video version of the film states:

'Achieve, be excellent . . . and be afraid.' When the esteemed Blue Ribbon club of Cradle Bay High takes its slogans too far, things in the small coastal town begin to go wrong. Newcomer Steve Clark finds fast allies in Gavin, an overly imaginative paranoid and Rachel, a 'bad girl' with a razor-sharp tongue and a body to match. But when some 'dark sinister force' begins turning the school's curricularly challenged into the soulless, academic elite, these three 'outsiders' join in a desperate, dizzying race to avoid becoming insiders—and losing their individuality forever.[7]

The only ones who are worried about such "strange" behavior of peer conformity and academic achievement, however, are the remaining burnouts and rebels at the school. The parents, teachers, and administrators are more than happy to see the troubled students finally get their acts together, join school activities, and apply themselves academically. The only adult character to suspect that something is terribly wrong with the Blue Ribbons is the school janitor. (While in the urban school films a student who aspired to be a janitor would be resoundingly criticized, it is not uncommon for school janitors to be the wisest and most admired adult characters in the suburban school films; see also *The Breakfast Club* and *Not Another Teen Movie*.) Most of the Blue Ribbons, however, dismiss the janitor as a worthless laborer. His concerns are not taken at all seriously, except by the student-hero Steve Clark.

As a moody adolescent who is having a tough time adjusting to his new life in Cradle Bay, Steve Clark resists the efforts by his parents and the school psychologist to become a Blue Ribbon. As it turns out, he is right to be suspicious. The Blue Ribbons are a creation of the school psychologist, who implants computer chips into the students' eyes and brainwashes them to behave like perfect little students who never rebel, never question authority, never make mistakes, and never fail.

Unable to recruit Steve and his girlfriend voluntarily, the Blue Ribbons capture them and take them to the psychologist's clinic. As the psychologist tells Steve moments before he attempts to implant a computer chip into his eyes: "Adolescence is a mine field. But soon you'll be fully equipped to walk right through . . . It's time to leave mediocrity behind." Steve and his girlfriend manage to escape from the clinic before the psychologist can implant the computer chips. They meet up with another uninfected student who is worried that they have already been brainwashed into Blue Ribbons. To be sure, he gives them a test—"What is the capital of North Dakota?" He is relieved when they don't know the answer. Their ignorance is a sure sign that they are not Blue Ribbons.

Meanwhile, the janitor has learned that a mechanical device that emits a high-pitched noise in order to repel rats also happens to torture the Blue

Ribbons (due to a malfunction of their implanted computer chip). The janitor collects dozens of the devices, loads them into the back of his truck, turns them on, and drives to the psychologist's clinic, where the Blue Ribbons have gathered. The Blue Ribbons begin screaming in agony as the noise emitters disrupt their programming. They climb onto the truck to destroy the devices and the janitor sacrificially drives his truck over a cliff, killing them all.

All, that is, except one. One Blue Ribbon somehow survives. In the last scene of the film we see him again years later. He is training to become a teacher so that he can continue the psychologist's original project to implant the devices and change the behavior of disaffected and rebellious high school students. His teacher training takes him to a high school where Hollywood filmmakers just might approve of such behavior modification—an impoverished inner-city public high school.

In *Disturbing Behavior* (and many other suburban school films) academic success is the last thing on the minds of the student-heroes. Obedience to authority, conformity to the expectations of parents, teachers, and peers, and academic achievement clearly do *not* provide a solution to the problems in their lives. Rather, obedience, conformity, and academic achievement pose a direct threat to their identities. We have turned 180 degrees from the lessons of the urban school films.

If the students in the urban school films were to treat academic achievement with the disinterest or contempt expressed by the students in the suburban school films, they would be promptly kicked out of school (and out of the movies) and continue to suffer in their culture of poverty. The students in the suburban school films, however, are *rewarded* for such behavior. They win acclaim for their heroic action, they become popular in school, and they win the attention of their love interest. Furthermore, in spite of their lack of attention to academic matters, the middle-class suburban students tend to maintain their middle-class status. Rather than reflecting a political critique of the educational system, these films reinforce dominant notions of what it means to be a middle-class suburban adolescent in the United States.

American culture has very different conceptions of poor urban and middle-class suburban youth. Because of these different conceptions of adolescence and social class, the school plays a much different role in the urban and suburban school films. What middle-class American culture wants most for poor urban adolescents is a rejection of the culture of poverty and the attainment of a middle-class lifestyle and financial independence through hard work. Therefore, the school is central to this project of turning urban adolescents into responsible and gainfully employed adults. The occupational future of the "at risk" youth in the urban school films is in jeopardy if they do not abide by the lessons of their middle-class teachers.

On the other hand, because future gainful employment is generally assumed for the middle-class youth, what middle-class American culture wants most for the middle-class suburban adolescent is a stable and self-assured adult identity that is strong enough to resist peer pressure, thoughtless conformity, and self-destructive impulses. Since the ability of the students in the suburban school films to attain a middle-class lifestyle is rarely questioned (even when they reject the school), academic achievement is rarely a feature of the plot as it is in the urban school films.

Furthermore, the hostile attitude toward academic achievement in the suburban school films is representative of an ambivalence that middle-class Americans feel about utilitarian individualism. While there are cultural expectations that Americans should be rational, hardworking, and achievement-oriented, there is also a sense that the personal costs of such achievement can be too great. While not a high school film, 1967's classic film about cultural alienation, *The Graduate*, reflects this attitude beautifully. Ben, the recent college graduate in the film, confesses to his very conventional and financially successful father, "I'm just worried . . . about my future. I want it to be . . . different."

Middle-Class Conformity in American Culture

Don't you find it ridiculous that from day one they tell us to be unique. They tell us to be individuals. Then they give us a standardized test that makes us one faceless herd?

—Kyle in *The Perfect Score* (2004)

I suggest that these suburban school films reflect an American middle-class fear that conformity to the expectations of an achievement-oriented culture will eclipse the expressiveness and creativity of individuality. In the 1950s sociological classic *The Lonely Crowd*, David Riesman warned against the new American cultural and psychological character developing in the ascendant "new" middle class of corporate managers and bureaucrats. Riesman worried that the "other-directed" character of the new middle class depends upon others for approval and guidance rather than looking inward and charting an autonomous course:

What is common to all the other-directed people is that their contemporaries are the source of direction for the individual—either those known to him or those with whom he is indirectly acquainted, through friends and through the mass media.[8]

Similarly, C. Wright Mills wrote a withering critique of the new "white-collar" middle classes that were emerging as the dominant American social class in the postindustrial era. Mills argued that conformity is the hallmark of life in the corporate and bureaucratic world of employment. Unlike the earlier entrepreneur or farmer, the white-collar employee lives a drab life of suburban conformity and a lack of individuality:

The twentieth-century white-collar man has never been independent as the farmer used to be, nor as hopeful of the main chance as the businessman. He is always somebody's man, the corporation's, the government's, the army's; and he is seen as the man who does not rise. The decline of the free entrepreneur and the rise of the dependent employee on the American scene has paralleled the decline of the independent individual and the rise of the little man in the American mind.[9]

Riesman and Mills shared a fear that such cultural trends brought on by the rise of the new middle class implied that Americans were becoming a different sort of people—less autonomous, less competent, and less free. A middle class that is dependent upon corporate bosses and bureaucratic rules, that is passionate only about their status vis-à-vis their middle-class neighbors, and that looks to others for approval and direction is a middle class in trouble. In other words, the new middle class is caught up in the "rat race," trapped against its will in the "red tape" of bureaucracy, and preoccupied with "keeping up with the Joneses." Such cultural clichés capture the middle-class existence that developed in the latter half of the twentieth century. However, this is not a cultural critique relevant only to the 1950s. While the protest movements of the 1960s and 1970s encouraged the growth of nonconformity and the critical questioning of many middle-class values, the middle class in the 1980s and 1990s returned the national culture to values similar to those that were criticized by Mills and Riesman. For instance, a more recent cultural critic, Barbara Ehrenreich, notes that the middle-class "yuppies" of the 1980s, while they believed themselves to be unique individuals, unexpectedly found themselves to be conformists:

But many in the middle-class could see some part of themselves, some emerging constellation of tastes (for coarse-grain mustard, linen suits, or frequent workouts), and realize that they themselves had been labeled, caricatured, and fingered as part of some larger conformity emanating from beyond their individual will and judgment.[10]

While Mills bemoaned the possibility that the white-collar workers were content with such a life of conformity, that they were "cheerful robots,"

Riesman argued that the overwhelming psychological state of the new middle class was one of anxiety. Indeed, the cultural contradictions in the new middle class are enough to cause a severe case of diffuse anxiety. On the one hand, the spirit of American individualism and free expression remain cultural values, yet the work and domestic lives of the middle class seem to encourage conformity, obedience to authority, competition for status among peers, and the censorship of unpopular ideas.

I suggest that this anxious tension is still a problem facing today's middle class. In spite of (or perhaps because of) the corporate rat race, the red tape of bureaucracy, and the quest to match the consumption of the Joneses, there is, among the middle class, a powerful underlying longing for independence, creative self-expression, and rebellion. In other words, there is also a tendency in American culture to express Riesman's "inner-directed" character type—one who has a strong sense of individuality, autonomy, and creativity. Perhaps this tension finds some measure of at least temporary resolution in entertainment, such as Hollywood films. For instance, the antagonists in the suburban high school films are none other than the characters who were the utilitarian middle-class heroes of the urban school films—the teachers. While the middle-class teachers offered utilitarian salvation to the urban poor, in the suburban school films these cowboys wear black hats. Teachers are once again representatives of middle-class American culture, but this time that culture offers not salvation, but oppression. It is up to the student-hero (the expressive individual) to defeat this symbol of conventional, utilitarian, and conformist authority.

We Don't Need No Education: Middle-Class Teachers as Antagonists

In addition to the generally hostile or indifferent attitude toward learning in these suburban school films, teachers (and adults in general) are treated with either hostility or indifference. Far from representing the middle-class civility and values of the urban school teacher-heroes, teachers are depicted in many of the suburban school films as, at best, benign fools, or, at worst, ruthless enemies. As representatives of a stale and oppressive middle-class future of corporate, bureaucratic, and suburban conformity, the middle-class teachers in the suburban school films are definitely *not* characters to be emulated.

Rather than offering needed assistance to the students, the teachers in the suburban school films (to the extent to which teachers are featured at all) are often depicted as a direct threat to the students. In contrast to the songs that refer to the urban high school students as dangerous jungle animals, the film soundtracks to *Disturbing Behavior* and *The Faculty* feature Pink Floyd's song of adolescent rebellion, "Another Brick in the Wall (Part II)," which implies that it is the teachers who are dangerous, not the students.

Rather than depending upon and cooperating with an adult authority figure in order to achieve academic goals, the students in the suburban school films must form their adult identities *in opposition to* adult figures. We saw how in *Disturbing Behavior* adult characters can threaten the identity and independence of youth. There are other films, too, where adults are antagonists to the student-heroes. One of the most explicit is *Teaching Mrs. Tingle*.

Far removed from the teacher-hero role in the urban school films, Mrs. Tingle is a mean-spirited, bitter, and terrifying presence in her history classroom. She routinely insults and humiliates her students, grades them harshly, and delights in the abuse of her power. Leigh Ann Watson is a bright lower-middle-class student from a single-parent home. She is one of the best students in school, but she has not been able to impress the stubborn Mrs. Tingle. In order to escape her small town and to attend college, Leigh Ann is in desperate need of an academic scholarship. To win the scholarship, she needs to graduate first in her class. All that stands in her way is Mrs. Tingle.

Leigh Ann's final history project, an impressively detailed re-creation of a diary of a seventeenth-century accused Salem witch, is assessed brutally by Mrs. Tingle, who favors the sycophantic Trudie (Leigh Ann's academic rival). Leigh Ann's hopes for a college education seem dashed. Meanwhile, Luke, an academically challenged burnout, steals a copy of Mrs. Tingle's final exam and offers it to Leigh Ann. Leigh Ann refuses to accept the exam, but Luke stuffs it into her backpack just before Mrs. Tingle walks into the room. Mrs. Tingle discovers the exam and seems pleased to have caught the "smartest girl in school" cheating.

In order to help set things straight, Luke, Leigh Ann, and Leigh Ann's best friend, Jo Lynn, go to Mrs. Tingle's house that night to plead on Leigh Ann's behalf. Nevertheless, Mrs. Tingle has no sympathy for Leigh Ann. In desperation, Luke raises a crossbow (the final history project of another student in class) to threaten Mrs. Tingle. He yells, "Time to teach Tingle a lesson . . . You can't keep treating people the way you do!" Mrs. Tingle struggles with Luke, the crossbow drops, and Jo Lynn picks it up and fires it at Mrs. Tingle, who is knocked unconscious. The three students then tie Mrs. Tingle to her bed, conspire to frame her in a sex scandal, and plan to use the incriminating photographs as blackmail against her. Mrs. Tingle spends most of the movie tied up as she and her student captors wage psychological warfare on each other.

Eventually, Leigh Ann finds Mrs. Tingle's grade book and changes Trudie's final grade to a B and her own to an A. She delivers the grade book to the counselor's office, and the grades are posted. When Trudie sees the grades, she is incredulous about her B. Meanwhile, Mrs. Tingle manages to escape from the bed and ties Luke to the bedposts. After a violent struggle with Leigh Ann, Mrs. Tingle attempts to kill her with the crossbow. Rather than hitting Leigh Ann, however, Mrs. Tingle accidentally shoots Trudie, who had come to Mrs. Tingle's house to complain about her B in history. As a result of this violent outburst, the principal fires Mrs. Tingle. Mrs. Tingle finally learns her lesson.

Ultimately, none of the students is punished for his or her behavior. Leigh Ann graduates first in her class and wins the academic scholarship that allows her to attend college. Assaulting your teacher, holding her captive, and blackmailing her seem to have the desired effect. Contrasted with the tragic outcome for the students who held a policeman hostage in the urban school film *Light It Up*, the happy ending of *Teaching Mrs. Tingle* speaks volumes about Hollywood's representation of urban and suburban school students.

The Evil High School Football Coach

In addition to the occasional rogue history teacher, high school football coaches are often portrayed as antagonists in the suburban school films (see *Lucas*, *All the Right Moves*, *Dazed and Confused*, and *Varsity Blues*). Rather than an adult figure who cares for the players and mentors them into adulthood, the typical coach in the suburban school film is a cruel and heartless man (frustrated by his own limitations in life) who crushes the spirit of his players and is ultimately defeated by a heroic student unafraid to stand up for himself. (*Remember the Titans* and *Radio*, which play more like urban school films with a coach-hero, are exceptions to this trend.) These high school football films celebrate the rejection of adult authority and the personal growth of adolescents as they learn to express their emerging adult identities.

Varsity Blues depicts football as a sacred activity that binds together a small Texas town and its high school.[11] The quarterback is revered around town as a larger-than-life hero (he even has his own billboard), the players are granted many entitlements as local celebrities, the players' fathers live vicariously through their sons, and the coach is an obnoxious egotist who cares only about winning. In spite of the American middle-class respect for tradition, authority, adherence to rules, and achievement, *Varsity Blues* suggests that sometimes you have to disobey authority, break with tradition, learn that winning is not everything that matters, and, as the promotional material for the film states, "make your own rules."

Moxon (Mox) is the brainy backup quarterback for the West Canaan Coyotes under the leadership of Coach Bud Kilmer, a local legend who has twenty-two district championships under his belt. Disliked by the coach, Mox rides the bench for most of the season with little interest in the game. (During one game he surreptitiously reads Kurt Vonnegut's *Slaughterhouse Five*, the paperback slipped within his football playbook.) His father, like most of the players' fathers, is a former Coyote who is obsessed with football and with his son's performance on the field. He asks Mox to pray for playing time each week. Mox, however, couldn't care any less about playing in the games. He is counting down the last games of the season and anxiously awaiting a hoped-for acceptance to Brown University. Mox loves football for the purity of the game, but he despises what it has become—a system that values winning at any cost and that eats up players and spits them out without regard for their best interests. He hates that football means more to the residents of West Canaan than it means to the players. And he hates that Coach Kilmer cares only for his own glory.

Coach Kilmer is a hard-nosed coach who demands the strict obedience of his players and ruthlessness on the field. "Don't show weakness!" he exclaims to his players. "Inflict pain!" He inflicts his own pain upon the players by coercing them to play hurt. In spite of several concussions, he insists that Billy Bob continue to play as a key offensive lineman. Lance Harbor, the star quarterback with an athletic scholarship waiting for him at Florida State, has an injured knee. Rather than letting the knee heal, however, Coach Kilmer has been injecting painkillers into it to keep Lance playing. Coach Kilmer is so driven to win that he disregards the long-term health consequences to Lance. Inevitably, Lance's knee is badly damaged in a game (jeopardizing his athletic scholarship to Florida State and his future football career). With Lance sidelined, Mox is required to play in his place. Mox plays well and wins game after game, although he does so by calling his own plays and not Coach Kilmer's. Kilmer, however, threatens to tamper with Mox's transcripts and to block his academic scholarship to Brown if he doesn't obey.

In the game that will decide the district championship, the running back Wendell injures his leg. At halftime Coach Kilmer tells the trainer to do anything he can to get Wendell back in the game. Mox is livid that Kilmer would sacrifice Wendell's health for Kilmer's glory. Mox stands up to Kilmer and threatens to quit playing if Wendell receives the painkiller. The rest of the players rally around Mox. "The only way we are going back on that field is without you," says Mox. Coach Kilmer, in humiliation, leaves the locker room and does not return for the second half of one of the most important games of his career. Meanwhile, inspired by Mox's locker room speech that asks them to play "like gods" for the love of the game, the players return to the field. Without Coach Kilmer, the team wins in dramatic fashion. It is the last football game that Mox ever plays. He receives the academic scholarship and enrolls in Brown University in the fall. The football legend Kilmer, thoroughly defeated, never coaches football again.

As the student-hero, Mox rejects adult authority, rebels against the expectations that his parents and the rest of town have of him, and breaks free from the shackles of the school to emerge as an independent hero. However, rather than being punished for his mutiny, Mox is rewarded for it. Under Mox's leadership the team triumphs, independent from school authority. The triumph, however, is the winning of the championship. Winning, Coach Kilmer's goal, is also the goal of the players. The triumph is not in their rejection of Kilmer, but in their winning without him. While poor urban school students need a middle-class adult as a guide in order to achieve their goals, middle-class suburban students (and, in this case, middle-class rural students) achieve their goals independently. Rather than challenging the status quo, however, these goals are often consistent with the goals the rejected adult authorities had for these students in the first place. The middle-class youth don't invent new goals. Rather, they travel their own path to achieve conventional ones. In the words of sociologist Robert Merton, these suburban school student-heroes are "innovators"— deviants who accept culturally defined goals, but pursue unconventional paths to achieve them.[12]

Adults as Fools

Adults are not antagonists in every suburban school film. They are often simply absent. In many cases, however, adults play the fool. Adults are often amusing secondary characters who suffer humiliation as the smooth-operating adolescents run circles around them. Whether adults are absent, antagonists, or fools, however, the resulting message is the same—adults are not required for middle-class suburban school students to discover their identity.

In *Ferris Bueller's Day Off*, Ferris Bueller is a confident, charming, and charismatic upper-middle-class high school senior who, from time to time, takes a day off from school because, as he says, "life moves pretty fast. If you don't stop and look around once and a while, you could miss it." Ferris is not about to miss out on life. And life, apparently, does not happen in high school, which, according to Ferris, is "a little childish and stupid." The only two teachers depicted in the film deliver their lectures with such a monotonous drone that it takes all the life out of their subjects and makes the school day nearly unendurable for the bored-to-death students. Ferris, however, is loved by nearly everyone—his parents, all the students and teachers in the school, and many others in the community at large. He is a bit of an operator at the school (he hacks into the school computer to change his record, he can get kids out of summer school, et cetera), but he never gets caught. His sister, however, is frustrated that everyone is fooled by Ferris's charms.

Ferris is pushing the limits on his school absences (nine so far in his final semester). One morning Ferris fools his gullible parents into believing he is sick. They forbid him to attend school, ignoring his mock protestations that he needs to attend school because it is an investment in his future: "I want to go to a good college so I can have a fruitful life." It is clear through his sarcasm that Ferris does not believe that his high school experiences will play any role in his future success, of which he has little doubt.

Mr. Rooney, the dean of students, is skeptical of Ferris's illness. Fed up with the student's cons, he makes it his mission to reveal Ferris as the "dangerous character" that he is. Mr. Rooney complains to his secretary that Ferris "jeopardizes my ability to effectively govern the student body." At each step of the way, however, Ferris thwarts Mr. Rooney's attempts to catch him.

Ferris orchestrates the release of his girlfriend from school (by faking the death of her grandmother) and convinces his neurotic friend Cameron to "borrow" his father's 1961 Ferrari. Ferris and his friends make the most of their day off. They go to the top of the Sears Tower and gaze out at the city. They observe the manic gestures of the traders at the Chicago Board of Trade. They con their way into a reservation for lunch at an exclusive French restaurant. They attend a Cubs game (where Ferris catches a foul ball). They lovingly absorb the masterpieces at the Art Institute of Chicago. They watch the German American Day parade (and Ferris takes center stage on one of the floats). Meanwhile, Mr. Rooney hunts the city for Ferris.

While Mr. Rooney searches for him unsuccessfully at the teen-filled video arcade of a local pizza parlor, Ferris and his friends are partaking in very adult (and upper-middle-class) activities in fancy restaurants, art museums, skyscrapers, expensive cars, and financial markets. Ferris and his friends will soon be successful upper-middle-class adults, but on this day off from high school they are simply rehearsing for that inevitability. While they act like adults with ease and confidence, however, Mr. Rooney acts like a childish fool. Mr. Rooney plays the bumbling slapstick fool to Ferris's cool and controlled hero. In the course of searching for Ferris, Mr. Rooney suffers the indignities of soda spit in his face, an attack by a dog, the loss of a shoe in a puddle of mud, ripped pants, a kick to the face, a towed car, and a lost wallet. Ferris, on the other hand, escapes all consequences for his faked illness, lies to his parents, absence from school, and the eventual destruction of the priceless Ferrari.

After leaving the pizza parlor, Mr. Rooney goes to Ferris's home, drugs their attack dog, breaks in, and is assaulted by Ferris's startled sister. Injured and humiliated, Mr. Rooney waits outside the home for Ferris's return from truancy. Meanwhile, on an adventure of her own, Ferris's long-suffering sister is also struggling to prove that Ferris is conning his parents. Ferris races home to beat his parents' return from work, only to find Mr. Rooney waiting at the door. Ferris's sister, inside the house, faces a choice to either let Ferris be caught and punished by Mr. Rooney or to let him in the house before his parents learn of his ruse. Almost incredibly (perhaps due to her anger at Mr. Rooney's corrupt authority), Ferris's sister allies with Ferris and lets him off the hook at the last minute. Score one for the adolescents. All the adults are either fooled or defeated in humiliation. Without passion, soul, or wisdom, the adults are mere pawns in Ferris's game. Ferris is the untarnished adolescent hero whose confidence and charm transcend the limitations of his youth. In part, Ferris's convincing success is due to the talents of the actor who portrayed him, Matthew Broderick. In an ironic but rather predictable turn of cinematic events, however, thirteen years after *Ferris Bueller's Day Off* Matthew Broderick played the role of the bumbling, foolish, and humiliated teacher with a student nemesis in the 1999 suburban school film *Election*.

Students as Heroes: The Possibilities of Youth

In contrast to the antagonistic and foolish roles that teachers and parents play in suburban school films, the students almost universally play the role of the hero. The student-heroes express themselves in opposition to the tyranny of the middle-class establishment. The endless possibilities of youth, creativity, and freedom are alive in the hearts of the student-heroes as they battle the forces of conformity, status hierarchy, and restrictive social conventions. The students are heroes for different reasons in different movies, but heroes nonetheless. For the most part they are heroes when they discover and express their individuality regardless of what their parents, their school, or their friends expect of them. More specifically, they are heroes:

◆ When they break down the social barriers of race or social class.

◆ When they criticize and escape the culture of popularity at their high school.

◆ When they stand up to parents and teachers and prevail as independent youth.

1. Breaking Down the Walls of Race and Class

A number of suburban school films depict students who cross the boundaries of race or class in the pursuit of romantic love (or, in the case of *Remember the Titans*, in the pursuit of friendship).[13] These films suggest that no social divide is strong enough to keep two adolescents from expressing their love for each other. These student-heroes transcend the barriers of the social world to express their true feelings, regardless of the social consequences. No film better represents this dynamic than *Pretty in Pink*.

Andie Walsh lives on the wrong side of the tracks. In fact, the train runs right by her house. Her mom left the family years ago, and her dad is unemployed. She attends Meadowbrook High, a large high school that serves the students of a very wealthy community. However, the school reserves some spaces for the working and lower-middle-class kids on the other side of town. There is a severe social divide between the "richies" and the students who are bused to the school. At lunch the rich students hang out inside the school wearing clean, tailored, pressed, and bright preppy pastels. The kids from the wrong side of town hang out in the courtyard, smoke cigarettes, and wear grungy, baggy, and dark clothing. Andie and her working-class friends withstand abuse and ridicule from the wealthy students in the school.

In spite of the social divide, Andie develops a crush on Blane, a rich guy who doesn't act as aloof as the other "richies." Blane's friend Steff, however, can't believe that Blane would stoop to date such a "mutant" as

Andie. Andie's devoted friend Duckie (also from the wrong side of the tracks) has a secret crush on Andie. He is devastated that Andie would date Blane, whom he considers to be as conceited and selfish as the other rich students. On the night of Blane and Andie's first date, they attend a party at Steff's house. They are not received warmly. Blane's rich and snobby friends ridicule Andie and criticize Blane for bringing her into their social world. Frustrated, Andie and Blane leave the party and attend a club frequented by Andie's friends. Their reception at the club, however, is not friendly, either. Blane offers to drive Andie home, but she is ashamed to reveal to Blane the modesty of her house: "I *don't* want you to take me home . . . I don't want you to see where I live!"

In spite of her shame, he does drive her home. While dropping her off he surprises her by asking her to the prom (she had been waiting for *someone* to ask her). They kiss passionately before Andie goes inside to talk to her dad, who observed the kiss through the window. In spite of her feelings for Blane, Andie is cautious about their ability to overcome the chasm between their social class positions. Andie's dad quizzes her when she enters the house:

Mr. Walsh: Who is this guy?

Andie: His name's Blane. He's a senior. He's so beautiful. Umm. He's a . . . richie.

Mr. Walsh: A whatie?

Andie: A richie. It's kind of stupid. It's just, his family has a lot of money.

Mr. Walsh: Is that a problem?

Andie: No. It's just weird. His friends have a lot of money. He has a lot of money. He drives a BMW. I am not really sure they can accept me.

Mr. Walsh: What does that mean? You like him. He likes you. What his friends think shouldn't make a difference.

Andie: Yeah, but it's not just his friends. It's my friends, too. It's everybody. I'm not real secure about it.

Mr. Walsh: So take the heat . . . It's worth it.

Andie: Is it?

Mr. Walsh: Well, isn't it?

Thanks to the pep talk from her dad, Andie forges ahead with her emotional investment in the relationship with Blane. Blane, however, is getting more resistance from his friends. Steff gives Blane an ultimatum: "If you want your little piece of low-grade ass, fine. Take it. But if you do, you are not going to have a friend." Confused, Blane stops calling Andie and breaks off their date to the prom. Andie, however, is not about to let the rich snobs ruin her prom. She stiches together a homemade pink dress and goes to the prom by herself. Just before entering the dance she runs into the heartbroken Duckie, who is also attending alone. Happy to find each other, they pair up and enter the dance together. Blane, looking glum and sitting by himself, brightens when he sees Andie. As he goes to talk to her, the insufferable Steff intercepts him, but Blane finally stands up to Steff and follows his heart.

Blane apologizes to Andie and, in front of the long-suffering and lovesick Duckie, confesses his love for her: "I always believed in you. I just didn't believe in me. I love you. Always." Blane walks away and Andie is left speechless. Duckie, the poor sap, makes an incredible sacrifice. He urges her to follow Blane and to take advantage of this romantic moment. "You're right," Duckie admits, "he's not like the others."

The movie ends happily ever after with Blane and Andie embracing in the parking lot. They are both depicted as heroes for dismissing the class-based concerns and prejudices of their friends and listening to their own hearts. The courage to express their feelings honestly in spite of the rigid social and economic barriers between them demonstrates that the power of individual wills can overcome the obstacles of social class. It is worth noting that racial and class inequality only become issues in these subur-ban school films when they interfere with romantic attachments. Once the barriers of irrational prejudice and clannish balkanization are broken— once love prevails—the issues of race and class in the suburban school films disappear. As in the urban school films, Hollywood once again priv-ileges individual-level solutions to social problems rather than addressing them structurally. This, too, is typical of American culture in general.

2. Overcoming the Culture of Popularity

I really think it's in my best interest if I went out with someone more popular.

—Beth in *Better Off Dead*

In addition to shattering the barriers of race and class, the students in the suburban school films are heroes when they attack the culture of popu-larity that governs the social organization of their schools. The social divide between the popular and the unpopular students is even more gap-ing than the social divide between different races and social classes. The culture of popularity is often graphically depicted in the suburban school films. In these films the hierarchical organization and exclusivity of student cliques, the mindless conformity to the expectations of the "leading crowd,"[14] and the cruelty inflicted upon the less popular students are resoundingly criticized. The student antagonists of these films judge people according to their level of social popularity. The student-heroes demand that students be judged not by the social clique they belong to, but by the content of their individual character. Perhaps the film that best represents this tendency to attack the culture of popularity is the dark comedy *Heathers*.

The three most popular girls at Westerbrook High School are all named Heather. They are wealthy, they're snobby, and they rule the school. Their popular male counterparts are the football jocks Kurt and Ram. Veronica Sawyer is also a "Heather," although she has mixed feelings about her own popularity and the way it has separated her from her old friends. For instance, the Heathers ask Veronica to write a forged love letter to the obese and lonely Martha "Dumptruck." When Martha approaches the football player whose signature Veronica forged on the fake love note, she is humiliated in front of everyone in the lunchroom. Ashamed of herself, Veronica begins to wonder why she associates with such a cruel crowd.

Jason Dean (J. D.), a new student at the school, stands up to the harassment of Kurt and Ram. He pulls a gun on them in the lunchroom and fires blanks, scaring them nearly to death. Veronica takes an immediate liking to J. D., and the two of them begin a romance. J. D. is incredulous about the crowd she hangs out with. Veronica explains to J. D., "I don't really like my friends . . . It's like they're people I work with and our job is being popular and shit." Increasingly frustrated with her friends, and feeling trapped in the conformity to their expectations, Veronica begins to have fantasies of killing Heather #1. As she confesses to her diary, "Killing Heather would be like killing the Wicked Witch of the West . . . Tomorrow I'll be kissing her aerobicized ass, but tonight let me dream of a world without Heather, a world where I am free."

J. D. and Veronica plot to make Heather #1 suffer. They break into her house the morning after a big party and concoct a hangover "cure" that will make her vomit. J. D. suggests giving her a mug of drain cleaner, which Veronica dismisses as a bad joke. Nevertheless, J. D. pours the poison into one mug as Veronica mixes milk and orange juice in another. Veronica mistakenly takes the poisoned mug up to Heather's room. Heather drinks the drain cleaner, collapses, and dies. To cover their crime, J. D. and Veronica compose a suicide note.

Heather's "suicide" becomes big news at the school, and she becomes even more popular in death. In the meantime, Kurt and Ram have been spreading lurid rumors about Veronica. Veronica and J. D. plot their revenge against the popular jocks. They plan to lure the two to a clearing in the woods, have them remove their clothes (under the impression that they are about to have sex with Veronica), shoot them with what Veronica thinks will be bullets that only stun them (when, in fact, J. D. knows they are lethal), and then plant a note framing them in a gay suicide pact. After unwittingly killing them, Veronica begins to develop a guilty conscience: "Dear diary, my teen angst bullshit has a body count. The most popular people in school are dead." She decides that her "Bonny and Clyde days are over" and she breaks up with J. D.

J. D., however, has a lust for killing his high school peers. In fact, he hatches a plan to kill all of the students in the school in a mass "suicide." After the death of Heather #1, J. D. convinces Heather #2 to take her place in the power structure of the school's social world. He blackmails her into starting a petition to gather the signatures of all the students in the high school (ostensibly to get a popular band to play at their prom). Heather #2 takes to her new role with relish. She wears in her hair Heather #1's red scrunchie, the symbol of social power and popularity. She also inherits Heather #1's cruelty. After Martha "Dumptruck" attempts, but fails, to kill herself by walking into auto traffic, Heather #2 jokes, "Just another case of a geek trying to imitate the popular people of the school and failing miserably."

J. D. plans to blow up the entire school and to frame it as a mass suicide, using the faked petition as a collective suicide note. (J. D.'s attempt to plant bombs in the school while wearing a black trench coat is eerily prescient of the Columbine tragedy.) As J. D. tells Veronica, "The only place different social types can get along together is in heaven." Veronica, however, foils J. D.'s plans. She shoots him and prevents the bombs from detonating beneath all of the students gathered for a pep rally in the school gym. J. D., hurt and bleeding, stumbles outside and detonates a bomb strapped to his chest.

In the final scene of the film, Veronica approaches Heather #2, takes away her red scrunchie, and ties it into her own hair, announcing that there is a "new sheriff in town." It doesn't take us long to figure out how Veronica will use her new power. She approaches Martha "Dumptruck," now in a wheelchair, and says:

> My date for the prom kind of flaked out on me, so I thought if you weren't doing anything that night we could go to the video store and rent some new releases or something. Maybe pop some popcorn.

"I'd like that," says Martha. "So would I," replies Veronica.

In an earlier version of the script the school is destroyed and the jocks and the nerds finally co-mingle in a heavenly prom, with their petty earthly cliques finally dissolved.[15] In the actual ending, however, Veronica, as the student-hero, begins a new social regime at the school without divisions between different social groups. She garnered the individual strength to stand up to the toxic popularity of the Heathers, the homophobia of the jocks, and the cynical destructiveness of J. D. She finally discovered her true self and resisted the pressures to conform to any social group. She is finally in a world where she is free of "Heathers," a world where individuals are valued for their personality, not their popularity.[16]

3. The Triumph of Youth: "When You Grow Up, Your Heart Dies"

Finally, the students of the suburban school films are heroes when they stand up to parents and teachers and prevail as youth. We have seen evidence of this in *Pump Up the Volume*, *Teaching Mrs. Tingle*, *Disturbing Behavior*, *Varsity Blues*, and *Ferris Bueller's Day Off*. No movie better dramatizes this heroism of youth against the adult world than John Hughes's 1985 classic, *The Breakfast Club*. In fact, *The Breakfast Club* is perhaps the quintessential suburban school film. It expresses all of the suburban school film themes discussed so far: The heroes are students, parents are mostly absent, school officials are depicted as antagonists and fools, the walls of social class and social cliques are torn down, and academic and athletic achievement are criticized.

The film begins with the following voice-over, the reading of an essay written to the dean of students, Mr. Vernon, as punishment during a Saturday detention at Shermer High School in a wealthy suburb of Chicago:

> We accept the fact that we had to sacrifice a whole Saturday in detention for whatever it was we did wrong—and what we did was wrong—but we think you're crazy to make us write an essay telling you who we think we are. What do you care? You see us as you want to see us . . . as a brain, an athlete, a basket-case, a princess, and a criminal. Correct? That's the way we saw each other at 7:00 this morning. We were brainwashed.

The five students who report for Saturday detention are Claire, the rich and popular "princess," Andrew, the popular "athlete," Brian, the nerdy "brain," Bender, the gruff and burned-out "criminal," and Allison, the enigmatic "basket-case." Claire and Andrew seem to know and like each other, but for the most part the five students don't understand and don't like each other. As Brian notes in the essay he wrote above for the dean of students, they had been brainwashed. They'd been falsely led to believe that the differences between them as students were greater than the differences between young people and adults.

They each belong to a different social group at school, and they are forced against their will to spend this day together for transgressions they each have committed against the authority of the school. Their hostility for each other is palpable from the beginning. Bender in particular is the lightning rod for disputes between the students. He antagonizes Claire and Andrew by provocatively inquiring about their sexual experiences. Andrew, in turn, attacks Bender by suggesting that he is nothing but a worthless burnout.

There is no adult savior in this film to help the students to find themselves, to realize their personal potential, or to usher them into adulthood. Over the course of the film the five students discover their own identities and the identities of their peers *in spite of* the authority of the school. Set entirely in the high school library during one day's detention, the movie is essentially group therapy that helps the students to tear down the differences that divide them and to come to terms with their own personal problems—problems that are a different sort entirely from those of students in the urban school films. While the urban school students all had to overcome their culture of poverty and prove themselves academically, these suburban students have to deal with the problems of popularity, peer pressure, virginity, bad parents, high academic expectations, and personal identity.

Mr. Vernon has absolutely no legitimate authority in the eyes of these students. His rants against their worthlessness only serve to bond them together as students, in spite of their differences. Richard Vernon's character is deliberately portrayed as an antagonist and a fool. For instance, immediately after declaring that he will "not be made a fool of," he turns to reveal to the students that a sanitary toilet seat cover is hanging out of the back of his pants. Richard Vernon believes that the students in his high school have turned on him. He complains to Carl, the wise janitor, that the students in his school get more and more arrogant each year. Carl, who knows better, responds, "Bullshit, man . . . The kids haven't changed, you have."

Slowly, the students begin to overcome their differences and unite in opposition to the corrupt and buffoonish Mr. Vernon. Their bonding is cemented over their collective use of illicit drugs. The five escape from their library prison briefly to travel to Bender's locker, where he has a stash of marijuana. After they bond over the drugs, the five students begin to share their intimate secrets and reveal their souls to each other. Mostly, they vent their anger toward their parents. Brian reveals the intense pressure he feels to keep a high grade point average. A failing grade in shop class drove him to consider suicide with a flare gun. Andrew confesses that he hates his father for the pressure he puts on him to excel at sports.

Allison confesses to being a compulsive liar and to having parents who ignore her. Claire complains that her parents hate each other and use her as a pawn to hurt the other. Bender reveals that his father abuses him physically. In exasperation Andrew asks if they will all end up like their parents. Allison's answer summarizes the fear that they all have of the future, as adulthood inevitably overtakes them: "It's unavoidable. It just happens . . . when you grow up, your heart dies."

In addition to complaints about their parents, the students complain about the pressures they feel from their friends and the rigidity of social cliques at school. When Claire confesses that she probably won't be friendly to the "weird" Brian and Claire in school on Monday, Bender attacks her. Claire, however, says it isn't so simple: "I hate having to go along with everything my friends say . . . you just don't understand the pressure they can put on you." The collective confessional continues and soon, with their anger, fears, and frustration purged, they begin to understand each other and themselves a little better.

By the end of their detention the students like each other much more than they had eight hours earlier. They *will*, it seems, all be friends in school on Monday morning. After Claire gives Allison a beauty makeover, Allison and Andrew become romantically involved (an all-too-common scene in suburban high school films that suggests women must conform to standard measures of beauty in order to attract men; see also *Clueless, Jawbreaker, She's All That,* and *Not Another Teen Movie*). In spite of their mutual anger, Claire approaches Bender, kisses him, and gives him her diamond earring. Brian, as the brain, agrees to write the punishment essay for all of them. He concludes with a statement that summarizes their newfound solidarity and identity as youth who challenge the expectations of adults: "What we found out is that each one of is a brain, and an athlete, and a basket-case, a princess, and a criminal. Does that answer your question?"

Social Class, Symbolic Deviance, and Adolescent Identity

In these suburban school films rebellion against the expectations of parents, peers, and teachers helps middle-class youth define themselves as individuals and teaches them how to express their emerging adult identities. For the middle class in general, youth is often understood as a time when boundaries are tested, personal exploration is encouraged, and wild-oat sowing and mistakes are expected. A bit of independence, nonconformity, and rebellion is seen as healthy for the developing middle-class adolescent. As the father of high school rebel Morgan Hiller in *Tuff Turf* tells his son, "I expect you to make mistakes. That's what life is all about, for Christ's sake. How else are you going to learn who you are and what you believe in?"

As we have seen repeatedly in this chapter, students directly challenge the authority of school officials and consciously break the rules in order to discover and protect their own identities and interests. In some of the suburban school films the journey to find an identity is expressed by fulfilling an adolescent fantasy to actually destroy the school. One or more students destroy or attempt to destroy their high school in *Class of Nuke 'Em High, Rock and Roll High School, Heathers, Rock and Roll High School Forever*, and *Elephant*.[17] More commonly, however, the adolescents in these films rebel or deviate only mildly by engaging in casual sex and illicit drug use.

Casual sex between students is depicted in many of the suburban school films. For instance, Veronica and J. D. sleep together shortly after meeting each other in *Heathers*. Luke and Leigh Ann have sex when they are not *Teaching Mrs. Tingle*. The pursuit of sex (and love) is central to the plot of *Fast Times at Ridgemont High*. There are, in fact, too many instances of casual sex to mention. However, one movie in particular stands out as an example of how sex is treated in films that feature middle-class suburban students—*American Pie*.

American Pie created a sensation when it was released in 1999 (perhaps because of its depiction of a young man having intercourse with a homemade apple pie), but it really is not that different from any number of teen sex comedies. In many ways it harks back to *Porky's*, the 1981 film from Canada. *Porky's* is another sex comedy that created a stir (perhaps because of its infamous "shower scene" of high school girls after gym class). Both *Porky's* and *American Pie* open with a scene of the main character, an adolescent male virgin, in bed with an erection, only to be disturbed by a parent entering his room. Each movie traces the desperate attempts of the main character to lose his virginity, and each movie concludes with his long-awaited sexual initiation. It is significant that these two popular teen sex comedies are bookended by scenes of an adolescent boy's parent entering his room while he is sexually aroused and the boy ultimately losing his virginity. While based in high schools, these films are not about schooling. Instead, they are about an adolescent rite of passage as middle-class boys develop a sexual identity apart from their parents.

In the case of *American Pie*, the shame of still being virgins is too much for five sexually frustrated male high school seniors to bear. The main character, Jim, exclaims after one particularly bleak party that ended without sex for any of his friends, "You know we're all going to college as virgins. You realize this don't you? I mean, they probably have special dorms for people like us." The five friends create a pact to lose their virginity by the day of their graduation in three weeks. As Jim's friend Kevin proclaims, "We all get laid before we graduate . . . This is our very manhood at stake. No longer will our penises remain flaccid and unused." To cement their collective goal they offer a toast, "To the next step!"

Having agreed that the night of the prom provides their best chance at success, the five friends focus their amorous energies on that evening. They are all successful. Jim has sex with his date, a sexually aggressive "band geek." Kevin finally has sex with his girlfriend. Finch has sex with the mother of his high school nemesis, Stifler. And while Oz doesn't say if he "went all the way," he did spend an intimate night with his new girlfriend and he reports that they are "falling in love." In the final scene the five friends once again offer a toast. Once again they say, "To the next step." This time, however, they are toasting their future lives after high school. They are toasting the transition to adulthood, to which their loss of virginity was a symbolic rite of passage.

Casual drug use, too, is often depicted in suburban school films. Jeff Spicolli is stoned in every scene in which he appears in *Fast Times at Ridgemont High*. The five students in Saturday detention in *The Breakfast Club* overcome their differences and bond together as they get high on marijuana in the school library. In *Never Been Kissed* Josie Geller is an awkward twenty-five-year-old newspaper reporter posing undercover as a high school student. She has trouble fitting in until she breaks out of her shell after eating a pot-laced brownie. In *Clueless* drug use is frequently referred to, but a distinction is made between recreational drug use and drug abuse. As the character Cher explains, "It is one thing to spark up a doobie and get laced at parties. But it is quite another to be fried all day." In *Dazed and Confused* the students *are* fried all day.

The students in the suburban school films take lots of drugs and have lots of casual sex (or, at least, try to have lots of sex). But rather than being punished for such deviation from social norms and laws, they are rewarded for it. As the promotional material for *Fast Times at Ridgemont High* states, "Only the rules get busted" at Ridgemont High School. In *Risky Business* Joel is rewarded with admission to Princeton University for his business skills as a pimp. By consciously rejecting the rules, these students are distancing themselves from adult authority, celebrating their autonomy, and experimenting with their new identities. In many of these films drug use and casual sex are depicted as developmental signposts about what it means to be an adolescent in transition to adulthood. This particular understanding of youth, however, is very much dependent upon the social class of the adolescent.

While use of drugs is treated as a rite of passage in the suburban school films, it is likely to get the students in the urban school films kicked out of school, arrested, or killed. While the students in the suburban school films race to lose their virginity and are celebrated by audiences when they do so, casual sex often results in pregnancy and dropping out of school for the girls in the urban school films. (It should be noted that among the suburban school films, sex does result in a pregnancy in *How to Deal* and in pregnancy and abortion in *Fast Times at Ridgemont High* and *The Last American Virgin*.) Such freedom to express oneself without fear of punishment is a luxury not permitted poor urban youth, for whom a different standard of behavior is very often applied. Such deviance on the part of poor urban youth is not treated as permissively as it is for middle-class suburban youth, either in Hollywood films or in real life. While Hollywood (and Americans generally) thinks adolescents have a "get-out-of-jail-free" card, they are implicitly speaking about suburban middle-class youth. The "deviance" of poor urban youth is taken much more seriously than the youthful "mistakes" of suburban middle-class youth.

This asymmetric reaction to deviance by middle-class and lower-class adolescents is well recognized in the sociological literature. William J. Chambliss's classic article "The Saints and the Roughnecks" describes this dynamic well.[18] For two years Chambliss observed two groups of adolescent boys in Hannibal High School. The "Saints" were a group of eight young white men from upper-middle-class families. They were good students with college plans, they were involved with school activities, and they happened to be the most deviant kids in school. The Saints regularly skipped school, got drunk, drove recklessly, played dangerous pranks, and vandalized property. Their reputation in town, however, was that of obedient boys, good students, and youth leaders. For the most part the Saints had access to cars and were careful to commit their deviant acts out of town in order to preserve their upstanding reputations. Should they ever be pulled over by the police, the Saints were always polite and deferential. On the few occasions when they were caught acting delinquently, the community at large understood the boys' actions as the sowing of their wild oats—harmless fun for young middle-class men with promising futures.

The community at large, however, did not treat the adolescent Roughnecks with such leniency. They were a group of six lower-class white boys at Hannibal High School who also acted deviantly. The Roughnecks would drink, fight, and shoplift. Without access to their own automobiles, however, the Roughnecks would commit such delinquent acts in Hannibal, with greater visibility than the Saints' delinquency. While Chambliss points out that the Saints actually engaged in more delinquent acts than the Roughnecks, it was the Roughnecks (from poorer families, with fewer resources and less status) who had the reputation in the school and in town as criminals and gang members with bleak futures. The police assumed that the Roughnecks were criminals with bad attitudes, and the Roughnecks confirmed their suspicion by acting defiantly when questioned by the police.

Because of their location in the social hierarchy, the Saints were labeled as "good kids" in spite of their deviant acts. As members of prominent families with plenty of resources, the Saints were expected to follow in their parents' footsteps. The community assumed that they must be good kids and their futures must be bright. Their occasional "mistakes" were dismissed as the excesses of youth. These acts were not enough to relabel the Saints as delinquents. Indeed, six of the Saints graduated from college and are living the bright futures others had predicted for them. The Roughnecks, on the other hand, did not enjoy the privileges afforded to the Saints. Nor did they experience bright futures. Their lower social class status made them suspicious to the middle-class residents of Hannibal, and their subsequent acts merely served to cement their label as delinquents. Their deviant acts were not viewed in light of their *adolescence*, but were seen by the school, by the police, and by the community at large as definitive statements about their worth and merit as *lower-class* adolescents.[19]

A similar dynamic is at work in these high school films. When the students of lower socioeconomic status act deviantly (drugs, fighting, sex), they are condemned and treated as serious violators of middle-class expectations. When the students of middle- and upper-middle-class status act deviantly (mostly drugs and sex, but sometimes fighting), their actions are excused, ignored, or treated as normal expressions of adolescence.

The Paths to Adulthood: Social Class and Adolescent Strategies to Independence

Social class differences affect not only perception of deviance, but also perceptions of students' relationship to school and their transition to adulthood. In her 1989 book, *Jocks and Burnouts: Social Categories and Identity in the High School*, Penelope Eckert argues that American high schools are often organized around two dominant social categories of students: the "Jocks," whom she defines as students who are involved in school activities, cooperate with school authorities, do well academically, and largely come from the middle classes; and the "Burnouts," students who reject the school, have an antagonistic relationship to school authorities, struggle academically, and largely come from the working and lower classes:

> Studies of adolescents in school frequently isolate as two dominant categories those who share the goals of the school and those who form a counter-school culture . . . This basic division into pro- and anti-school categories is a social process common to virtually all public schools, and it generates and institutionalizes differences among adolescents on the basis of responses to the school.[20]

Since students from the middle classes are more likely to attend a four-year college than their working-class counterparts, their adolescent years are extended longer, and they remain dependent upon adults for a longer period of time. Middle-class students are dependent upon adult "sponsorship" to get into college and to reproduce their middle-class lives. They are also dependent upon the school for most of their social relationships. Jocks, therefore, identify closely with the school for both personal and professional reasons. Burnouts, however, are less dependent upon the school for access to both future jobs and social networks. Lower-class students are less likely to have parents who have been to college, are less likely to attend college themselves, and tend to assume adult responsibilities (full-time work, marriage and children, et cetera) much earlier than students from the middle classes. Burnouts, then, are more likely to reject the school and to resent the authority that it has over them.

Eckert argues that middle- and lower-class students pursue different strategies of transition to adulthood. The middle-class "Jocks" tend to accept the legitimacy of adult authority, cooperate with that authority, and negotiate for their own adult autonomy within the framework of that authority in the high school. The lower-class "Burnouts," however, tend to demand adult autonomy on their own terms:

> Burnouts seek freedom in absence of adult supervision and view school activities as one more sphere of control. They view the freedoms dispensed within this sphere as vestiges of childhood patterns, because they are acquired at the cost of submission.[21]

To the extent to which the urban school films feature troubled poor and working-class students (similar to Eckert's "Burnout" category) and the suburban school films feature privileged students from the middle classes who do well in school (somewhat resembling Eckert's "Jock" category), Hollywood inverts Eckert's thesis about social class and adolescent transitions to adulthood. In poor and urban high schools Hollywood asks Burnouts to become Jocks and to cooperate with the school in an attempt to attain utilitarian independence. In middle-class suburban high schools Hollywood asks Jocks to become Burnouts and to express their identities free of adult authority. While in reality poor youth become independent earlier in life, the films suggest they should be dependent longer. While in reality middle-class students delay their adulthood until after graduation from college, the films suggest they should assert their independence while still in high school.

The yardstick Hollywood uses to measure "adulthood" varies between the urban and suburban school films. Adulthood is defined as the attainment of educational and occupational *independence* in the urban school films (utilitarian individualism) and as the attainment of an adult *identity* in the suburban school films (expressive individualism). In the urban school films the students are criticized when they express themselves as individuals (by deviating from the norm, leaving school, having sex, getting pregnant, doing drugs, and so forth). Hollywood's lesson is that they should delay such adult identities. They are asked not to leave school, but to be more dependent upon it; to not yet focus on work, but finish school first; to avoid sex and drugs; and to obey authority and conform to middle-class standards. Adulthood in the urban school films implies getting the skills and credentials one needs to support oneself and to be a responsible middle-class adult.

In the suburban school films, however, the students are tired of being adolescents and of being dependent upon adults. They feel suffocated by their dependence on the school and their parents. They long to "grow up"—to get out of school, to be in a relationship, to experiment with sex and drugs, and to explore their identities. They don't believe in the skills and credentials the discredited adults are offering them. They take their middle-class lives for granted. Earning a living is not the primary concern facing them as soon-to-be adults. Rather, adulthood in the suburban school films means finding and expressing your identity as an individual.

Conclusion: The Cultural Contradiction of Individualism and Conformity

Just as the urban school films reflect a middle-class fantasy that the problems in urban schools can be rectified by a middle-class savior and the adoption of middle-class values by poor urban students, the suburban school films reflect a middle-class fantasy that suburban adolescents can avoid the stultifying effects of American middle-class life if they discover who they are as individuals and learn to express themselves in spite of pressures to conform. The mythic fantasy in the urban school films is that conformity to adult middle-class expectations is a prerequisite for independence. The fantasy in the suburban school films is that *nonconformity* to adult expectations is a prerequisite for group acceptance.

For instance, in *Pump Up the Volume* the iconoclastic "Hard Harry" becomes beloved by a student body that ignored well-behaved Mark Hunter. In spite of his multiple transgressions during his day off from high school, Ferris Bueller is idolized by the entire school (with the exception of Mr. Rooney). In *Teaching Mrs. Tingle* Leigh Ann Watson is publicly honored as the valedictorian and given a free pass to college in spite of her crimes. John Moxon does things his own way and becomes a beloved local hero in *Varsity Blues*. In *Heathers* Veronica Sawyer makes time for friendship with the outcast Martha "Dumptruck," but she still gets the powerful red scrunchie. The five detainees from *The Breakfast Club* will say hello to each other in school on Monday. They are now, as it were, members of the same club. Furthermore, they are members of a club that includes us, the audience. We, too, identify with and accept the student-heroes. Hollywood's fantasy tells the audience that J. D. in *Heathers* was wrong to be cynical. Heaven is *not* the only place that different social types can get along. Just as the lone teacher-heroes in the urban school films are ultimately beloved by their students, the lone student-heroes in the suburban school films are ultimately beloved by the students in all of the school's social cliques. Nonconformity, ironically, fosters social acceptance.

As Kai Erikson has noted, cultures always have contradictory potential. Cultures exist along an "axis of variation" in which "the idea and its counterpart become natural partners in the cultural order of things."[22] Drawing upon the work of Tocqueville, Robert Bellah and his co-authors specifically note the contradictory tendency in American culture between individualism and conformity. This tension is particularly strong among members of the middle class, who search for meaning and identity in their individual achievements. However, the meaning of their achievements (and, by extension, the understanding of their self) is measured by how their achievements stack up against those of others. Expanding upon Schneider and Smith's work on the middle-class culture of individualism, Bellah, et al., write:

> Middle-class individuals are thus motivated to enter a highly autonomous and demanding quest for achievement and then left with no standard against which achievement is to be measured except the income and consumption levels of their neighbors, exhibiting anew the clash between autonomy and conformity that seems to be the fate of American individualism.[23]

Americans, however, are uneasy living with such contradictory tendencies in their culture. Perhaps the anxiety that is the hallmark of the new middle class in postindustrial America attempts to find some resolution in the fantasies found at the movies. The middle-class student-heroes of the suburban school films resist conformity and struggle to assert their individuality and independence. What these student-heroes in the suburban school films have accomplished is what many middle-class Americans implicitly long for—escape from a world of status competition, envy, coldness, exclusion, and conformity. They seek refuge in a world of cooperation, mutual admiration, acceptance, kindness, and free expression. In many ways these suburban school student-heroes have found meaningful relationships and a sense of belonging that is the fantasy of the middle-class American who longs for a return to the structure and values of a close-knit community, as symbolized by the ideals of small-town America.[24] It is fittingly ironic, however, that the small-town ideal that many middle-class Americans long for is *not* based on the acceptance of individual difference and free expression. The small-town ideal, as much as modern consumer culture, suburban sprawl, or the bureaucratic office, requires conformity to achieve acceptance. It is simply one of the many contradictions of American culture that the meaningful relationships and sense of belonging that Americans long for happen to challenge the ideals of individualism and free expression that they also hold dear. It is also one of the many contradictions expressed (and cinematically resolved) in high school films.

Notes

1. Emerson, Ralph Waldo. 1883. "Self Reliance." In *Essays*. Boston: Houghton, Mifflin, and Co., pp. 51–52.
2. Thoreau, Henry David. 1960. *Walden*. New York: Signet, p. 39.
3. One of the few exceptions to this is *Bill and Ted's Excellent Adventure*. The plot revolves entirely around Bill and Ted's travels through time so that they can bring historical figures back to 1988 to help them with their oral history report.
4. Dalton, *The Hollywood Curriculum*. Dalton draws upon Henry Giroux's work on critical pedagogy: Giroux, Henry A. 1992. "Resisting Difference: Cultural Studies and the Discourse of Critical Pedagogy." In *Cultural Studies*. Lawrence Grossberg, Cary Nelson, and Paula A. Treichler, editors. New York: Routledge, pp. 199–212.

5. Dalton, *The Hollywood Curriculum.*
6. One notable exception is *The Perfect Score* (2004). The plot revolves around six high school seniors who break into the headquarters of the Educational Testing Service in order to steal the answers to the SAT exam. This is a rare suburban school film in that it acknowledges the importance of academic achievement. However, the movie does so by criticizing standardized testing and celebrating the creative deviance of middle-class students who find a way to beat the system. In their deviance, the students come to terms with their identities and discover what is truly important in their lives—and it turns out that the SAT is not one of those things. None of the six decides to use the stolen answers.
7. Quoted from the back of the 1998 MGM Home Entertainment VHS packaging.
8. Riesman, *The Lonely Crowd*, p. 21.
9. Mills, *White Collar*, p. xii.
10. Ehrenreich, *Fear of Falling*, p. 238.
11. In many ways the film echoes Douglas Foley's observations about the symbolic role high school football plays in defining American culture. Foley argues that the "great American football ritual" symbolizes the ways in which Americans learn contradictory messages about race, class, and gender that are embedded in our culture. Foley, Douglas. 1990. *Learning Capitalist Culture: Deep in the Heart of Tejas.* Philadelphia: University of Pennsylvania Press.
12. Merton, Robert. 1968. *Social Theory and Social Structure.* New York: Free Press.
13. See, for instance, *Cry Baby, Crazy/Beautiful, Grease, Valley Girl, Some Kind of Wonderful, The Karate Kid, The Breakfast Club, Say Anything, She's All That, Can't Buy Me Love,* and *10 Things I Hate About You.*
14. Coleman, *The Adolescent Society.*
15. Bernstein, Jonathan. 1997. *Pretty in Pink: The Golden Age of Teenage Movies.* New York: St. Martin's Griffin.
16. In a more recent example, *Mean Girls* (2004) has the same theme as *Heathers*, but it is told less darkly. Cady Heron is the new girl in a suburban public high school. She makes friends with the "plastics," the beautiful, popular, and "mean" girls of the school. She simultaneously is friendly with the outcasts. She conspires with the outcasts to infiltrate the plastics in order to learn their secrets and to use these secrets against them. She successfully defeats the "queen bee," but she is seduced by the powerful status of the plastics and becomes the new queen bee. She neglects her studies and becomes consumed with appearances, popularity, and being cruel to others. Predictably, she

realizes the error of her ways at the homecoming dance. She is elected queen, but she uses the opportunity to make a speech denouncing cliques and popularity. She breaks her tiara into many pieces and says, "Everybody looks like royalty tonight." She distributes the broken pieces of the crown to all sorts of students—popular, pretty, and otherwise. By the next semester there are no cliques and students of different social types are getting along. I almost expected to see Cady invite Martha Dumptruck over to watch movies.

17. In *Over the Edge* (1979) students attempt to destroy their junior high school. Also, the school is destroyed in *Carrie* (1976), but it is not included in this sample since I exclude horror films.

18. Chambliss, William J. 1973. "The Saints and the Roughnecks." *Society* 11, no. 1: 24.

19. Such unequal application of social sanctions upon "deviant" adolescents is still true today. In the films as well as in reality the deviance of white middle-class suburban adolescents is often evaluated in the context of their youth, while the deviance of nonwhite poor urban youth is often evaluated in the context of their race and class. For instance, in 2000 Californians overwhelmingly passed Proposition 21, the Gang Violence and Juvenile Crime Prevention Act. It allows prosecutors much more discretion to circumvent the juvenile justice system and to charge juvenile offenders (as young as fourteen) as adults and to sentence them adult prisons. By leaving the decision to charge youthful offenders as adults up to the discretion of the prosecutor, the potential for the unequal application of justice is heightened. Even before Proposition 21, poor and nonwhite youth were much more likely to be charged with crimes than middle-class white youth. And when charged with similar offenses, nonwhite youth are at least twice as likely to be charged as adults than white youth. (Nieves, Evelyn. 2000. "California Proposal Toughens Penalties for Young Criminals." *New York Times* (March 6); and Huizinga, D., and D. Elliott. 1987. "Juvenile Offenders: Prevalence, Offender Incidence, and Arrest Rates by Race." *Crime and Delinquency* 33: 206–223.) The supporters of Proposition 21 maintained that the juvenile justice system would remain in place to rehabilitate those youth who could be "saved." However, they used racially and class-coded words to make the distinction between those who could be saved (and treated as juveniles) and those who were beyond hope (and punished as adults). As former California governor Pete Wilson wrote in an op-ed piece in the *San Francisco Chronicle*, "The objective of the proposition is to focus the juvenile justice system's resources on those who can be saved while protecting the public from members of vicious street gangs who are both willing

and capable of random, senseless violence" (quoted in Nieves). When polled, California voters were much more likely to support the initiative when it was described as punishment for "gang-related felonies such as home-invasion robbery, carjacking, witness intimidations and drive-by shootings" than when it was described as an initiative that would "increase penalties, change trial procedures and require reporting" for juvenile felonies (Nieves). The strategic use of language that was likely to invoke in the minds of voters images of offenders who are poor nonwhite urban youth (*gangs, home-invasion robbery, drive-by shootings*) helped ensure its passage.

20. Eckert, *Jocks and Burnouts*, pp. 21–22.
21. Ibid., p. 165.
22. Erikson, *Everything in Its Path*, p. 82.
23. Bellah, et al., *Habits of the Heart*, p. 149. They draw upon Schneider, David M., and Raymond T. Smith. 1973. *Class Differences and Sex Roles in American Kinship and Family Structure*. Englewood Cliffs, NJ: Prentice Hall.
24. Ibid., p. 282.

Challenging the
Culture of Privilege

Class Conflict in the Private School Film

The [private] school—rather than the upper-class family—is the most important agency for transmitting the traditions of the upper social classes, and regulating the admission of new wealth and talent. It is the characterizing point in the upper-class experience. In the top fifteen or twenty such schools, if anywhere, one finds a prime organizing center of the national upper classes.[1]

—C. Wright Mills, *The Power Elite*

You go to one of the best schools in the country, Rushmore. Now for some of you it doesn't matter. You were born rich and you are going to stay rich. But here's my advice for the rest of you—take dead aim at the rich boys. Get them in your cross-hairs and take them down. They can buy anything. But they can't buy backbone. Don't let them forget that.

—Herman Blume in *Rushmore*

"Take dead aim at the rich boys." That is exactly what Hollywood does in the elite private school films. In the urban school films Hollywood depicts a class struggle between the morally challenged urban poor and their virtuous middle-class saviors. In the suburban school films middle-class students struggle with each other and their adult nemeses in an attempt to find their true selves. In the private school films the issue of social class once again emerges as a central theme. This time, however, it is poor, working, and middle-class students who do battle with the pompous power elite. Other scholars have noted that Hollywood's view of the wealthy is generally negative and has been growing more negative over the past twenty-five years.[2] The depiction of the upper class in these elite private school films offers support for this observation.

Nearly all of the schools in the elite private school film sample are board-ing schools. As Peter Cookson and Caroline Persell argue in *Preparing for Power: America's Elite Boarding Schools*, the boarding school is an institu-tion that is about much more than a formal education. Parents who send their children to a boarding school expect more than what the school has to offer in the classroom. The boarding school is, in many ways, what Goffman called a "total institution." That is, nearly every aspect of board-ing school life is controlled. There are few areas of life in a boarding school where a student can escape the watchful eyes of the institution. Nearly everything—the curriculum, mealtimes, bedtimes, dress, et cetera—is strictly regulated. As Cookson and Persell note, there is a hidden curricu-lum at work here: "Students discover that power and pain are inseparable and that to a large degree the price of privilege is the loss of autonomy and individuality."[3] The loss of individuality is an important step in the socialization into elite culture. The elite boarding school is not there to serve the individual scholar, but to help create an upper-class community. As C. Wright Mills writes in *The Power Elite*:

> What holds the upper class together is not only wealth and power, but shared beliefs and shared lives. A sense of collective identity, however, does not de-velop naturally; it must be forged out of actual encounters.[4]

In many ways this function is seen as offensive to members of the middle class. It favors collective identity over that of individualism. It favors the school over the family. It fosters a belief in the entitlement of the privi-leged. And it makes cracking the glass ceiling of the American upper class all the more difficult for individuals from more humble origins. It is no wonder, then, that the elite private school films condemn the privilege of the upper classes and feature individual heroes from the working and mid-dle classes who deserve the rewards of their labor, not those who effort-lessly inherit such rewards.

This chapter shows that in the elite private school films the importance of academics once again enters the picture. Unlike the suburban public school films in which academics were mostly absent, learning is an im-portant element of the private school films. Unlike the urban public school films, however, academics are *not* the key to success or happiness in the private school films. Rather than offering salvation to troubled youth, the high expectations of academic success are often considered *burdensome* to the wealthy students. In the elite private school films the upper class is depicted as morally bankrupt and focused only on superficial measures of status. The heroes of the films are individual representatives of nonelite social classes who exhibit individuality, integrity, well roundedness, and academic merit. These middle-class values help to defeat the upper-class culture of privilege in these films. I argue that the elite private school films reflect dual aspects of American culture. On the one hand they echo the urban school films to the extent that social institutions are ultimately shown to be fair and meritocratic—that success in America is open to all, not just the privileged. On the other hand, they express some of the themes of the suburban school films—specifically, the idea that there is more to life than narrow academic achievement and the pursuit of social status. Ultimately, you must figure out who you are and be true to your self.

The Catholic and Christian school films (smaller in number), however, do not resemble the elite private school films. As I will explain later in this chapter, the characteristics of the Catholic and Christian school films depend upon the social class characteristics of the students depicted. For the most part, these private religious school films resemble the suburban public school films—middle-class students struggle against the school and adult society in order to discover and express their authentic selves. However, if the students in the film are mostly poor, then the film is more likely to resemble the urban public school films, with a middle-class teacher "saving" the students from a culture of poverty.

"Just Because You Are Accepted, Doesn't Mean You Belong"[5]

So states the promotional material to *School Ties*, the 1992 film (set in 1959) that epitomizes Hollywood's treatment of elite private schools. In *School Ties*, David Greene is a working-class Jewish boy from Scranton, Pennsylvania. He is a successful student and a football hero at his local public school, where he has led his team to the state championship. Saint Matthew's Academy, an elite private boys' boarding school, recruits David for his senior year to play quarterback for their struggling football team. David accepts the scholarship and leaves his family and friends in gritty and industrial Scranton to live at Saint Matthew's in serene and bucolic New England. His parents are proud of him—they want him to take advantage of the tremendous educational opportunity and to possibly gain admission to Harvard University. David is not expected, however, to leave his past behind. His father urges him to remember where he comes from: "You show respect and get to Temple . . . no excuses." Yet David is reluctant to reveal that he is Jewish in such a blue-blooded Protestant environment where there are no other Jews and anti-Semitic comments are uttered routinely by students.

David is in awe as he first enters the grounds of Saint Matthew's—it is, to him, an entirely other world. It is overwhelmingly populated by white, Protestant, wealthy, and privileged students. He is impressed by the lush green lawns, the church steeple, the majestic old brick buildings, the elegantly dressed students, the expensive automobiles, the sporting dogs, and the air of casual sophistication that permeates the grounds. While drinking in the rarefied atmosphere he incredulously asks the football coach, "Jesus, this is a high school?"

Indeed, it is a high school, but an exceptionally elite high school. Saint Matthew's has produced two American presidents and is considered to be a "pipeline to Harvard." All who work and study at Saint Matthew's are well aware of the school's elevated status. Headmaster Bartram addresses the students on the first day of school:

> Welcome to the finest preparatory school in the nation . . . You, my boys, are among the elite of the nation and we strive here at Saint Matthew's to prepare you for the heavy responsibilities that come with favored position.

One of the students who is quite comfortable with his favored position in life is Charlie Dillon. He is, as he proclaims himself, a big man on campus. He comes from a wealthy family, and several family members are prestigious alumni of Saint Matthew's. His older brother had been a star football player at Saint Matthew's and is now a successful student at Harvard and a new inductee into the Saint Matthew's football hall of fame. Had it not been for the last-minute recruiting of David Greene, Charlie would have played quarterback for Saint Matthew's in his senior year. Charlie is dating (or claims to be dating) the well-pedigreed Sally. However, Sally, who says she is "just friends" with Charlie, falls in love with David. The pressure to succeed academically, athletically, and socially is overwhelming to Charlie. Without Sally and without glory on the football field, Charlie feels a sharp loss in status, one that is made more painful in the shadow of his successful older brother.

At an alumni party to celebrate Saint Matthew's victory on the football field over their archrival (thanks to David much more than Charlie), Charlie serendipitously learns that David is Jewish. Eager for revenge, Charlie soon spreads the word to the other students and to Sally, aware that such a revelation would shock the wealthy, conservative, and socially insulated Protestants and turn the tide of admiration away from his Jewish rival. As a result of this news Sally breaks up with David and his friends ostracize him. Some are disgusted that a Jew lives among them; others feel betrayed that David hid the truth from them.

The success of his revenge upon David notwithstanding, Charlie is still anxious about his chances of getting into Harvard. To improve his odds he cheats on a history test. David witnesses Charlie consult a crib sheet during the exam. After class the teacher finds the sheet on the floor and announces that if the violator does not confess the whole class will fail. He leaves it to the members of the class to come to a resolution on the matter. David approaches Charlie in private and tells him that if he doesn't confess, he will turn Charlie in. Instead, Charlie turns the tables on David and announces to his classmates that it was *David* who cheated. It is his word against David's. Charlie hopes that the old-boy network and anti-Semitism will work in his favor.

Charlie's privileged position seems at first to pay off. The class votes to clear Charlie of the charges and to indict David. The decision, however, is not unanimous. Several students have begun to realize that their rejection of David was bigoted and irrational. With his conscience bothering him, one of these students, Rip, informs the headmaster that he, too, saw Charlie cheat. As a result, David is redeemed and asked by the headmaster to remain at the school in spite of the awkward situation. David agrees to stay, but he is not happy about how he has been treated by the students or the administration. He tells the headmaster, "You used me for football. I'll use you to get into Harvard."

Charlie is expelled from the school. Not even his family connections to the school can protect him. Charlie, however, knows that his privileged position in society is likely to be preserved regardless. As Charlie is leaving campus on his final trip home, David sees him in the backseat of his father's luxury car. Charlie rolls down the window to speak to David:

Charlie: You know something—I'm still going to get into Harvard. In ten years no one will remember any of this. But you'll still be a Goddamn Jew.

David: And you'll still be a prick.

In *School Ties* the classroom drama of history exams and the hope of admission to an elite college animate the plot. Success in these academic matters, however, is not the climax of the film as it was in the urban school films. In fact, the single-minded pursuit of academic success and the high social status that results is considered somewhat dangerous. The pressures to achieve lead to disastrous results for Charlie. Furthermore, Charlie's smug upper-class entitlement, anti-Semitism, and unethical behavior leave his character with few redeeming qualities. On the other hand, David, the proletarian hero, remains true to his faith, exhibits personal integrity in the face of an unjust attack, and honestly earns his success in both football and academics.

School Ties is not the only elite private school film with these themes. Nearly all of the elite private school films (but not the Catholic or Christian school films) feature academic content, a concern that a narrow focus on academics is burdensome, the moral bankruptcy of the rich, a working- or middle-class hero, and a celebration of the middle-class values of individualism, well roundedness, merit, and personal integrity.

Academic Matters

In spite of the academic focus, the heroes of the elite private school films are not teachers, as they were in the urban public school films. The heroes of the elite private school films are almost always students—working- or middle-class students in particular. These students have trouble blending into the exclusive world of the elite private high school. They must overcome the prejudices of the privileged and prove that they belong. They often do so by demonstrating their academic qualifications.

In *Finding Forrester,* Jamal Wallace is a poor African American student from a single-parent household in the Bronx. He plays basketball with his friends and brings home C's from his local public high school. However, he studies in secret, has test scores through the roof, and reads and writes at every possible moment he has free. The public school authorities take notice of his astronomically high test scores, and an elite private school in Manhattan, Mailor-Callow, offers him a full academic scholarship (and they wouldn't be disappointed if he decides to play basketball for them as well).

The school is a bit snobby, with a pompous and condescending writing teacher, Robert Crawford. Mr. Crawford is suspicious of Jamal. Mr. Crawford does not believe that Jamal's high-quality work is his own. He can't conceive that a poor black basketball player could write so well— "He's a basketball player! From the Bronx!" Nonetheless, the writing is Jamal's. His academic achievements are authentic, but they are not due to the efforts of the school. Jamal does have a mentor, but he is not a schoolteacher.

Jamal has serendipitously struck up a friendship with William Forrester, a famous author who wrote a best-selling novel many years ago and never wrote another (heavy shades of J. D. Salinger). William Forrester is an eccentric man who lives alone and suffers from agoraphobia. William helps Jamal with his writing, and Jamal helps William to interact with the outside world again. With William Forrester's permission, Jamal uses the title of an old Forrester short story to help him get started on a story of his own. William, however, urges Jamal to never reveal their friendship to anyone. Jamal uses the story to enter a writing contest at school. Mr. Crawford, recognizing the title, accuses Jamal of plagiarism. Jamal keeps his promise to William and does not tell Mr. Crawford that he had permission to use the story's title.

Jamal's story is disqualified from the school's writing contest. The school authorities, nervous that Jamal will be athletically disqualified, offer Jamal a deal—if he wins a key play-off game, they will drop the charges against him. Disgusted with the moral bankruptcy of the school, Jamal misses two key free throws, deliberately losing the game. On the day the stories in the contest are to be read aloud at the school, William Forrester unexpectedly shows up. His rare public appearance and dramatic reading to the crowd impress Mr. Crawford. William Forrester then announces that the story he read that day was not his own, but Jamal's:

> I spoke here today because a friend of mine wasn't allowed to. A friend who had the integrity to protect me when I was unwilling to protect him. His name is Jamal Wallace . . . I helped him to find his own words by starting with some of mine and in return he promised never to say anything to anyone about me.

Mr. Crawford is humiliated as the school trustees go over his head and award the writing prize to Jamal. Jamal receives a standing ovation from his peers.

At first it would appear that this film has much in common with the urban school films. There is an academic focus, and a poor student is apparently saved by a white middle-class mentor (William Forrester). There are, however, important differences. The school and the teacher are discredited. The school is depicted as an elite institution that values status much more than it values learning. The school sees Jamal primarily as an athlete who can bring glory to the school on the basketball court. Mr. Crawford does not believe Jamal deserves to be at the elite school. As a result, the school and Mr. Crawford lose their authority in Jamal's eyes and in the eyes of the audience. Regardless, Jamal doesn't need the school to have a bright future. Jamal is not dependent upon the school, Mr. Crawford, or even upon William Forrester. In fact, just the opposite is true.

As an underprivileged, black, and academically gifted student from a social world far removed from that of the elite school, it is *Jamal* who has the lessons to teach. The school eventually learns these lessons and changes as a result. Mr. Crawford's humiliation symbolizes this transformation. In many ways, Jamal is the savior of both the school and of William Forrester. Only after he develops a friendship with Jamal does William emerge from his shell and reconnect with the things and people that matter to him in life. Jamal enters the world of the rich, the famous, and the elite and leaves it a better place. It was William who was lost, not Jamal. After all, the title of the movie is *Finding Forrester*, not *Finding Jamal*.

The Burden of Academic Achievement

There is another important difference between the treatment of academics in the urban public school films and the elite private school films. While academic achievement was the celebrated goal of the urban public school films, it is often considered an oppressive burden in the elite private school films. Academic and occupational success is considered to be important in the private school films, but only if they are pursued in balance with other life goals. The narrow focus on academic and professional achievement often results in tragedy.

For instance, in *Dead Poet's Society* the Welton School is "the best preparatory school in the United States." Neil Perry is the son of a strict, demanding, and status-conscious father who has aspirations that Neil will become a successful medical doctor.[6] Neil, however, would like to pursue his own interests in and out of the classroom. He has an interest in exploring a career in the theater. He enjoys poetry. He looks forward to serving as the assistant editor of the school yearbook. His overbearing father, however, insists that Neil drop all extracurricular activities and devote himself entirely to his rigorous academic schedule—"After you finish medical school and you're on your own, then you can do as you please. Until then you do as I tell you. Is that clear?"

Neil auditions and wins the lead in a local production of *A Midsummer Night's Dream*. Neil has never been happier than he is in the theater. He shines as an actor. His father watches his dazzling performance on opening night, but he still disapproves of the path Neil has chosen—"I've made a great many sacrifices to get you here, Neil, and you will not let me down." He withdraws Neil from Welton, takes him home, and intends to enroll him in military school. Distraught, Neil kills himself with his father's handgun. Rather than blaming Neil's suicide on the intense pressures, high expectations, and narrow restrictions that parents and teachers put on the students, the school responds to Neil's suicide by firing the only humane teacher it has, the iconoclastic Mr. Keating, whose only sin was to encourage his students to follow their hearts.

In *School Ties,* the intense academic pressure also results in tragedy. Not only is the pressure a catalyst for Charlie Dillon to cheat on his history test, but it also causes the nervous breakdown of another student, McGivern. McGivern is from a family that has had five generations attend Princeton University. The pressure to follow his family's footsteps is enormous. His chances of admission to Princeton, however, seem to rest on his French grade. Unfortunately, the demanding French teacher, Mr. Cleary, treats McGivern harshly in French class. McGivern rhetorically asks his friends, "When the guy from Princeton says they might be willing to accept a C in French and you are failing French, then life is pretty much over, don't you agree?"

During an oral exam in French class Mr. Cleary ridicules McGivern's hesitant French. McGivern knows the material, but his nerves in the face of Mr. Cleary's criticism cause him to perform poorly. To escape the humiliation, McGivern runs out of the classroom in the midst of his exam—his future admission to Princeton apparently doomed. He does not return to the dorm that night. Instead, he returns to the classroom and repeatedly recites the French assignment. His friends search the campus and find him in the classroom, half conscious and half muttering in French. He is taken away in an ambulance, never to return to school.

The urban public school films treat academic achievement as a panacea to the problems of poor students. I argued in chapter 3 that the urban school films reflect a middle-class fantasy that the culture of poverty can be broken through hard work and academic success. Middle-class teacher-heroes must teach these values to poor students. The suburban school films, on the other hand, tend to ignore academics entirely or to treat academic achievement with hostility. The suburban school films, I suggested in chapter 4, reflect a middle-class frustration with following conventional paths to pursue conventionally defined "success." The middle-class student-heroes react against utilitarian individualism and seek to find and express their true selves.

The elite private school films tend to strike a middle ground. Academic success is valued, but not if it requires the exclusion of other life experiences to achieve. The poor, working-class, and middle-class students in the elite private school films recognize that an elite private education is valuable because it can help them to become upwardly mobile. They are, to a certain extent, utilitarian individuals. David Greene, for instance, plans to use the prestige of the private school to get into Harvard. At the same time, the heroes of the elite private school film reject the solitary focus on achievement and express themselves in opposition to the expectations of elite society. To do otherwise invites disaster. The elite private school films tend to celebrate both utilitarian and expressive individualism among their nonelite protagonists. Members of the elite, however, are consistently depicted as the morally bankrupt antagonists. There is no redemption for the rich in these films.

The Moral Bankruptcy of the Rich

Just as adults were either the fools or the antagonists in the suburban public school films, it is the rich who are portrayed as fools or enemies in the elite private school films. Charlie's anti-Semitism and lack of integrity in *School Ties*, Mr. Crawford's racist suspicions of Jamal in *Finding Forrester*, and the school's heartless response to Neil's suicide in *Dead Poet's Society* only begin to explore this theme. Another example of the bankruptcy of the rich in elite private school films can be found in 2002's *The Emperor's Club*.

Mr. Hundert teaches the history of Western civilization at the prestigious Saint Benedict's Academy for boys. He is fond of saying that "a man's character is his fate." He uses countless examples from the ancient Greeks and Romans to prove this point. Sedgwick Bell is a new student at Saint Benedict's Academy. He is the rich and privileged son of a U.S. senator. Sedgwick is an impetuous and immature brat who is unenthusiastic about learning. He goofs off in class, plays practical jokes on others, believes that winning is all that matters, and introduces pornographic magazines to the other boys. He frustrates and fascinates Mr. Hundert, who approaches Sedgwick's education as a personal challenge.

Mr. Hundert goes to Washington, DC, to meet with Sedgwick's dad and to discuss Sedgwick's attitude problem. After their meeting, Sedgwick's dad calls Sedgwick to tell him to get his act together. As a result, Sedgwick begins to take his studies more seriously. He begins to study in earnest for the annual Mr. Julius Caesar contest—a Saint Benedict's tradition in which the top three students in Mr. Hundert's Western civilization class wear togas and compete against each other on the topic of Roman history. Sedgwick improves his academic performance significantly, and Mr. Hundert is proud of his progress. After the final qualifying quiz to narrow the contestants down to the top three, Sedgwick is just one point shy of qualifying. Mr. Hundert sacrifices his own values of integrity and character by changing Sedgwick's grade so that he is among the finalists—edging out the meritorious Martin Blythe, whose father won the Julius Caesar contest years ago.

Sedgwick shocks Mr. Hundert by cheating during the final contest. He had taped cheat sheets to the inside of his toga. Mr. Hundert catches Sedgwick cheating toward the end of the contest but keeps the information private (Sedgwick's father and other dignitaries are in the audience). Mr. Hundert resolves the situation by asking Sedgwick a question that he knows that only the other remaining contestant, Deepak Mehta, will know. Deepak becomes Mr. Julius Caesar.

After this episode Sedgwick returns to his juvenile behavior and poor academic performance. Mr. Hundert is disappointed in Sedgwick and ashamed of himself for having believed in him. As it turns out, Sedgwick did not require good grades, academic accolades, glowing recommendations, or even "character." Sedgwick's future was already guaranteed. As Mr. Hundert explains, "Although his father's influence guaranteed him a place at Yale, it was with a profound sense of failure that in the spring of 1976 I handed Sedgwick Bell his diploma."

Twenty-five years later Sedgwick Bell becomes the CEO of one of the biggest corporations in the United States. He promises to make the largest-ever single donation to Saint Benedict's if, and only if, the recently retired Mr. Hundert agrees to officiate a rematch of the Mr. Julius Caesar contest in order to "recover his academic honor." Mr. Hundert would like to think that Sedgwick has reformed his ways. He attends the event and hosts the contest. Sedgwick seems to do quite well and is on his way to victory when Mr. Hundert once again catches him cheating—this time via a high-tech earpiece and a classics graduate student in the back of the room feeding him the answers. Once again, Mr. Hundert doesn't blow Sedgwick's cover. Instead, he asks a question that he knows neither Sedgwick nor the confederate graduate student will know the answer to (about an obscure ruler who was the subject of Mr. Hundert's very first history lesson). Deepak knows the answer, and he is once again crowned Mr. Julius Caesar.

Sedgwick Bell accepts the defeat graciously, but then announces to the crowd that he is running for the U.S. Senate and that educational excellence will be his platform. Mr. Hundert is disgusted with Sedgwick's hypocrisy. He is angry and embarrassed that as one of his students, Sedgwick acquired no noble virtues or principles. He tells Sedgwick, "I failed you as a teacher . . . all of us at some point are forced to look at ourselves in the mirror and see who we really are." Sedgwick, however, has no interest in or capacity for self-reflection. He responds to Mr. Hundert not as the senatorial candidate whose platform is educational excellence, but as the smug and entitled rich jerk who has had his whole life handed to him on a silver platter: "Who gives a shit about principle and your virtues? I live in the real world."

Sedgwick Bell may have become a rich and successful businessman and politician, but as far as his high school history teacher is concerned, he is a morally bankrupt failure. The *true* value of an education, according to these elite private school films, is found in the honorable pursuit of knowledge. Otherwise, utilitarian success is nothing but an empty victory.[7]

Revenge of the Middle Class: The Triumph of Well Roundedness, Integrity, and Merit

Rather than celebrating narrow academic achievement and the maintenance of high social status, it is a virtue in these elite private school films to exhibit balance by being a well-rounded human being, to exhibit integrity by being true to one's self, and to exhibit merit by earning rewards rather than inheriting them or cheating. These middle-class values defeat the culture of privilege that corrupts the upper class.

Well Roundedness

The hero of *Rushmore* is Max Fischer, the son of a barber who is at the elite Rushmore Academy on an academic scholarship. Max is a precocious young man who loves Rushmore, has many diverse talents, and develops a friendship with Herman Blume, a rich and unhappy industrialist who was quoted at the beginning of this chapter. Herman Blume has two spoiled and bratty sons who also attend Rushmore Academy. He dislikes his own children and admires Max because Max has the passion for life that Blume is lacking—a passion that money and privilege can't buy.

In spite of his passion for life and for Rushmore, Max is "one of the worst students in the school," as the headmaster says. The reason is that Max has many interests and pursues them all with gusto. He is the exaggerated picture of well roundedness. He is the school newspaper publisher, yearbook editor, French club president, model UN member, stamp and coin club vice president, debate team captain, lacrosse team manager, calligraphy club president, founder of the astronomy society, fencing team captain, junior varsity decathlete, second choral choirmaster, kung fu club yellow belt, trap and skeet club founder, Rushmore beekeepers president, Yankee racer founder, Piper Cub club flier, backgammon club president, alternate on the wrestling team, and director of the Max Fischer Players.

Max's academic performance suffers as a result of his involvement in so many diverse activities. In fact, Max is put on "sudden-death academic probation" and is eventually expelled from school. Whereas in the urban public school films such a "failure" would have demanded drastic reformation of the student to focus on his studies, in *Rushmore* the expulsion serves as a sign of Max's salvation—only after leaving Rushmore does Max truly find and become comfortable with his true identity. At first, Max was devastated by the expulsion because he thought that Rushmore was his life. But by the end of the movie Max realizes that there is meaning to life beyond Rushmore (and Herman Blume realizes there is meaning to life beyond money). Blume's conventional "success" is starkly contrasted with Max's "failure." Yet Max is the role model and hero of this film.

Max transfers to the local public high school, Grover Cleveland. There he continues his hyperinvolvement in many different activities and begins to improve his grades (to an average of C–). He produces his most successful play, *Heaven and Hell*—a Vietnam War epic and a tribute to Herman Blume, a Vietnam veteran. He also begins dating a public school student, Margaret Yang. Max comes to terms with who he is and what he wants out of life. While at the elite Rushmore Academy, Max was overly conscious about his status in relationship to the other students. He lied and told people his dad was a brain surgeon. After attending Grover Cleveland he proudly introduces his dad as a barber. The message is that you don't need to pretend to be someone you are not—you can find and express yourself and find love wherever and whoever you happen to be. You should follow your heart and not be dependent upon any particular "Rushmore." Furthermore, there is much more to school, and to life, than academic or occupational success. Max's dad is a happy man who loves his life and his job. Before he met Max, Herman Blume was a successful yet miserable capitalist. Max may not be the best student—but he finds meaning and satisfaction in living a creative and balanced life.[8]

Integrity

In addition to living a well-balanced life, these elite private school films extol the importance of personal integrity. Being true to one's self is much more important than "success." The students who exhibit the most integrity in these films are the middle- and working-class students who challenge the culture of privilege and the moral bankruptcy in the elite private schools. They become the triumphant heroes of these films when they are able to defeat the rich antagonists with their personal integrity.

In *Scent of a Woman,* Charlie Simms is a smart kid from a humble family in Oregon. His mom and stepdad manage a convenience store. He is on an academic scholarship, the "Young American Merit Scholarship," to one of the most prestigious preparatory schools in the country, Baird. While Charlie is at the school due to his own merit, it is hinted that the wealthy students are there thanks to their parents' legacy, connections, and financial donations. Most of the rich kids at Baird go to Harvard after graduation as a matter of course. As a financial aid student, Charlie is not a full member of the club. His nonelite status is a stigma among the students at the school, and his pompous and arrogant "friends" condescendingly flaunt their wealth, as this exchange illustrates:

George: You goin' home to fucking Idaho for Thanksgiving?

Charlie: I'm from Oregon.

Harry: Charlie, how do you feel about skiing the white bosom slopes of Vermont?

Charlie: How much?

Harry: $1,200 . . .

Charlie: $1,200 is a little rich for my blood, Harry. [Charlie walks away]

George: What'd you do that for? You know he's on aid.

Harry: On major holidays it's customary for the lord of the manor to offer drippings to the poor.

Harry and his rich friends pull a stunt embarrassing the headmaster and damaging his new car, an expensive Jaguar. Charlie and George were serendipitously in a position to see who was responsible for the stunt. The headmaster asks them both for information, but they both claim to not know who was responsible. The headmaster talks to Charlie alone. He subtly threatens that if Charlie does not name names, he will withdraw a special recommendation he has made on Charlie's behalf to the Harvard admissions committee; Charlie will also face possible expulsion. Charlie has the Thanksgiving weekend to come to a decision. There will be a public meeting of the judiciary committee to settle the matter on the Monday after the holiday.

George is particularly intent on keeping Charlie from talking. As a rich kid George knows the code—that rich guys don't rat each other out. He's not sure, though, if Charlie will play by their rules. He tries to make the situation clear to Charlie:

> *George: You're on scholarship from Oregon. At Baird! You're a long way from home, Chas.*
>
> *Charlie: What's that got to do with anything?*
>
> *George: I don't know how it works there. But how it works here—we stick together . . . above all, never leave any of us twisting in the wind.*
>
> *Charlie: What does that have to do with me being on scholarship?*
>
> *George: I'm just trying to bring you up to speed, kid.*

Charlie is not comfortable telling tales on his fellow students. But he's also not sure if he is a part of the "we" that George speaks of. He fears that the rich guys will stick together and sacrifice him, the commoner. Nevertheless, he doesn't want to be a snitch. He has too much integrity. Charlie goes away for the Thanksgiving weekend to take a part-time job caring for a blind army veteran, a colonel named Frank. Over the weekend Frank helps him talk through his ambivalent feelings and helps him to discover his identity and his values (and Charlie helps Frank to embrace life and aborts a planned suicide attempt). Charlie confirms his decision not to sell his soul in order to buy his future into Harvard.

Meanwhile, the rich and morally bankrupt George is preparing to sell his soul. George's rich father is putting pressure on George to name the culprits. George goes back on his pledge to keep quiet. In the public disciplinary hearing, George, with his father by his side, indicts his friends without much conviction. Charlie is needed to confirm the suspects. He does not do so. He is about to be kicked out of school for covering up a crime when Frank unexpectedly shows up as Charlie's advocate. Frank gives a rousing speech on Charlie's behalf that convinces the committee to let Charlie off the hook:

> If you think you are preparing these minnows for manhood, better think again! Because I say you are killing the very spirit this institution proclaims it instills. What a sham! . . . the only class in this act is sitting next to me and I'm here to tell you that this boy's soul is intact. It's non-negotiable . . . he won't sell himself out to buy his future. That's called integrity!

Neither Frank nor Charlie is from the elite social world that sustains Baird. As a middle-class outsider, Frank attacks the hypocrisy of the school—that George, with his deep-pockets father, can remain in school even though he sacrificed his integrity and sold out his friends, while Charlie, who has so much more to lose, maintained his integrity and refused to sell his soul. Frank says that this personal integrity is the leadership quality the school should be promoting, not the self-interested moral bankruptcy of wealthy snitches who protect themselves at the expense of others.

In lieu of a father with elite connections, Charlie relies on Frank, a middle-class outsider, to make his case that integrity matters. The wealthy,

Frank reveals, have no soul. Members of the middle class, however, do what is right, even at the expense of their own interests. Integrity triumphs over the corrupt old-boy network.[9]

The Triumph of Merit

In addition to living a well-balanced life full of integrity, the nonelite student-heroes of these elite private school films exhibit academic merit. While their rich peers may fall back on the social connections and the privileges of their families to get through school, the poor, working-class, and middle-class heroes rely upon their own honest talent and effort for their scholarly accomplishments. We have seen evidence of this already in several of the films discussed thus far in this chapter. *School Ties* offers yet another illustration of the value of merit and how Hollywood treats it as morally superior to the inherited "success" of the privileged classes.

Before Charlie Dillon learns that David Greene is Jewish, the two have a heart-to-heart conversation about life in the elite world of Saint Matthew's. After McGivern has a nervous breakdown and leaves campus in an ambulance, David is stunned. He had never imagined that a student could have such a negative and emotional response to a failing grade. The rich and privileged Charlie responds with an explanation of the way things are for him and his friends from elite families:

> Good grades, the right schools, right colleges, right connections—these are the keys to the kingdom. None of us ever goes off and lives by his wits. We do the things they tell us to do, then they give us the good life.

David, as an invited guest to this elite world, is still in disbelief. He does not feel the external pressure that Charlie feels. He wants to get into Harvard, but his life is not depending upon it. Charlie respects David for his authenticity and his down-to-earth attitude: "I envy you . . . because if you get what you want you'll deserve it and if not, you'll manage . . . You are who you are. That's really what draws people to you, David."

This exchange captures much of what these elite private school films are all about—Charlie, from a rich family at an elite school with a bright future, is envious of a working-class kid from Scranton. The envy that Charlie feels is because he knows that David *deserves* the success he's had. David (as a student and as a football player) is entirely responsible for his achievements in life. Charlie, on the other hand, cannot be certain that the same is true for him. Charlie is riding a wave that his family set in motion long ago. His "success" is not due to his own talents and effort, but his lineage.

Charlie's cynical attitude about the entire process of elite socialization in which he is enmeshed echoes the lesson that several of these elite private school films teach. The education of these wealthy students is not about integrity, not about following your heart or living by your own wits. The elite boarding school experience is merely a step along the path of upper-class "success" that has been predetermined by those who came before. With Charlie's defeat and humiliation at the end of the movie, Hollywood is expressing another fantasy of the middle class—that meritorious individuals can break into the upper class, and that the undeserving rich will suffer the consequences of their unethical behavior. Furthermore, Charlie's admiration for David reveals something else that is at the heart of these elite private school films. Not only does David deserve the success he has achieved, but he is comfortable with who he is. Charlie is envious that David has an independent identity he can be proud of. Charlie may be rich, but he is lost. David, however, is both academically successful (a utilitarian individual) and comfortable with himself (an expressive individual).

The Anomaly of the Catholic School Film

Roughly 10 percent of American schoolchildren attend some sort of private school. About half of all private school students are enrolled in Catholic school. Nevertheless, Hollywood's imagination seems to be more stimulated by the elite private boarding school (only 1 percent of all private school students are enrolled in such schools) than any other type of private school.[10] Still, there are a handful of Catholic school films (*Heaven Help Us, The Trouble with Angels, Sister Act 2, Girls Just Want to Have Fun, The Chocolate War, The Craft, The Dangerous Lives of Altar Boys*) and one Christian school film (*Saved!*) in the sample. These private religious school films, however, are of an entirely different type than the elite private school films.

This may be due to the fact that a very different sort of student enrolls in private religious schools than elite private schools. Catholic school students are predominantly from the middle class. The average Catholic school student has parents who have only somewhat higher incomes and educational attainment levels than the average public school student. While there is significant racial and class diversity among Catholic school students, the very poor and the wealthy are under-represented.[11] The Catholic school students in Hollywood's stories are also largely from the middle class.

Although they are technically "private" schools, the religious schools in Hollywood films are rarely the setting for academic drama or a conflict between social classes. Due to the predominant middle-class composition of the students in the religious school films, these films are reminiscent of the suburban public school films in which student-heroes oppose the authority of the school in their efforts to find themselves and express their identities apart from their parents and peers.[12] In the rare instance, however, when a religious school films depicts an urban school that serves poor students, the plot more closely resembles the public urban school films with a teacher-hero saving the students from a culture of poverty. In order to illustrate how the social class of the students (and not necessarily the public or private nature of the school) determines how Hollywood chooses to tell high school stories, we will examine two typical examples: *The Dangerous Lives of Altar Boys* represents the middle-class suburban Catholic school film, and *Sister Act 2* represents the urban lower-class Catholic school film.

The Dangerous Lives of Altar Boys

Francis Doyle and Tim Sullivan are the altar boys who live such "dangerous lives." They are best friends in a suburban Catholic school. With two other friends they aspire to create an original comic book, *The Atomic Trinity*. The archnemesis of the superheroes in *The Atomic Trinity* is their strict and mean geometry teacher, Sister Assumpta, or, as they prefer to call her, "Nunzilla."

Neither Tim nor Francis has a healthy home life. Tim's parents are divorced, and both are alcoholics. Tim is a bright but rebellious teenager. Francis's parents fight most of the time. He, too, is rebellious, and the two of them get into lots of trouble at school. Just as in the suburban public school films, the parents of the students are mostly absent, and the school officials are either antagonists or fools. For instance, in contrast to Sister Assumpta's cruelty, Father Casey is mostly submissive and ineffective, without much moral authority. He is bored and indifferent to his job. He gives bland and generic advice to students without any appreciation for the actual problems they face. When Francis goes to him for advice about sin, the priest gives him platitudes and empty assurances that he will "do the right thing." Father Casey even consults a Magic 8 Ball for guidance.

Without legitimate guidance from adults, Tim and Frances organize mischief in order to express their dissatisfaction with the school and their lives in general. For instance, they steal the statue of Saint Agatha, the school's holy mascot. Sister Assumpta is furious. She suspects Tim and Francis stole it, but she can't prove it. The two boys have an even more ambitious prank in mind, however. They want to steal a cougar from a local zoo and put it in Sister Assumpta's office.

Francis, however, begins to doubt the feasibility of the cougar plan and complains that Tim only acts out in such rebellious ways because he is bored. In response Tim says, "At least I'm doing something. What do you do, Francis?" Indeed, what *does* Francis do? This is the major question that the movie confronts. As in most of the suburban public school films, this movie is about a middle-class teenager's angst and coming of age. He struggles to make sense of life and to find himself somewhere within the confusion. The movie is not about learning. It is not about class conflict (all of the characters are solidly middle class). It is about confused middle-class youth and their search for adult identity.

Where this film differs slightly from most of the suburban public school films, however, is in its darker tones.[13] Francis's search for identity is deeply existential, and not nearly as superficial as that of most of the characters in the suburban public school films. For instance, while walking back from a reconnaissance trip to the animal park, Tim and Francis come across a dying dog that has been hit by a car. Francis says, "Someone has to help it! They have to come get it." Tim, angry at Francis's faith in others, says emphatically, "There is no '*they*.' *We* are 'they'!" Tim knows that it is he who must make decisions and take responsibility. No one (no school authority or family member) will either rescue the dog or rescue Francis or Tim. Tim knows that it is *he* who must take action.

Later Tim and Francis return to the zoo to carry out the theft of the cougar. After successfully sedating the cougar, Tim bravely enters the cage. However, he is unaware that there are two cougars in the zoo's display. The second cougar emerges from a den and attacks and kills Tim. Francis speaks at Tim's funeral, held at the school's church. It is Francis who brings meaning to this tragic event—not the nun, the priest, or Tim's family. Francis rises above the shallow morality of the school and the adult authorities to speak the truth about Tim and about life. This event has forced Francis to find himself and to grow up. As in the suburban public school films, however, he needed no adult guidance to do so. In fact, he had to overcome adult obstacles to find and express his true self.

Sister Act 2

By contrast, in *Sister Act 2* the depiction of the Catholic school takes on the unmistakable characteristics of the urban public schools in Hollywood's imagination. As with *The Dangerous Lives of Altar Boys*, it is not the privateness or the Catholicness of the school that makes its mark on the film. Rather, the film's plot takes its cue from the socioeconomic characteristics of the students in the school. Just as with the urban public schools, *Sister Act 2* takes place in an impoverished inner-city school that serves a predominantly poor and nonwhite population. And, as in the urban public school film, the hero is a middle-class adult outsider who is new to teaching. Over the course of the film the students learn from their teacher-hero the value of hard work, middle-class values, and the virtue of following your dreams.

The teacher-hero is "Sister Mary Clarence," an imposter nun. She is actually a Las Vegas headliner. However, she leaves her lucrative career in order to help her nun friends (see *Sister Act 1*) solve the problems in the Catholic high school they operate in San Francisco, Saint Francis Academy. The nuns, new to education, are trying, as they say, "to do good in the 'hood." Doing good, however, is proving harder than they had bargained for. The students are out of control, loud, disobedient, and apathetic inner-city kids. Mr. Crisp, the administrator for the archdiocese, wants to close the school for financial reasons. "It is worth more as a parking lot than a school," he explains to the principal, a well-meaning but ineffectual priest. Only Sister Mary Clarence, it seems, can save the students and save the school.

Sister Mary Clarence is assigned to teach the music class. After encountering the hostility of the students, however, she almost quits. The ungrateful students ignore her, ridicule her, and play pranks on her. She is, nonetheless, persistent. "You must have faith," she is told by another teacher. Sister Mary must have watched many of the urban school films discussed in chapter 3, because she decides that there is only one strategy to pursue—to get the students to care about education and to exercise a work ethic. She preaches to her students, "If you don't have an education you don't have anything . . . If you want to be somebody. If you want to go somewhere you better wake up and pay attention." In addition to inspiring her students, Sister Mary helps the other nuns to clean up the school (literally and figuratively). All that was needed, apparently, was a new coat of paint and some new attitudes.

The students begin to absorb Sister Mary's lessons and start to believe in themselves. As a result, the student choir dramatically develops very polished musical skills. The other nuns are so impressed that they enroll the choir in an all-state music competition. They travel to the competition, but the students momentarily lose faith in their own abilities after seeing the quality of the competing choirs. Sister Mary gives them an inspirational pep talk, and they end up winning the contest unanimously.

The board of trustees is so impressed that they decide not to close the school after all.

Once again, a middle-class teacher-hero combats the educational establishment, overcomes administrative obstacles, is able to "get through" to students suffering in a culture of poverty, and teaches the students the middle-class values and attitudes they need in order to achieve academic success—a feat that no one else had been able to achieve previously. The fact that this is a private Catholic school is barely relevant to the story. The fact that the students are poor and in need of salvation, however, is all that Hollywood needs to know in order to structure the plot.

Inequality, Education, and American Culture

As the elite private school films suggest, the United States is a deeply unequal society. No more than 25 percent of the adult population in the United States has a college degree. Nearly half of all income earned in the United States goes to only 20 percent of the population. Even more dramatically, approximately 70 percent of all the wealth in the United States (property, savings, stocks, bonds, and so forth) is owned by just 10 percent of the population.[14] Americans, however, tend to accept such social class inequality without questioning its legitimacy. While Americans do not believe in equality of outcomes, they do believe strongly in equality of opportunity. That is, as long as all individuals, regardless of social background, have equal opportunity to prove themselves in school and on the job market, then the resulting unequal outcome of educational attainment, income, and wealth is considered to be fairly determined.[15]

Americans can be particularly offended if they believe that the system is not fair. If poor people encounter blocked opportunities, for instance, Americans of all social classes generally believe the obstacles should be removed. By the same token, Americans are outraged if it is perceived that the privileges and social status of the wealthy are not earned in a fair contest. In spite of the general acceptance of inequality, there is a strain of populism in the American character that is suspicious of "fat cats" and the legitimacy of their wealth. In a 1992 poll, 45 percent of a random national sample believed that the rich have too much power and influence in the

United States. Sixty-seven percent believed the rich "use their wealth mostly to protect their own positions in society." A sizable minority (37 percent) did not believe that the rich worked hard to achieve their wealth.[16] Americans do not have much patience for those who do not earn their keep. The legacy of the work ethic remains strong.

The attitude of the average American toward the extremes of inequality in the United States can perhaps best be described as ambivalent.[17] Such ambivalence does not result in political attempts to redistribute income as has been the case in many other industrialized nations. In part, this is because average Americans like to think that someday perhaps they, too, may be rich. In a random national poll taken in 1999, 55 percent of young Americans aged 18 to 29 believed it was either "somewhat likely" or "very likely" that they would someday be rich.[18] If one is not born rich, however, how is this likely to happen? Through hard work in school, of course.

The institution of the school figures prominently in both Americans' acceptance of economic inequality and their commitment to equality. According to a 1998 Gallup poll, 63 percent of Americans believe that wealth should be more evenly distributed in the population. However, only 16 percent of Americans believe that the answer is in providing more job opportunities for the poor. Instead, 67 percent of Americans believe the answer to income inequality is to provide better education and job training.[19] If the school is the key to upward social mobility, however, Americans have a peculiar relationship to it.

On the one hand, as utilitarian individuals, academic success in school is required to climb the socioeconomic ladder. Economists speak to the utilitarian individualism of the American character when they explain that schooling is a rational path to achieve success in the competitive marketplace.[20] The purpose of schooling, in effect, is to build "human capital," specific skills to be used in the job market, so that the national economy can function smoothly and the individual can experience upward mobility.[21] Schooling is a competitive race and the point is to finish first, as Benjamin Franklin would have certainly advocated. The primary purpose of school is not intellectual stimulation, but to provide a practical means of upward mobility in a market economy. The government should provide equal opportunities for all students, but it is up to individual students to take advantage of such opportunities. If they fail, they deserve their poverty.

On the other hand, schooling in the United States means much more than a tool to achieve utilitarian ends. As expressive individuals, Americans also see the school as a place where human growth occurs and where creativity and self-expression are encouraged. School is not just an institution to measure achievement, but also a place to experience personal growth and celebrate human dignity and diversity. Americans see school as an institution where students discover their own identities, their relationship to others, and their relationship to society.[22]

In other words, there is an expressive function to schooling as well as a utilitarian function. These two functions, however, are often at odds with each other. Schooling in the United States is seen both as a private commodity to be consumed by individuals who hope for social mobility in the marketplace as well as a public good that fosters citizenship, community, free expression, and democracy in civil society.[23] As we have seen in previous chapters, Hollywood helps Americans to resolve this tension by emphasizing different educational functions depending upon the social class of the student. In the urban school films the utilitarian function of the school was celebrated. In the suburban school films the educational setting was more of an arena for the expressive function. In the case of the elite private school films the school has both an expressive *and* a utilitarian function. According to Hollywood, these functions of the elite private school should benefit only those students who truly deserve them.

The elite private school films reflect a belief that success in school and happiness in life should be the result not of *ascribed* characteristics (inherited characteristics rooted in one's group membership, such as race, class, or gender) but of *achieved* characteristics (the hard work and talent of individuals). Sociologists have long debated whether achievement has replaced ascription as the process through which individuals attain educational and occupational status in the United States. There is some evidence that through the twentieth century, the role of ascription has declined in relation to individual achievement.[24] Perhaps this is one reason why so many of the elite private school films (nearly half of the elite private school films in this sample) are period pieces that depict an earlier era when the privileges of membership in the upper class could be asserted without having to legitimate them through individual hard work and effort.

In spite of the historical trend in favor of achievement, however, the ascribed characteristics of race, class, and gender continue to play a powerful role in determining the educational and occupational success of individuals in the United States. Therefore, I argue that Hollywood's depiction of the meritorious student-hero in the elite private school films reflects another middle-class fantasy—a projection of the ideal that hardworking individuals with integrity, regardless of their social background, do not need privileged connections to elite networks in order to become upwardly mobile. This fantasy reflects a deep desire to believe that the system *is* fair—that in spite of the deep chasm between the "haves" and "have nots" in this country we nevertheless *do* live in a meritocracy; that schools and employers accurately evaluate individual ability and fairly promote students and workers on the basis of their objective performance; that achievement is earned, not inherited; and that those who try to subvert this principle of fairness are rightly punished.

There is a tension in the elite private schools between the material value of an elite education and the resentment of such an education by those individuals normally denied access to it. These films resolve such tension by both emphasizing the utilitarian value of an elite private education (it can be an avenue of upward social mobility for meritorious members of the working and middle classes if they have access to it) and by stressing the importance of expressive individualism (there is more to life and more to school than achievement; one must be comfortable with one's self). These films suggest that access to an elite education should not be dependent upon wealth. The rich exercise their collective privilege by trying to buy access to educational status and happiness. In Hollywood's cinematic fantasy, however, the rich are doomed to fail without individuality, well roundedness, integrity, and merit. The hero of these films is always a nonelite student who succeeds as both a meritorious academic scholar and an expressive individual. In Hollywood, achievement trumps ascription every time.

Notes

1. Mills, C. Wright. *The Power Elite*. New York: Oxford University Press, pp. 64–65.
2. Powers, Rothman, and Rothman, *Hollywood's America.*
3. Cookson, Peter, Jr., and Caroline Persell. 1985. *Preparing for Power: America's Elite Boarding Schools*. New York: Basic Books.
4. Mills, *The Power Elite*, pp. 64–65.
5. Quoted from the front cover of the 1998 Paramount Home Video VHS packaging.
6. Some observers have claimed that Neil's parents are middle class. See, for instance, Giroux, Henry A. 1993. *Living Dangerously: Multiculturalism and the Politics of Difference*. New York: Peter Lang. Indeed, Neil says his parents are not "rich" and his father admits to having "sacrificed" for Neil's education. However, we never learn about his father's occupation. Nevertheless, the style of their clothing, car, and home suggest that the family is at least upper middle class. If not rich, Neil

certainly represents the striving of the middle class to become upwardly mobile through accomplishment in elite institutions. He also represents the folly of such blind ambition if one ignores the calling of one's soul.

7. For instance, in 2003's *Igby Goes Down,* Igby is a smart but troubled teen from a very rich and dysfunctional family. He spends the entire movie getting kicked out of, running away from, or avoiding enrollment in private schools. Having watched his rich father self-destruct in mental anguish, he is not interested in following the rules of the upper-class "system": "My father went through the system and the system told him what he was supposed to want. He achieved everything. And then, in his forties, he flipped." Igby, and the other heroes of these films, would rather follow their hearts and be true to themselves than find their fortunes.

8. Another lesson about living a balanced life is found in *Dead Poet's Society.* The character of the English teacher, Mr. Keating, is similar to that of the teacher-heroes in the urban public school films. But from what do these talented, intelligent, hardworking, and rich boys need to be saved? Apparently, they need to be saved from the conformity and lockstep attitude of elite society, from the drudgery of traditional learning, and from the complacency of their comfortable taken-for-granted lives. Mr. Keating urges them to expand their horizons, to live life to its fullest, to challenge accepted ways of seeing the world, and to pursue their passions, even in the face of adversity. Mr. Keating wants his students to be expressive individuals—not the elite conformists the school is molding them to be.

9. It is remarkable how similar *Scent of a Woman* is to *Finding Forrester.* In both cases the working- or middle-class student with academic gifts is not fully accepted in the elite institution. The nonelite student is at the school because of merit, but school officials attempt to exploit his lower status. A troubled and mysterious outsider enters the picture to mentor the nonelite student, who is up against overwhelming odds. In each case the mentor is an alcoholic who has had much success in life, but who has since fallen far. The mentor unexpectedly comes to the aid of the student during a public trial or contest where the lower-class student is being judged. The hero makes a speech that shames the school—that shows how the student has integrity and was willing to risk his status in order to maintain that integrity. The elite private school is discredited. The student is redeemed, and the adult hero moves on to other challenges, both having learned a lesson.

10. See Henig, Jeffrey R., and Stephen D. Sugarman. 1999. "The Nature and Extent of School Choice." In *School Choice and Social Controversy:*

Poltics, Policy, and Law. Stephen D. Sugarman and Frank R. Kemerer, editors. Washington, DC: Brookings Institution Press; and Cookson and Persell, *Preparing for Power.*

11. For data on Catholic school students, see Bryk, et al., *Catholic Schools and the Common Good.*

12. This is also true in the case of the one private Christian school film, 2004's *Saved!* As in most of the suburban public school films, *Saved!* is characterized by the lack of attention to academic work, the heroism of students, the corruption of adult authorities, and the defeat of the popular kids by the social misfits and outsiders. Also, the drama predictably culminates the night of the school's prom, when the true natures of the various characters are finally revealed.

13. There are a couple of exceptions among the suburban school films. *River's Edge* and *Over the Edge* each are darker depictions of the struggles adolescents go through. *River's Edge* in particular is unique among the suburban public school films—it depicts apathetic, amoral, and emotionally numb teens who help to cover up the murder of a friend by another friend. *Over the Edge*, while it focuses on junior high school students, also depicts disaffected and violent youth who rebel against the adult authorities in their suburban town.

14. See Marger, *Social Inequality: Pattern and Processes*, for data.

15. Hochschild, Jennifer. 1981. *What's Fair? American Beliefs About Distributive Justice.* Cambridge, MA: Harvard University Press.

16. Roper Starch Worldwide. January 1992. Cited in Ladd, Everett Carll, and Karlyn H. Bowman. 1998. *Attitudes Toward Economic Inequality.* Washington, DC: The American Enterprise Institute.

17. See Hochschild, *What's Fair?*; and Ladd and Bowman, *Attitudes Toward Economic Inequality.*

18. Newsweek Poll, Princeton Research Center, 1999.

19. Gallup Organization. 1998. "Have and Have-Nots: Perceptions of Fairness and Opportunity—1998." Gallup Special Report.

20. Turner, Ralph. 1960. "Sponsored and Contest Mobility and the School System." *American Sociological Review* 25: 855–867.

21. Becker, Gary S. 1975. *Human Capital: A Theoretical and Empirical Analysis with Special Reference to Education.* Chicago: University of Chicago Press.

22. Dewey, John. 1966. *Democracy and Education.* New York: Free Press.

23. Carnoy, Martin, and Henry M. Levin. *Schooling and Work in the Democratic State.* Stanford: Stanford University Press.

24. Hurn, *The Limits and Possibilities of Schooling.*

Cinematic Study Abroad

High School Films in Comparative Perspective

We've got no choice but to keep moving forward . . . Run!
—Nanahara to his girlfriend Noriko in *Battle Royale* (Japan, 2000)

When I'm a man I'll return and we'll talk about everything.
—Antoine to his parents in *The 400 Blows* (France, 1959)

Are the cinematic patterns of the American high school films any different from the patterns found in foreign films that depict adolescents and schooling? Are these American school films actually an indication of something about American culture or are they merely following the standard plot structure of films around the world? To help answer this question I contrasted the American films to a sample of foreign school films.[1] There are forty-one foreign films in the sample; fifteen countries are represented in all. It should be noted that the limited sample of foreign school films does not allow me to make any representative claims about the cinema or cultures of other countries. Such a claim is far beyond the scope of this book.[2] The important point to note is that in contrast to the American high school films, the themes and patterns observed in the sample of foreign school films are consistently different enough to suggest that the American films *do* represent something unique about American culture.

Against the relief of the more pessimistic foreign school films with morally complicated characters and ambiguous endings, the American high school films tend to resolve the dramatic tension in neat fashion, look optimistically toward the future, depict an unambiguous triumph of the individual, and suggest that social problems can be solved and society can be reformed in order to accommodate the needs and wishes of all individuals.

To illustrate this contrast, it is helpful to first look in depth at one foreign school film that typifies many of the themes expressed among the films in the foreign school sample. The Japanese film *Battle Royale* (2000) depicts a deteriorating Japanese society in the near future in which eight hundred thousand students are boycotting school. *Battle Royale* begins as members of ninth-grade "Class B" are preparing to go on their annual field trip (used to bribe the students back to school). Instead of the field trip, however, the students are gassed into unconsciousness, kidnapped by the army, and taken to a deserted island, where they are required to fight for their lives in a brutal and violent game. It is clear in the first five minutes that this is not your average American high school film.

The adults, in fear of the nation's youth, have attempted to reassert control over society and to quell the rising rebellion of the young by passing the draconian Millennium Education Reform Act. The abducted students of Class B are about to participate in one element of the new act, the Battle Royale. Each year a randomly selected class of students is isolated on an island with the instructions to kill each other until only one "winner" is left alive. Their host, and the contest referee, is the teacher they had in seventh grade, Mr. Kitano. While the students are gathered to learn the rules of the "game," Mr. Kitano tells them:

> This country is absolutely no good anymore . . . you guys mock grown ups. Go ahead and mock us. But don't forget life is a game. So fight for survival and find out if you are worth it.

The students are each given a pack with some food and one weapon in it. All have a necklace locked around their neck that constantly monitors their location and activity. It also tells the authorities when they are dead. If they attempt to take the necklace off it detonates, killing them. If there is no winner after three days, all the students are killed. In addition to the regular class of forty students participating in the game, there are two "transfer" students—one, as it turns out, won a previous Battle Royale and the other signed up just "for fun."

Some students take to the game eagerly, killing their friends without hesitation. Others attempt to gather the students together to resist the rules of the cruel game. Still others are simply depressed about the grim situation and kill themselves. The film focuses on the character of Nanahara. He is an angry boy who is filled with doubt about adult society. His mother left him when he was younger, and his father killed himself. He was raised in a foster home. His heart is not in the game, but he will try to survive: "I've never really trusted adults . . . But I'll keep fighting, even though I don't know how, until I become a real adult." More importantly, he devotes himself to defending his girlfriend, Noriko.

Nanahara and Noriko befriend Kawada, the previous winner of a Battle Royale and a viciously effective fighter. Kawada is kind to them because he, too, had devoted himself to protecting his girlfriend in his first Battle Royale. The three of them form an alliance. Kawada kills many students, but Nanahara and Noriko take refuge in a cabin through most of the battles. After much carnage, Nanahara, Noriko, and Kawada are the last three left alive on the island. As it turns out, Kawada has the ability to safely disable the monitoring necklaces. Kawada fools Mr. Kitano into thinking that he has killed Nanahara and Noriko and has once again won the contest. After the army leaves their headquarters to collect the students' bodies, the three survivors return to confront Mr. Kitano alone. Nanahara kills Mr. Kitano, and the three survivors escape the island on a boat. En route back to the mainland, however, Kawada dies of the injuries he suffered in the battle. Noriko and Nanahara return home safely only to find that they are wanted for the murder of Mr. Kitano. Fugitives from the law, they must go underground to avoid capture. The film ends with the two "winners" of the game running for their lives in civilization just as they had run for their lives in the Battle Royale.

This is certainly not the happy ending that we have come to expect in most of the American high school films. Noriko and Nanahara are the student-heroes, but they are not victorious as the student-heroes of the American films are. Noriko and Nanahara must remain constantly on the run from the oppressive adult authorities of society. The spirit of the movie may side with the youth, but the youth do not triumph. Neither, however, do the adults. The distrust and fear that are the premise of the movie remain at the end. There is no resolution to the dramatic tension that fueled the plot. Furthermore, unlike the American school films, *Battle Royale* offers little hope for the future. We do not know what will become of Noriko and Nanahara. While they were clever enough to avoid death in the Battle Royale, it is not certain that they can survive back home. We last see them running away from all they know in order to stay alive. Had this film been a production of Hollywood, the two surviving students would likely have emerged triumphant as they revealed the arrogance and brutality of the school authorities and adult society. They would have been celebrated as individual heroes who defeated the system and made the world a better place. Instead, there is no victory, no redemption, and no lessons learned about middle-class values, the power of an individual, or the illegitimate privilege of elites.

The Cultural Distinctiveness of American Films

In *A Certain Tendency of the Hollywood Cinema, 1930–1980*, Robert Ray argues that American films tend to neatly resolve tension and contradictions in the story:

> This reconciliatory pattern, itself derived largely from earlier American forms, increasingly became the self-perpetuating norm of the American Cinema. Movies that refused to resolve contradictory myths typically found themselves without the large audiences expected by the industry; as a result, directors of such films found themselves without chances to work.[3]

This often results in the proverbial "happy ending" of the typical American film, an ending in which the tension that drove the plot is released and the characters and themes are no longer in opposition to each other. Either one pole is eliminated or a compromise is reached between opposing sides. The audience leaves feeling content and pleased that a satisfying resolution has been reached. If, as I have argued, the contradictions in these films mirror the contradictions in American culture, then perhaps the tidy resolutions of the American films help in a small way to smooth out some of the rough patches that perplex Americans in their everyday lives.

For instance, we have seen how in the American urban school film the utilitarian middle-class achievement ideology is at odds with the apathy and hostility of poor students. By the end of the film, this tension in resolved in favor of the achievement ideology. The relationship between the teacher-hero and the students transforms the students' culture of poverty into a culture of individual achievement. In the suburban school film there is a tension between the freedom of individual self-expression and the acceptance of that individuality by social groups such as friends, family, and the school. By the end of the film, this tension is resolved in such a way as to preserve both the expressive individualism of the students and their membership in a community. In the private school film there is a tension between the elitism of an exclusive education and the claims of equality by the middle- or working-class protagonist. By the conclusion of the private school film this tension is resolved by maintaining the prestige and benefits of a private school education yet transforming the institution of the school so that it recognizes merit and integrity and establishes equality of opportunity for all.

These tendencies speak to much more than the dynamics of storytelling. The American film is unique because American culture is unique. A glimpse into the American cinema gives us a glimpse into the American soul. The optimism, hard work, personal freedom, faith in the individual, and belief in the ultimate fairness of the system that characterize American culture also characterize American film. In reality, Americans may not necessarily be optimistic and rugged individuals working hard in a meritorious system in which the good guys triumph against the odds. However, this is often how Americans *believe* themselves to be. This is the myth we tell ourselves. By contrast, the sample of foreign school films throws into relief these mythic tendencies in American high school films.

Characteristics of the Foreign School Films

In contrast to the neat and tidy resolutions of the American films, the foreign school films tend to leave the viewer with a tension that is still highly strung. Rather than a resolution to the contradictions in the story or within the characters, the foreign school films often end in discord. The main characters frequently fail to resolve their problems. Their futures remain clouded and their relationships to others remain troubled. Happy endings are far less common and tragic endings far more common in the foreign school film sample than in the American school sample. Finally, and most significantly, the individual is still the focus of the foreign school film, but the individual's relationship to society is dramatically different. Rather than battling the odds and successfully changing the social world, as in the American school films, the individual "hero" of the foreign school film confronts and then tries to escape the oppressive social world. In some cases the individual is defeated. In other cases the individual is happy to have escaped. But rarely does the individual succeed in transforming the antagonistic social forces. The following sections provide examples of each of these trends among the foreign school films.

The Unresolved Tension in Foreign School Films

Unlike the American school films, the foreign school films in the sample often end without having resolved the tension that fueled the action in the story.[4] These movies often end with as much doubt and confusion about the characters and their predicaments as when the film began. The ambiguous endings of the foreign school films certainly do not reflect the fantasies of conflict resolution and the triumph of the individual that are the consistent characteristics of the American high school films. In particular, the French films in the sample are the most likely to leave the tension unresolved. A typical example of this trend can be seen in *Wild Reeds* (France, 1994).[5]

Wild Reeds takes place in a French boarding school in 1962. It highlights the lives of four students—Maite, the daughter of a communist teacher at the school, François, who is discovering his homosexuality, Serge, his friend and first lover, and Henri, a French Algerian anticommunist. The four students struggle with the pains of growing up, the trauma of war, the anxiety of school, and the heartbreak of love. It is not a carefree adolescence that is depicted. Maite summarizes her feelings this way: "I hate being young. It's a huge burden. I want to shut my eyes and wake up much later, with a life of my own that I choose."

The film revolves around a love rectangle between these four students. Maite and François "date," but there is no sexual relationship between them. Henri unexpectedly falls in love with Maite. François and Serge sleep together and François promptly falls in love with Serge. Serge, however, tells François that he must forget the night they slept together. Serge wants nothing more than to inherit the family farm, marry a woman, and raise a family. He denies his homosexuality and develops a crush on Maite.

The sexual tension among the four is heightened by political tension. Serge's brother, who was opposed to the war in Algeria, fought there against his will and was killed. Serge blames Henri and other French Algerians for his brother's death. As an anticommunist and a French Algerian, Henri is furious that the French are not doing more to preserve the colony. His father was killed by a terrorist bomb, and his mother is struggling in exile in Marseilles. His political beliefs cause trouble for him at school—particularly in the classroom of Mrs. Alvarez, the communist teacher and mother of Maite.

Henri has been kicked out of several schools and, now that he is twenty-one, is free to leave school at any time. This is his last chance to earn a diploma. After a dispute with another teacher over the political situation in Algeria, however, Henri drops out. In anger and frustration he burns the communist posters around town, and he goes to the Communist party headquarters in town with the intention of burning it down as well. Before he can set it on fire, however, he sees Maite in the building. She invites him in, and the two develop an attraction toward each other in spite of their severe political differences.

In the midst of all of this sexual, romantic, and political confusion, these students are faced with their high school final exams. The final few scenes of the movie take place after Henri has dropped out of school. The other three are waiting to learn if they have passed their final exams and qualified to graduate. They are quite anxious to learn the results. To relieve the tension, the four of them go to the river to relax and to swim. Here Serge rejects François's desperate appeals for his love; meanwhile, the odd political pair of Henri and Maite make love along the riverbank. Rather than resolving any tension, these final scenes see only further anxiety, confusion, and pain develop. Maite and Henri despise each other's politics, yet they seem to be falling in love. Nevertheless, Henri leaves abruptly to catch a train to Marseilles. François has a crush on Serge, but he rejects him for heterosexuality. Serge has a crush on Maite, but she rejects him for the suddenly absent Henri.

After Henri leaves, the confused Maite sobbingly embraces and kisses François, with jealous Serge looking on. François, Maite, and Serge then walk silently back toward school to learn the outcome of their final exams. We see them walking farther and farther away from the camera when the screen fades to black and the movie ends. The viewers never learn if Maite and Henri will see each other again, if François and Serge will find love with each other or with anyone else, or if any of them graduate from high school! The political, academic, personal, and sexual tension remains as thick at the end of the film as at any other point. Serge sets the tone for the end of the movie when he tells François, "The death of a brother is tough. I thought I'd die. But there's something even tougher. Tougher than war. It's that life goes on."

In contrast to the unresolved tension at the end of most of the foreign school films in the sample, the American high school films tend to leave the viewer with very few unanswered questions. The tension is almost always resolved in the American school film. For instance, even the serious and tragic drama *Rebel Without a Cause* (1955) has a happy ending that resolves the dramatic tension. Jim Stark is an angry and frustrated teenager whose family moves from town to town as they attempt to escape the trouble that Jim creates for himself. Jim's parents bicker with each other, they have difficulty communicating with Jim, and they attempt to buy his love with gifts. His mother is cold and domineering, and his father is a fearful and ineffective man whom Jim does not respect. The normally reticent Jim opens up to a police officer who attempts to help him. He wishfully complains to the officer, "If I had one day when I didn't have to be all confused and didn't have to feel that I was ashamed of everything. If I felt like I belonged someplace . . ."

Over the course of the film (during Jim's first day at a new high school), Jim gets into trouble after a deadly drag race; he develops a crush on Judy, a popular girl at his high school; and he develops a friendship with Plato, a psychologically troubled boy with rich but absent parents. Plato looks up to Jim and Judy as substitute parents. The three of them hide in an old abandoned mansion, playing family as they evade the gang whose leader was killed earlier in the drag race. The members of the gang catch up to them at the mansion and Plato, who has his father's handgun for protection, frantically runs from the gang members. Jim catches up to him and tries to calm him down. The movie ends tragically when the police shoot and kill Plato as he attempts to run away from them with the gun in his hand (they are unaware that Jim had removed the bullets).

Jim is devastated that Plato is dead. Nevertheless, there is a resolution to the tension that had driven Jim's rebellion. In his anguish, Jim embraces his father. His father consoles Jim and, for the first time, effectively communicates with him: "Jim, you can depend on me. Trust me. Whatever comes we'll face it together . . . Stand up. I'll stand up with you. I'll try to be as strong as you want me to be." This time, the family won't run away from their problems. They will stand and face them together. They will, it seems, finally give each other the love and support they need. Jim introduces his parents to Judy, and the two couples walk arm-in-arm away from the scene of Plato's death—a happy ending after all.

The future for Jim is much brighter than it had been earlier in the film. He has repaired the relationship with his parents, found a girlfriend, and finally gained the emotional support of his father. The viewer leaves the film feeling optimistic about Jim's second day at school. With the significant tension resolved by the end of most of the American high school films, the audience has a fairly clear view of what the future holds for the protagonists. The future for the protagonists in the foreign school film, however, is not nearly as clear or as bright.

A Murky Future in the Foreign School Film

What does the future hold for the characters in these foreign school films? Since the tension is not resolved, it is difficult to tell what direction the lives of these characters will take. In the American school films the protagonists graduate from high school, find their true selves, repair significant relationships, fall in love, or prove their worth to others. These accomplishments set the stage for the next chapter of their lives, chapters that the viewer can easily imagine—graduation from college, gainful employment, a happy marriage and family, and a healthy self that is filled with confidence and self-esteem.

For instance, in the American film *All the Right Moves*, Stef is a high school senior who lives in a severely depressed Pennsylvania coal-mining town that he and his girlfriend, Lisa, are desperate to escape. He is a talented football player and is dependent upon an athletic scholarship to get him out of town and to earn a college degree in engineering. A severe conflict with the football coach (who is also trying to get out of town), however, seems to doom Stef's dream of going away to college and living a better and upwardly mobile life. The stubborn Coach Nickerson throws Stef off the football team and tells college recruiters that Stef has an "attitude problem." As a result, Stef loses any chance at a college scholarship. Feeling defeated, he goes to work on a demolition crew in town. He seems destined to re-create the lives of his parents in the depressed coal-mining town.

The movie does not end with Stef resigned to reproduce his parents' working-class lives, however. Nor does it end with Stef fleeing town toward an uncertain future. Rather, an improbable turn of events gives this story a happy ending. Coach Nickerson is offered a job coaching football for a college in California. Feeling guilty for having sabotaged Stef's future, Coach Nickerson has a sudden change of heart and offers Stef a full scholarship to play football for him in California—at a school that just happens to have an excellent program in engineering. Stef and Lisa have their ticket to a better life after all.

The viewer of the foreign school film, however, has a much more difficult time predicting how the postscript of these films might be written. Rather than resulting in a happy ending, the foreign school film ends with uncertainty and doubt about the future. Instead of unambiguous lessons about right and wrong, the foreign school film is more likely to close with moral confusion and complexity. As Serge in *Wild Reeds* notes, life goes on and it is a painful struggle. A film that typically represents this unclear future is the Swedish film *Torment* (1944).[6]

Torment takes place in a strict religious boys' high school in Sweden. The students are just two weeks away from graduating, and they are excessively worried about their final exams and grades. They steal every opportunity to study, including the moments they are "singing" in the church choir. One teacher in particular sends chills down the spines of these boys. He is the Latin teacher, whom they call Caligula. He is mean to the students to the point of sadism. He relishes finding weakness among his students and exploiting it. He seems to enjoy handing out demerits and suggesting that a last-minute misstep may prevent some students from graduating. A kind and elderly teacher learns of Caligula's terrifying methods. He approaches Caligula, but even this speech does not change his behavior toward the students:

Ever heard of a teacher's calling? It means we are called, it should come to us naturally. It's absurd to call yourself a teacher on academic qualifications alone. You don't understand any more about boys than the man in the moon. There's something called a heart, a smile, kindliness, understanding. But, on my word, you haven't enough of these to feed a flea . . . A tormentor of men. That's what you are!

Widgren is the favorite target of Caligula's irrational wrath. Widgren is a goodhearted student who wants nothing but to write, play his violin, and fall in love. Caligula, however, has Widgren so scared that he is on the edge of a nervous breakdown. Widgren also has problems at home. His parents are ashamed of the "black mark" he received in Latin and they are upset that his graduation is in jeopardy. Widgren is fearful of Caligula, yet also hopeful that he will somehow find happiness and purpose in his life.

Walking home one night, Widgren runs into a woman, Bertha, who is very drunk and in obvious need of assistance. He cares for her and takes her back to her apartment. She is grateful for his kindness. Widgren is attracted to the woman and spends the night with her. He quickly falls in love with her in spite of a mysterious problem that she alludes to in great fear. She speaks vaguely of a terrifying man who threatens her, but she refuses to name him. Widgren soon learns that the man tormenting Bertha is none other than his nemesis at school, the Latin teacher Caligula. Bertha tells Widgren that she is afraid that Caligula will kill her. Indeed, not long after she expresses this fear, Widgren finds Bertha dead in her apartment with Caligula standing above her body. Widgren accuses Caligula of killing Bertha. The medical examiner, however, finds that the death was the result of alcohol abuse and heart disease. Caligula goes to the headmaster of the high school and charges Widgren with false accusations and with improper relations with a girl of questionable repute. Widgren angrily responds, "You tormented her to death! You drove her to drink!" In his rage, Widgren punches Caligula and is immediately expelled without any chance of graduating. Mortified, Widgren leaves home. He says to his parents, "I won't be around to shame you. I'm leaving."

Widgren goes to stay at Bertha's old apartment. The headmaster learns where he is staying and, feeling sorry for Widgren, stops by and offers to help. Caligula, hiding in the hallway outside Bertha's apartment, is paranoid that they are talking about him. After the headmaster leaves, Caligula approaches Widgren and whines, "no one cares about me." Widgren ignores his sorrowful pleas for pity. The movie ends as Widgren turns out the lights in the hallway, picks up Bertha's cat, leaves Caligula behind in the dark, and walks toward town. Just as in *Wild Reeds*, there is no resolution to the dramatic tension in the story. Therefore, the audience's view of the future of these characters is clouded. Where is Widgren headed? Will he accept the headmaster's offer of assistance? Will he return to his parents' house? Will he go to another school and graduate? Will he yet again encounter Caligula? Will Caligula keep his job and torment other boys? All we are certain of is that life goes on and that it is indeed a struggle.[7]

It should be noted that there are a few foreign school films in which the dramatic tension *is* resolved at the end of the film. Yet, unlike their American counterparts, the tension of the foreign school film is often resolved through tragedy, not triumph. While the American films almost always end with an upbeat and hopeful message about the future, the foreign school films that offer a view of the future often offer a view that is depressingly bleak.[8]

The Tragic Ending of the Foreign School Film

While not the most common ending among the films in the foreign school sample, the tragic ending is, nevertheless, much more common in the foreign school sample than in the American school sample. Whether it is repressed sexuality, Nazis, teen angst, mental illness, cruel teachers, or heartbreak, the student characters in these foreign school films are unable to overcome oppressive social forces.[9] The dramatic tension is sometimes resolved with the death of the protagonist. For instance, *To Play or to Die*, a 1991 film from Holland, represents this trend with particular despair.

Kees is the teenage only son of a wealthy couple. His parents leave town for a couple of days in order to attend a wedding. Rather than staying with his aunt, Kees asks to stay home. He tells his parents he wants to have a friend from school over to the house. His parents look shocked. Kees is a shy, quiet, nerdy, and contemplative student who doesn't have many friends. The other boys at school make fun of Kees relentlessly. One boy in particular, Charel, abuses Kees without mercy. He copies his homework, insults him, and taunts him. Kees, however, does not resist Charel's abuse. He does not complain to anyone at school about Charel. After he is victimized by a humiliating prank, he tells on all of the boys who harassed him, with the notable exception of Charel. Kees's intense gaze at Charel in the locker room after gym class suggests to the viewer that Kees has a crush on Charel.

In geometry class Kees gives Charel a note that presumably invites Charel over to his house that night. Charel agrees and arrives at the appointed time. After copying Kees's homework Charel sexually teases him. He asks him if he has ever "done it" and asks about the whereabouts of his parents. Learning that they are gone for the night, he makes suggestive sexual remarks to Kees, hinting that they might have sex.

The two boys go up to Kees's room, where Kees introduces Charel to his gymnast's rings. Kees demonstrates the techniques of the rings and Charel wants to try them. Charel is certain that he, the jock, can perform at least as well as the nerdy and awkward Kees. When he has difficulty on the rings, however, Charel is embarrassed and challenges Kees to a "real sport"—boxing. Charel shadowboxes until Kees puts up his arms in defense. Charel then pummels Kees, bloodying his lip. Kees fights back "like a girl" and pulls Charel's hair. Charel responds by hitting Kees and knocking him to the ground. Charel pins Kees to the floor and makes him beg for mercy. Charel finally stops hitting Kees and leaves the house. Hurt and humiliated, Kees has an emotional tantrum on the floor. His anger, confusion, and emotional pain are palpable.

Physically and psychologically wounded, Kees wanders downstairs and broods alone. In spite of his anger and despair Kees is sexually aroused. He masturbates, presumably while fantasizing about Charel. Kees's parents call to tell him they will be home later than expected. Kees begs them to come home soon. Meanwhile, some children who are playing outside accidentally throw a soccer ball through the window of the dining room. Kees picks it up and hallucinates that the basketball is Charel's severed head, which proceeds to insult him and spit in Kees's face. Overwhelmed, confused, and humiliated, Kees leaps headfirst down the staircase, killing himself.

To Play or to Die is a dark and tragic story. There is despair, confusion, anger, masochism, and loneliness. There are no apparent answers to these problems short of nihilism. Unlike the suburban American high school films in which the nerdy, unpopular, or lonely student triumphs over the popular kids, finds and expresses his or her true self, and is accepted for it, *To Play or to Die* offers no hope for the marginalized individual. The obstacles facing Kees—abusive peers, an indifferent school, absent parents, depression, and struggles with his sexual identity—defeat him. Unlike the protagonists in the American high school films, Kees is unable to confront and overcome the social forces bearing down on him. For Kees, along with the characters of Polly in *Lost and Delirious*, Jean Kippelstein in *Au Revoir Les Enfants*, and Miranda in *Picnic at Hanging Rock*, death is the only escape from the oppressive burdens they face. As Mrs. Tunheim says in *The Other Side of Sunday*, "When you are dead you are free."

Most of the protagonists in the foreign school film sample, however, do not die. Instead, they confront the challenges they face at school and at home and then run away from them. In contrast to the American high school films in which the protagonist confronts a serious obstacle and then successfully overcomes that obstacle and resolves the conflict that drove the plot, the foreign school films often end with the protagonist failing to resolve the conflict and seeking freedom through an escape from social burdens.[10]

Running Away from Society

We have already seen how Widgren flees in *Torment*, Henri leaves in *Wild Reeds*, and Nanahara and Noriko run in *Battle Royale*. These examples only scratch the surface of this escapist theme among the foreign school films. A clear example of this trend is François Truffaut's classic coming-of-age story, *The 400 Blows* (France, 1959). Unwanted by his parents, unhappy at school, and treated poorly by state authorities, the central character, Antoine, is searching for a place he belongs. Yet he fails to find his self, his identity, his home, or his freedom. He runs away from his parents and away from school and ends up as a ward of the state. In the final scene of the movie he runs away from the state juvenile detention center. Will he be free now that he has left home, dropped out of school, and escaped the reach of the state? The lost look on his face in the final haunting freeze-framed shot suggests not. Antoine could not reconcile the conflicts he had at home, at school, or with the state authorities. His only response was to run. Where he ends up, however, the viewer never knows. Such an ending is common among the foreign school films.

For instance, in *The Disenchanted* (France, 1990), Beth is a seventeen-year-old high school student who is unhappy with her life. Beth's teacher is worried that she will perform poorly on her final exams because she gets carried away with her romantic enthusiasm for poetry. Beth gives a romantic and dramatic presentation of Rimbaud's poetry in class, but ignores the nuts and bolts of the curriculum. For Beth, the importance of an education is the emotional fire it ignites in her soul. For her teachers, however, this approach is misguided and counterproductive. It does not prepare her for the exams.

Things are not any better for Beth at home. Her mother is bedridden at home with a fatal illness. As a result, Beth is in charge of the household, including the care of her younger brother. The family does not have much money. They do, however, have a benefactor. "Sugardad" is Beth's mother's doctor and lover. He gives the family money, but Beth, who hates and distrusts him, rips it up. Beth's mother, however, wants Beth to sleep with "Sugardad" in exchange for a large sum of money he has promised. Beth resists this distasteful request.

Beth has a boyfriend, but he is manipulative and violent. When she meets her boyfriend to break up with him, he begins to attack her. A middle-aged bystander, Alphonse, intervenes and protects Beth. Attracted to Beth, he gives her his business card and invites her to stop by his apartment anytime. Without much else going for her in her difficult life, Beth visits Alphonse that night. They flirt and talk all night. He offers to take her out to dinner the following night. They agree to meet by the Seine.

The next day Beth makes the difficult decision to sleep with "Sugardad" for the financial benefit of her family. After she sleeps with him, he gives her a check, and she sullenly hands it over to her mother. She then announces that after she passes her final exams she will leave home. That night, she goes to meet Alphonse at the appointed time and place for their date. She sees him standing by the river, waiting for her. He does not see her. She stops and contemplates her future. Instead of meeting up with Alphonse, the movie ends abruptly as Beth runs away through the streets of Paris.

Once again, we find an unclear and unsettled future with very little dramatic tension resolved. As in the American high school films, Beth is looking to find her identity and to define her future. Yet, unlike the American school films, she does not succeed. As with Antoine in *The 400 Blows*, Beth runs away from her unhappy life in search of an undefined something else. We don't know if she ever finds it. Rather than overcoming her abusive boyfriend, the challenge of school, and her unhappy family life, Beth flees these oppressive social forces.[11]

Conclusion: Returning from Study Abroad

In the American high school film the individual hero stands outside of the community in order to help save or transform that community. In the urban school film, for instance, the middle-class teacher comes from a different social world (with different values) to save the urban school students from their culture of poverty. In the suburban school film the unpopular student (or otherwise unique individual) defeats the culture of popularity and creates a social space where all can be accepted for who they are. In the private school film the working- or middle-class hero successfully challenges the culture of privilege in the elite private school, creating an institution that respects merit and integrity. In each of these American subgenres of the high school film, the individual hero affects the larger community. These films reflect a common American cultural belief that individuals have the power to make a difference—the power to change society.

The foreign school films also focus on the trials and tribulations of the individual, but the individual's relationship to society is much less powerful than in the American films. In some cases, as we have seen, the character is tragically defeated by social forces. More often, however, the main character of the foreign school film confronts and then runs away from the oppressive social world. The hero does not transform the social world as in the American school film. Instead, he or she attempts to escape it.

This different perspective, I suggest, highlights a particularly American cultural orientation of optimism (particularly among the American middle class) and a persistent faith in the power of the individual in the face of social institutions. In their 1991 follow-up to *Habits of the Heart*, Bellah and his co-authors note that after World War II there was a particularly powerful mood of optimism in the United States. While the postwar years have certainly presented many challenges to the "American Century" and provided plenty of reasons to be pessimistic, a peculiar American optimism remains.[12] Americans have lost some faith in their institutions and politicians, yet they remain hopeful and upbeat about their personal fortunes. As Alan Wolfe found in his survey study of the American middle class:

> Americans are usually thought of as an optimistic people, emphasizing the positive, quick to turn away from despair. They may have become cynical and resentful toward politicians, but, by the same token, they have always been, and continue to be, hopeful about their own prospects . . . Optimism is so pervasive in middle-class America that many found unimaginable that "our society is going to continue to decline and decline."[13]

Such optimism does not necessarily correspond with real conditions. The optimistic and happy endings of the American school films are not very accurate reflections of American society. That is, our lives are not as tidy and happy as the lives of the characters in these high school films. However, it is noteworthy that these films, with happy endings and neatly resolved conflicts, are the stories that we choose to tell to ourselves about ourselves. That is, the *image* of who we are as Americans, how we understand ourselves to be, is reflected in the cultural products we produce and consume.

While the foreign school films tend to depict the individual at the mercy of oppressive social forces, the American school films ultimately suggest that oppressive social forces are at the mercy of the individual. Whether it is the cowboy of the urban school classroom, the expressive individual fighting against suburban conformity, or the meritorious underdog of the elite private school, the American films end with the happy triumph of the individual. The myths of American culture are echoed and reinforced in American film. These myths of the capitalist ethic, the rugged individual, the drummer who marches to his or her own beat, and the fairness of social institutions, help to conceal the structural sources of inequality and oppression in society. In the American high school films the system is fair, the individual is free, and hard work is rewarded. If not, then it is the task of the heroic individual to defeat the system or to reform it. The counter example of the foreign school films helps us to see that, rather than conforming to standard requirements of movie plots, the American high school films clearly bear the unmistakable stamp of a unique cultural view of the individual and society.

Notes

1. There are far fewer foreign films in the sample than domestic films. This is due in part to the limited availability of the films in the United States. Also, I speculate that the larger number of American high school films has something to do with the American preoccupation with adolescence as a unique stage of life and with education as a key to upward social mobility and identity formation. In order to increase the number of foreign films in the sample, the selection criteria were loosened somewhat to include films that featured junior-high-aged students. Also, the school is not always at the center of the plot in the foreign school films.
2. Such a project would require greater attention to the specific historical and cultural traditions within each of the fifteen countries represented and a much more representative sample of the films produced by each country.
3. Ray, Robert B. 1985. *A Certain Tendency of the Hollywood Cinema, 1930–1980*. Princeton, NJ: Princeton University Press, p. 57.
4. A recent exception to this among the American school films is the movie *Thirteen* (2003). It tells a bleak story of a psychologically troubled young teen who spirals rapidly down a hole of drugs, sex, and crime. While there is some reason for hope at the close of the film, it ends ambiguously with the main character circling on a merry-go-round. It was not included in my sample of films since the main characters are junior high school students. Another exception is the independent film *Ghost World* (2000), which tells the story of two disaffected teens during the summer after their high school graduation. It ends enigmatically with the main character, Enid, leaving town on a bus headed toward an unknown destination.

5. Some of the other films in the foreign school sample that leave the dramatic tension unresolved include *The Year My Voice Broke* (Australia, 1988), *Flirting* (Australia, 1993), *Battle Royale* (Japan, 2000), *The 400 Blows* (France, 1959), *The Disenchanted* (France, 1990), *A Nos Amours* (France, 1983), *All Things Fair* (Sweden, 1995), *Peppermint Soda* (France, 1977), *The Getting of Wisdom* (Australia, 1977), *Torment* (Sweden, 1944), *Sweet Sixteen* (Scotland, 2002), *July Rhapsody* (Hong Kong, 2002), and *The Fighting Elegy* (Japan, 1966).

6. In addition to the foreign school films mentioned in the previous section, *The Other Side of Sunday* (Norway, 1996), *Murmur of the Heart* (France, 1971), *Puberty Blues* (Australia, 1981), *Saint Clara* (Israel, 1995), *Maedchen in Uniform* (Germany, 1931), and *Big Girls Don't Cry* (Germany, 2002) leave the audience guessing about the future. The viewer receives very little guidance about the direction the story might take after the credits roll.

7. As the teenage Kati says at the end of *Big Girls Don't Cry* (Germany, 2002), "You don't need to find a solution for everything. Sometimes things just suck, but you have to keep going anyway."

8. A few of the American school films do end with the tragic death of the protagonist. They are relatively few in number, however—*Donnie Darko*, *Powder*, *187*, and *The Dangerous Lives of Altar Boys*. Also, in spite of the tragic endings, these films end with a feeling of hope and optimism, unlike the darker endings of the foreign school films.

9. *Picnic at Hanging Rock* (Australia, 1975), *Au Revoir Les Enfants* (France, 1987), *To Play or to Die* (Holland, 1991), *Heavenly Creatures* (New Zealand, 1994), and *Lost and Delirious* (Canada, 2001) all end tragically.

10. With only a few exceptions in which the student protagonists triumph through collective struggle—*If* (England, 1969), *Sarafina* (United States/England/France, 1992), and *Zero de Conduite* (France, 1933)—the protagonists in most of the foreign school films struggle alone.

11. While the French school films in the sample often end with the protagonists running away from the social forces that oppress them, this is not unique to French cinema. In addition to the already discussed films *Torment* (Sweden, 1944) and *Battle Royale* (Japan, 2000), the films *Fighting Elegy* (Japan, 1966), *The Getting of Wisdom* (Australia, 1977), *The Other Side of Sunday* (Norway, 1996), *Sweet Sixteen* (Scotland, 2002), and *The Year My Voice Broke* (Australia, 1988) all feature endings in which the protagonists flee the social forces they were unable to conquer.

12. Bellah, Robert N., et al. 1991. *The Good Society*. New York: Knopf.

13. Wolfe, *One Nation, After All*.

Film Fantasies as Cultural Myths

Applying the Sociological Imagination

Hollywood films have as much to teach us about our selves and our society as any other cultural artifact that Americans produce and consume. There are layers upon layers of cultural meaning just beneath the celluloid surface of the motion picture. Movies are big business and they are art. But that is not all that they are. They are, in a sense, modern-day folktales. They are the mythical stories that we tell to ourselves about who we are and what we believe. As such, motion pictures are social documents that map the terrain of our culture. Films emerge out of the imagination of an artist and the office of a businessperson and find their way into our neighborhoods and into our lives. We watch films, read about them, talk back to them, love or hate them, laugh and cry to them, tell our friends about them, argue about them, remember or forget them, and compare them to other films and to our own life experiences. Our collective reaction to films helps to create film genres that are thick with cultural meaning and which play themselves out again and again until they no longer resonate with a sizable audience.

C. Wright Mills taught us to exercise our "sociological imaginations."[1] He explained that to do sociology, one must understand the intersection of biography and history. That is, our individual biographies, the unique lives that we experience, are in very important ways influenced by the time and the place in which we live. We are not alone. The social, historical, cultural, and geographic landscape is as much a part of us as we are a part of it. Mills taught us to see our lives not as disconnected and isolated, but as a part of this larger matrix. Our "personal troubles" are not just our own. Personal troubles are in important ways also "public issues." For instance, while I may experience unemployment as a very intimate, personal, and unique experience, it also exists as a social issue that is much larger than my particular personal troubles. My individual life is not disconnected from the lives of millions of strangers. Nor is it disconnected from the larger cultural and structural forces that are outside of my immediate experience. To recognize our connectedness to the larger social world of which we are inevitably a part is to exercise our sociological imagination.

In much the same way, I have tried to understand Hollywood films as existing within this matrix. Films are more than individual expressions of an artistic vision. They are more than a businessperson's investment. Films exist in a social context. They both are shaped by and in turn shape the social world in which they are embedded. Films are not produced in cultural isolation. Nor are they consumed that way. They are social products and must be analyzed as a part of the social world.

The purpose of this book has been to carefully examine one type of modern-day folktale—the high school motion picture—and to help make sense of its multiple and often contradictory messages in the rich and complicated milieu of American culture. Films are fantasies, but they are fantasies that are firmly grounded within a specific social and cultural context. Applying a sociological imagination to the analysis of films helps to make sense of the relationship between art and society. What is immediately clear in this study is that there is no one single genre called the high school film. There are multiple subgenres of the high school picture, each with its own particular set of messages and meanings. The urban public school film, the suburban public school film, and the elite private school film each tells a very different story about individualism, inequality, education, and adolescence. Together, however, they speak volumes about the mysteries and contradictions of American culture.

As Kai Erikson has noted, cultures are filled with contradictory potential.[2] This is as true of American culture as it is of any other. Americans, for instance, hold contradictory beliefs about individualism, inequality, education, and adolescence. Americans believe that the individual is more powerful than society, yet we as individuals are dependent upon community. Inequality is considered to be both a social problem and a social necessity. Education is treated as both oppressive and emancipatory. Adolescence is viewed as both threatening and promising. The American high school film is just one lens through which we can get a glimpse of how Americans struggle with these contradictions.

The anthropologist Claude Levi-Strauss argued that myths are a way of reconciling cultural contradictions.[3] The structure of the myth is such that two opposing positions eventually find a compatible resolution. I agree with other sociologists who have studied film that movies are the myths of the contemporary world.[4] They are the medium that a culture uses to tell stories about itself to itself. In a small way Hollywood's representation of reality helps Americans to reconcile some of the contradictory elements within their own culture. For its part, the American high school film genre struggles to reconcile contradictory cultural beliefs about autonomy and dependence, individuality and conformity, and equality and inequality.

The urban school film, for instance, struggles to reconcile independence and dependence. These films feature poor students who suffer in a culture of poverty. The students do not believe in the achievement ideology or the ethic of hard work. These urban students are largely apathetic, violent, and hostile to school authorities. Most of the teachers and administrators have lost hope that any of these students can be successfully educated. Not everyone has lost hope, however. An idealistic teacher new to the school and often new to the profession believes that he or she can "get through" to these at-risk students. After rejecting traditional methods these teacher-heroes are able to touch the lives of the poor students and to open their eyes to the possibilities waiting for them in the middle-class world. After enduring several crises and having their faith tested, the teacher-heroes transform these students from culturally impoverished pessimists to optimistic young people with middle-class values and aspirations. The urban high school movies tend to end happily as the students finally begin to achieve some level of academic success. While the teacher-hero encourages the students to transcend their poverty—to become utilitarian individuals—they are ironically placed in a position of dependence upon the teacher-hero in order to achieve their middle-class goal of independence.

The suburban school film, on the other hand, struggles to reconcile individuality and conformity. While middle-class adults are predominantly the heroes of the urban school films, middle-class adolescents are consistently the heroes of the suburban school films. The suburban school films feature mostly middle-class students who struggle with their parents, families, and peers as they try to figure out who they are and what they want out of life. In contrast to the urban school films, there is almost no academic content to the suburban school films. Instead, these students take their academic achievement (and future occupational achievement) for granted. The adult authorities in the suburban high school films are not wise educational guides who usher adolescents into adulthood. Instead, these adults are often antagonists who interfere with the freedom and expressive individualism of the middle-class teenager. These suburban school films end happily when the teenage hero is able to assert his or her identity in opposition to the world of conventional middle-class adults or is able to defeat the culture of popularity that governs the peer relations at their high school. Ironically, the students who oppose conventional institutions end up achieving conventional success and the students who defeat the culture of popularity inevitably become the most popular students in school.

For its part, the elite private school film struggles to reconcile equality and inequality. The elite private school film is more likely than the suburban public school film to feature academic content. Unlike the urban public school film, however, academic achievement is not depicted as a strategy that leads to emancipation and independence. Instead, it is often considered to be a burden for upper-class students, who are under the pressure to legitimate and maintain their social class status. The heroes of these private school films are working- or middle-class students who enter the privileged world of the elite boarding school and teach their own lessons about academic merit, personal integrity, and the importance of living a balanced life. The antagonists are always members of the wealthy class. The working- or middle-class heroes of the elite private school films walk a tightrope between the lessons of the urban and suburban school films. On the one hand, they defeat the culture of privilege of the school as they assert their claims of equality, express their individuality, and resist the pressures of conformity in elite society. On the other hand, they exercise their academic talent and benefit from the unequal utilitarian rewards that the elite institution has to offer. These private school films also end happily as the integrity of the meritorious individual triumphs over the moral bankruptcy of the elite.

As for the few private Catholic and Christian school films, they more closely resemble either the suburban or urban public school films. Since the dramatic tension in these religious school films does not revolve around upper-class students at elite schools, they have very little in common with the other private school films. As in the real educational world, private religious schools are quite different from independent elite private schools. The dynamic of the plots and the relationships among the characters in the religious private school films depend not upon the type of school in which the story takes place, but upon the type of students who are represented in the film. If the school is populated primarily by middle-class students, then the film tends to resemble the typical suburban public school film. If the students are primarily poor and nonwhite, then the film takes on the defining characteristics of the urban public school film.

Finally, lest one think that these high school films say less about American culture and more about the medium of film and the nature of storytelling, we compared the American school film to school films from other countries. In contrast to the unambiguous and happy endings of the American high school films, the foreign school films tend to end without clear resolution of the dramatic tension in the plot. Instead of leaving the viewer feeling optimistic about the future of the main characters, the foreign school films leave the viewer with an uncertain or pessimistic view of the future. Instead of the triumph of the individual hero over antagonistic social forces, the foreign school films often end in tragedy. If the foreign school film does not end with the death of the protagonist, the individual hero often runs away from the social forces that he or she could not defeat. While the small sample of foreign school films in this study is not representative enough to make generalizable claims about the cinema of any foreign country, the sample does illuminate the sharp contrast between the American high school film and its counterpart abroad. Such a contrast indicates that the form and content of the American high school film reflects more than just the medium of film or the structure of storytelling. The American high school films do indeed reveal something unique about American culture.

Who Has Cultural Power?

Who has the power to tell the folktales that help to smooth out some of these contradictory elements of American culture? What social groups or institutions have the power to determine the messages conveyed in cultural products such as films? Feminist scholars have persuasively argued that Hollywood films tend to privilege the view of men. They argue that the movies are told from the point of view of the male gaze. As feminist scholar Laura Mulvey writes:

> The man controls the film fantasy and also emerges as the representative of power in a further sense: as the bearer of the look of the spectator . . . as the spectator identifies with the main male protagonist, he projects his look onto that of his like, his screen surrogate, so that the power of the male protagonist as he controls events coincides with the active power of the erotic look, both giving a satisfying sense of omnipotence.[5]

I would extend this critique to one of social class. The protagonists of the American high school films, almost without exception, represent middle-class assumptions, worldviews, and interests. However, the middle-class teacher or student is not explicitly painted in class terms. Rather, these film characters are taken for granted as "normal," rational, and sensible individuals. It is *assumed* that the audience will identify with and positively relate to the protagonist. These characters express individual autonomy, a capitalist work ethic, personal ambition, a faith in meritocracy, and free expression. But these are not neutral characteristics. They are characteristics with roots in a particular social class experience and perspective. It is precisely in the taken-for-grantedness of these characteristics as "normal," in the *invisibility* of class, that the perspective of the middle class holds such power in these Hollywood stories. The power to be defined as "normal" in a culture is intimately tied to the power to conceal and legitimate inequality—to justify the exclusion of the "deviant" from the status and rewards of society. There is cultural power in the privileged gaze of the middle class—and it is even more powerful if it is not recognized as a gaze that originates from a class position. Jack Zipes has made a similar argument about the class power behind the classic fairy tale:

> All the tools of modern industrial society . . . have made their mark on the fairy tale to make it classical ultimately in the name of the bourgeoisie which refuses to be named, denies involvement; for the fairy tale must appear harmless, natural, eternal, ahistorical, therapeutic. We are to live and breathe the classical fairy tale as fresh, free air. We are led to believe that this air has not been contaminated and polluted by a social class that will not name itself.[6]

In part, the middle-class perspective of Hollywood is due to the fact that artists and audiences are largely members of the middle class. But the reasons for this cultural hegemony go much deeper. As the producer of modern-day folktales, Hollywood has the power to represent the culture. Whether individuals in the Hollywood system are aware of it or not, they create such tales in a way that reinforces dominant cultural understandings about American life. Rather than merely representing "liberal" political positions, as Hollywood is often criticized for doing,[7] mainstream film studios actually tell folk stories that reinforce rather conservative myths of American culture, which in turn reinforce existing inequalities and support the status quo.

By extolling the power of the individual, celebrating the capitalist ethic, and advancing the myth of meritocracy, Hollywood's fantasies support a worldview that preserves class inequality—a worldview that assumes individuals have the power to change the world, that in the United States you are free to be whoever you want, that the poor are responsible for their own fate, and that those who work hard and obey the rules will be richly rewarded. It is not that the middle class has most of the power in the United States. The upper class certainly wields more economic and political power. However, it is a middle-class *sensibility* that dominates American culture. Such sensibilities protect the interests not only of the middle class, but of the wealthy as well. An emphasis on the individual work ethic and a belief in the fairness and openness of educational, political, and economic institutions serves to legitimate the wealth of the "haves" and to place the blame of failure on the "have nots."

As we have seen, the cultural hegemony of a middle-class perspective leaves its mark on all three subgenres of the high school film. The middle-class teacher-heroes of the urban school films defeat the culture of poverty and encourage utilitarian individualism among their poor students. The middle-class student-heroes of the suburban school films defeat the culture of popularity and exercise expressive individualism while maintaining their class position. The working- and middle-class heroes of the elite private school film exercise their utilitarian individualism by defeating the culture of privilege *and* exercise their expressive individualism by resisting the pressures of conformity in elite society.

Such expressions of American culture, however, are not unique to the high school film. While high school films offer us a particularly rich field in which to explore the ways our culture makes sense of education, inequality, and adolescence, the dominant lessons of this study can be applied to other genres of film as well. Whether it is the Western, the crime drama, the war movie, or the science-fiction film, the mark of American culture finds its way into the Hollywood film. And Hollywood films subsequently become a part of American culture.

Since this research did not talk to American moviegoers to see how they interpret and react to these films, there is more work to be done. A reception study to see how these high school films are viewed by a cross section of Americans could test many of the hypotheses about American culture that I have proposed in this book. Do Americans in general accept the dominant ideologies as they are represented in these films? Or do American film audiences actively reinterpret the messages of these films in such a way as to challenge the dominant ideology? Perhaps different groups in society react in different ways to the three subgenres discussed in this book. Only future research that collects data directly from film audiences will be able to offer answers to these questions.

The point of this book is not necessarily to be critical of the Hollywood system for perpetuating stereotypes or inaccuracies about inequality, young people, and education. The fault does not lie solely in the hands of a few studio executives. Yes, Hollywood has the power to represent our culture, but we, as members of this culture, are also participants in its creation and re-creation. As cultural artifacts, films depend both upon producers and consumers. To understand how Hollywood makes sense of youth, education, and inequality is to catch a glimpse of how *we* as a society implicitly make sense of these things. If we are to challenge these views—to engage in critical dialogue with American culture—it is necessary to exercise our sociological imagination. Only by looking at our own lives and at cultural artifacts in the rich complexity of social context can we begin to unpack the mysteries and contradictions of American life—and to change it.

Notes

1. Mills. C. Wright. 1959. *The Sociological Imagination*. New York: Oxford University Press.
2. Erikson, *Everything in Its Path*.
3. Levi-Strauss, *Myth and Meaning*.
4. Wright, *Sixguns and Society*; and Tudor, *Image and Influence*.
5. Mulvey, Laura. 1989. "Visual Pleasure and Narrative Cinema." In *Visual and Other Pleasures*. London: Macmillan, p. 20.
6. Zipes, *Fairy Tales as Myth*, p. 7.
7. Medved, Michael. 1992. *Hollywood vs. America: Popular Culture and the War on Traditional Values*. New York: HarperCollins.

Appendix:
High School Film Sample

The Suburban School
Films in the Sample

Rebel Without a Cause (1955)
High School Hell Cats (1958)
High School Caesar (1960)
Splendor in the Grass (1961)
The Last Picture Show (1971)
American Graffiti (1973)
Grease (1978)
Rock and Roll High School (1979)
Fast Times at Ridgemont High (1982)
The Last American Virgin (1982)
All the Right Moves (1983)
Risky Business (1983)
Valley Girl (1983)
16 Candles (1984)
The Karate Kid (1984)
The Breakfast Club (1985)
Weird Science (1985)
Better Off Dead (1985)
Tuff Turf (1985)
Teen Wolf (1985)
Just One of the Guys (1985)
Pretty in Pink (1986)
Ferris Bueller's Day Off (1986)
Dangerously Close (1986)
Hoosiers (1986)

Class of Nuke 'Em High (1986)
Lucas (1986)
River's Edge (1986)
Three O'Clock High (1987)
Can't Buy Me Love (1987)
Some Kind of Wonderful (1987)
Permanent Record (1988)
Heathers (1989)
Say Anything (1989)
How I Got Into College (1989)
Bill and Ted's Excellent Adventure (1989)
Cry Baby (1990)
Pump Up the Volume (1990)
Rock and Roll High School Forever (1990)
Buffy the Vampire Slayer (1992)
Dazed and Confused (1993)
Clueless (1995)
Powder (1995)
Mr. Holland's Opus (1995)
Angus (1995)
Foxfire (1996)
Can't Hardly Wait (1998)
The Faculty (1998)
Disturbing Behavior (1998)
Election (1999)
Varsity Blues (1999)
10 Things I Hate About You (1999)
Teaching Mrs. Tingle (1999)
She's All That (1999)
American Pie (1999)
Never Been Kissed (1999)
October Sky (1999)
Jawbreaker (1999)
Get Over It (2000)
Remember the Titans (2000)
Whatever It Takes (2000)
Ghost World (2000)
Bring It On (2001)
Crazy/Beautiful (2001)
My Horrible Year (2001)
Not Another Teen Movie (2001)
Orange County (2002)

The New Guy (2002)
The Hot Chick (2002)
Swimfan (2002)
Dumb and Dumberer (2003)
How to Deal (2003)
Freaky Friday (2003)
Better Luck Tomorrow (2003)
Radio (2003)
Blue Car (2003)
Elephant (2003)
Mean Girls (2004)
The Perfect Score (2004)
The Girl Next Door (2004)
Confessions of a Teenage Drama Queen (2004)
New York Minute (2004)
A Cinderella Story (2004)

The Urban School Films in the Sample

Blackboard Jungle (1955)
Up the Down Staircase (1967)
Halls of Anger (1970)
Conrack (1974)
Cooley High (1975)
Fame (1980)
Class of 1984 (1982)
Teachers (1984)
Wildcats (1986)
Stand and Deliver (1987)
The Principal (1987)
Summer School (1987)
The Beat (1988)
Lean on Me (1989)
Class Act (1992)
Zebrahead (1992)
Just Another Girl on the I.R.T. (1992)
Only the Strong (1993)
Dangerous Minds (1995)

The Substitute (1996)
High School High (1996)
Sunset Park (1996)
187 (1997)
The Substitute 2 (1998)
Detention (1998)
Light It Up (1999)
Cheaters (2000)
Our Song (2000)
Save the Last Dance (2001)
Real Women Have Curves (2002)
Detention (2003)
Love Don't Cost a Thing (2003)

The Private School Films in the Sample

The Trouble with Angels (1966)
The Prime of Miss Jean Brodie (1969)
Our Time (1974)
Up the Academy (1980)
Taps (1981)
Class (1983)
Private School (1983)
Making the Grade (1984)
Heaven Help Us (1985)
Girls Just Want to Have Fun (1985)
The Chocolate War (1988)
Dead Poet's Society (1989)
School Ties (1992)
Scent of a Woman (1992)
Sister Act 2 (1993)
The Craft (1996)
All I Wanna Do (1998)
Rushmore (1999)
Outside Providence (1999)
Cruel Intentions (1999)
Finding Forrester (2000)
O (2001)

Donnie Darko (2001)
The Smokers (2002)
Cheats (2002)
The Emperor's Club (2002)
The Dangerous Lives of Altar Boys (2002)
Igby Goes Down (2002)
Saved! (2004)

The Foreign School Films in the Sample

Maedchen in Uniform (1931, Germany)
Zero de Conduite (1933, France)
Goodbye, Mr. Chips (1939, England)
Torment (1944, Sweden)
L'Ecole Buissonniere (1951, France)
The 400 Blows (1959, France)
The Fighting Elegy (1966, Japan)
To Sir, With Love (1967, England)
If (1969, England)
Murmur of the Heart (1971, France)
Picnic at Hanging Rock (1975, Australia)
Peppermint Soda (1977, France)
The Getting of Wisdom (1977, Australia)
Boarding School (1977, Germany)
Puberty Blues (1981, Australia)
Porky's (1981, Canada)
Gregory's Girl (1981, Scotland)
A Nos Amours (1983, France)
Au Revoir Les Enfants (1987, France)
The Year My Voice Broke (1988, Australia)
The Disenchanted (1990, France)
Fight Back to School (1991, Hong Kong)
To Play or to Die (1991, Holland)
Sarafina (1992, United States/England/France)
The Slingshot (1993, Sweden)
Flirting (1993, Australia)
Wild Reeds (1994, France)
Heavenly Creatures (1994, New Zealand)

Saint Clara (1995, Israel)
All Things Fair (1995, Sweden)
The Other Side of Sunday (1996, Norway)
Show Me Love (1998, Sweden)
Battle Royale (2000, Japan)
Lost and Delirious (2001, Canada)
Volcano High (2001, South Korea)
Sweet Sixteen (2002, Scotland)
The Suicide Club (2002, Japan)
Big Girls Don't Cry (2002, Germany)
July Rhapsody (2002, Hong Kong)
Blue Gate Crossing (2002, Taiwan)
Evil (2003, Sweden)

Bibliography

Ayers, William. 1996. "A Teacher Ain't Nothin' but a Hero: Teachers and Teaching in Film." In *City Kids, City Teachers: Reports from the Front Row*. William Ayers and Patricia Ford, editors. New York: The New Press.

Banfield, Edward. 1968. *The Unheavenly City*. Boston: Little, Brown.

Bellah, Robert N. 1973. "Introduction." In *Emile Durkheim on Morality and Society*. Chicago: University of Chicago Press.

Bellah, Robert N., Richard Madsen, William M. Sullivan, Ann Swidler, and Steven M. Tipton. 1985. *Habits of the Heart: Individualism and Commitment in American Life*. New York: Harper and Row.

Bellah, Robert N., et al. 1991. *The Good Society*. New York: Knopf.

Becker, Gary S. 1975. *Human Capital: A Theoretical and Empirical Analysis with Special Reference to Education*. Chicago: University of Chicago Press.

Berliner, David C., and Bruce J. Biddle. 1997. *The Manufactured Crisis: Myths, Fraud, and the Attack on America's Public Schools*. White Plains, NY: Longman.

Bernstein, Jonathan. 1997. *Pretty in Pink: The Golden Age of Teenage Movies*. New York: St. Martin's Griffin.

Bourdieu, Pierre. 1977. "Cultural Reproduction and Social Reproduction." In *Power and Ideology in Education*. Jerome Karabel and A. H. Halsey, editors. New York: Oxford University Press.

Bryk, Anthony S., Valerie E. Lee, and Peter B. Holland. 1993. *Catholic Schools and the Common Good*. Cambridge, MA: Harvard University Press.

Bulman, Robert C. 2002. "Teachers in the 'Hood': Hollywood's Middle-Class Fantasy." *Urban Review* 34, no. 3 (September): 251–276.

Burbach, Harold J., and Margo A. Figgins. 1993. "A Thematic Profile of the Images of Teachers in Film." *Teacher Education Quarterly* (spring): 65–75.

Carnoy, Martin, and Henry M. Levin. *Schooling and Work in the Democratic State*. Stanford, CA: Stanford University Press.

Chambliss, William J. 1973. "The Saints and the Roughnecks." *Society* 11, no. 1: 24.

Chubb, John E., and Terry M. Moe. 1990. *Politics, Markets, and America's Schools*. Washington, DC: The Brookings Institution.

Coleman, James S. 1961. *The Adolescent Society*. New York: Free Press.

Coleman, James, et al. 1966. *Equality of Educational Opportunity*. Washington, DC: U.S. Government.

Considine, David M. 1985. *The Cinema of Adolescence*. Jefferson, NC: McFarland and Co.

Cookson, Peter, Jr., and Caroline Persell. 1985. *Preparing for Power: America's Elite Boarding Schools*. New York: Basic Books.

Corbett, Dick, Bruce Wilson, and Belinda Williams. 2002. *Effort and Excellence in Urban Classrooms: Expecting and Getting Success with All Students*. New York: Teachers College Press.

Crane, Diana. 1992. *The Production of Culture: Media and the Urban Arts*. New York: Sage.

Dalton, Mary. 1999. *The Hollywood Curriculum: Teachers and Teaching in the Movies*. New York: Peter Lang.

Darling-Hammond, Linda. 1997. *The Right to Learn: A Blueprint for Creating Schools That Work*. San Francisco: Jossey-Bass.

Denby, David. 1999. "High School Confidential: Notes on Teen Movies." *The New Yorker* (May 31): 94–98.

Deschenes, S., David Tyack, and Larry Cuban. 2001. "Mismatch: Historical Perspectives on Schools and Students Who Don't Fit Them." *Teachers College Record* 103, no. 4: 525–547.

Dewey, John. 1966. *Democracy and Education*. New York: Free Press.

Doherty, Thomas. 2002. *Teenagers and Teenpics: The Juvenilization of American Movies in the 1950s*. Philadelphia: Temple University Press.

Durkheim, Emile. 1984. *The Division of Labor in Society*. Translated by W. D. Halls. New York: Free Press.

Durkheim, Emile. 1973a. *Moral Education: A Study in the Theory and Application of the Sociology of Education*. New York: Free Press.

Durkheim, Emile. 1973b. "Individualism and the Intellectuals." In *Emile Durkheim on Morality and Society*. Chicago: University of Chicago Press.

Durkheim, Emile. 1973c. "The Dualism of Human Nature and Its Social Conditions." In *Emile Durkheim on Morality and Society*. Chicago: University of Chicago Press.

Eckert, Penelope. 1989. *Jocks and Burnouts: Social Categories and Identity in High School*. New York: Teachers College Press.

Ehrenreich, Barbara. 1989. *Fear of Falling: The Inner Life of the Middle Class*. New York: Harper Press.

Emerson, Ralph Waldo. 1883. "Self Reliance." In *Essays*. Boston: Houghton, Mifflin, and Co.

Epstein, Joyce. 1996. "Perspectives and Previews on Research and Policy for School, Family, and Community Partnerships." In *Family–School Links: How Do They Affect Educational Outcomes?* A. Booth and J. Dunn, editors. Mahwah, NJ: Lawrence Erlbaum Associates.

Epstein, Joyce L. 1987. "Parent Involvement: What Research Says to Administrators." *Education and Urban Society* 19, no. 2: 119–136.

Erikson, Kai T. 1978. *Everything in Its Path: Destruction of Community in the Buffalo Creek Flood*. New York: Simon and Schuster.

Farber, Paul, and Gunilla Holm. 1994a. "Adolescent Freedom and the Cinematic High School." In *Schooling in the Light of Popular Culture*. Albany: State University of New York Press.

Farber, Paul, and Gunilla Holm. 1994b. "A Brotherhood of Heroes: The Charismatic Educator in Recent American Movies." In *Schooling in the Light of Popular Culture*. Albany: State University of New York Press.

Farhi, Adam. 1999. "Hollywood Goes to School: Recognizing the Superteacher Myth in Film." *The Clearing House* 72, no. 3:157.

Fine, Michelle. 1991. *Framing Dropouts: Notes on the Politics of an Urban High School*. Albany: State University of New York Press.

Foley, Douglas E. 1990. *Learning Capitalist Culture: Deep in the Heart of Tejas*. Philadelphia: University of Pennsylvania Press.

Franklin, Benjamin, 1941. *The Autobiogrpahy of Benjamin Franklin*. New York: Walter J. Black.

Gallup Organization. 1998. "Have and Have-Nots: Perceptions of Fairness and Opportunity—1998." Gallup Special Report.

Gallup Organization. 2004. "36th Annual Phi Delta Kappan/Gallup Poll" (September).

Gans, Herbert J. 1988. *Middle American Individualism: The Future of Liberal Democracy*. New York: Free Press.

Geertz, Clifford. 1973. *The Interpretation of Cultures*. New York: Basic Books.

Gibson, Margaret A., and John U. Ogbu, editors. 1991. *Minority Status and Schooling: A Comparative Study of Immigrants and Involuntary Minorities*. New York: Garland.

Giroux, Henry A. 1992. "Resisting Difference: Cultural Studies and the Discourse of Critical Pedagogy." In *Cultural Studies*. Lawrence Grossberg, Cary Nelson, and Paula A. Treichler, editors. New York: Routledge, 199–212.

Giroux, Henry A. 1993. *Living Dangerously: Multiculturalism and the Politics of Difference*. New York: Peter Lang.

Giroux, Henry. 1996. "Race, Pedagogy and Whiteness in 'Dangerous Minds.'" *Cineaste* 22, no. 4: 46–50.

Gitlin, Todd. 1983. *Inside Prime Time*. New York: Pantheon.

Grant, Peggy A. 2002. "Using Popular Films to Challenge Preservice Teachers' Beliefs About Teaching in Urban Schools." *Urban Education* 37 (January 2002): 77–95.

Hall, Granville Stanley. 1904. *Adolescence: Its Psychology and Its Relations to Physiology, Anthropology, Sociology, Sex, Crime, Religion, and Education*. New York: D. Appleton and Company.

Harrington, C. Lee, and Denise D. Bielby. 2001. "Constructing the Popular: Cultural Production and Consumption." In *Popular Culture: Produc-*

tion and Consumption. C. Lee Harrington and Denise D. Bielby, editors. Malden, MA: Blackwell.

Heilman, Robert B. 1991. "The Great-Teacher Myth." *American Scholar* 60, no. 3: 417–423.

Henig, Jeffrey R., and Stephen D. Sugarman. 1999. "The Nature and Extent of School Choice." In *School Choice and Social Controversy: Politics, Policy, and Law*. Stephen D. Sugarman and Frank R. Kemerer, editors. Washington, DC: Brookings Institution Press.

Hill, David. 1995. "Tinseltown Teachers." *Teacher Magazine* (March).

Hine, Robert V., and John Mack Faragher. 2000. *The American West: A New Interpretive History*. New Haven, CT: Yale University Press.

Hine, Thomas. 1999. *The Rise and Fall of the American Teenager*. New York: Perennial.

Hochschild, Jennifer. 1981. *What's Fair? American Beliefs About Distributive Justice*. Cambridge, MA: Harvard University Press.

Hooks, Bell. 1996. *Reel to Real: Race, Sex, and Class at the Movies*. New York: Routledge.

Huizinga, D., and D. Elliott. 1987. "Juvenile Offenders: Prevalence, Offender Incidence, and Arrest Rates by Race." *Crime and Delinquency* 33: 206–223.

Hurn, Christopher. 1993. *The Limits and Possibilities of Schooling*. Boston: Allyn and Bacon.

Hutcheson, Ron. 2001. "Bush Calls for Faith-Based 'Assault on Poverty.'" *Sacramento Bee* (May 21): A15.

Johnson, LouAnne. 1992. *Dangerous Minds*. New York: St. Martin's Paperback.

Katz, Michael B. 1987. *Reconstructing American Education*. Cambridge, MA: Harvard University Press.

Katznelson, Ira, and Margaret Weir. 1985. *Schooling for All: Class, Race, and the Decline of the Democratic Ideal*. Berkeley: University of California Press.

Kett, Joseph F. 1977. *Rites of Passage: Adolescence in America, 1790 to the Present*. New York: Basic Books.

Kozol, Jonathan. 1991. *Savage Inequalities: Children in America's Schools*. New York: Crown Publishers.

Ladd, Everett Carll, and Karlyn H. Bowman. 1998. *Attitudes Toward Economic Inequality*. Washington, DC: The American Enterprise Institute.

Lareau, Annette. 1987. "Social Class Differences in Family-School Relationships: The Importance of Cultural Capital." *Sociology of Education* 60: 73–85.

Lee, Valerie E. 2001. *Restructuring High Schools for Equity and Excellence: What Works*. New York: Teachers College Press.

Levi-Strauss, Claude. 1978. *Myth and Meaning: Cracking the Code of Culture.* Toronto: University of Toronto Press.

Lewis, Jon. 1992. *The Road to Romance and Ruin: Teen Films and Youth Culture.* New York: Routledge.

Lieberman, Myron. 1993. *Public Education: An Autopsy.* Cambridge, MA: Harvard University Press.

Lipsitz, George. 1990. *Time Passages: Collective Memory and American Popular Culture.* Minneapolis: University of Minnesota Press.

MacLeod, Jay. 1995. *Ain't No Makin' It: Aspirations and Attainment in a Low-Income Neighborhood.* Boulder, CO: Westview Press.

Males, Mike A. 1999. *Framing Youth: 10 Myths About the Next Generation.* Monroe, ME: Common Courage Press.

Marger, Martin M. 2002. *Social Inequality: Pattern and Processes.* Second Edition. Boston: McGraw Hill.

McCarthy, Cameron, et al. 1996. "Race, Suburban Resentment, and the Representation of the Inner City in Contemporary Film and Television." In *Off White.* Michelle Fine, et al., editors. New York: Routledge.

Medved, Michael. 1992. *Hollywood vs. America: Popular Culture and the War on Traditional Values.* New York: HarperCollins.

Merton, Robert. 1968. *Social Theory and Social Structure.* New York: Free Press.

Mills, C. Wright. 1956. *White Collar: The American Middle Classes.* New York: Oxford University Press.

Mills, C. Wright. 1959a. *The Sociological Imagination.* New York: Oxford University Press.

Mills, C. Wright. 1959b. *The Power Elite.* New York: Oxford University Press.

Modell, John, and Madeline Goodman. 1990. "Historical Perspectives." In *At the Threshold: The Developing Adolescent.* S. Shirley Feldman and Glen R. Elliott, editors. Cambridge, MA: Harvard University Press.

Motion Picture Association of America. 2003. "The 2003 U.S. Movie Attendance Study."

Mukerji, Chandra, and Michael Shudson, editors. 1991. *Rethinking Popular Culture: Contemporary Perspectives in Cultural Studies.* Berkeley: University of California Press.

Mulvey, Laura. 1989. "Visual Pleasure and Narrative Cinema." In *Visual and Other Pleasures.* London: Macmillan.

Natriello, G., Aaron M. Pallas, and E. L. McDill. 1986. *Community Resources for Responding to the Dropout Problem.* New Brunswick, NJ: Rutgers University Press.

Natriello, Gary, Edward L. McDill, and Aaron M. Pallas. 1990. *Schooling the Disadvantaged: Racing Against Catastrophe.* New York: Teachers College Press.

Nieves, Evelyn. 2000. "California Proposal Toughens Penalties for Young Criminals." *New York Times* (March 6).

Oakes, Jeannine. 1985. *Keeping Track: How Schools Structure Inequality*. New Haven, CT: Yale University Press.

Palladino, Grace. 1996. *Teenagers: An American History*. New York: Basic Books.

Powers, Stephen, David Rothman, and Stanley Rothman. 1996. *Hollywood's America: Social and Political Themes in Motion Pictures*. Denver: Westview.

Purkey, Stewart C., and Marshall S. Smith, 1983. "Effective Schools: A Review." *Elementary School Journal* 83 (March): 427–452.

Putnam, Robert. 2000. *Bowling Alone: The Collapse and Revival of American Community*. New York: Touchstone Books.

Ray, Robert B. 1985. *A Certain Tendency of the Hollywood Cinema, 1930–1980*. Princeton, NJ: Princeton University Press.

Reed, Joseph W. 1989. *American Scenarios: The Uses of Film Genre*. Middletown: CT: Wesleyan University Press.

Riesman, David, with Nathan Glazer and Reuel Denney. 1961. *The Lonely Crowd: A Study of the Changing American Character*. New Haven, CT: Yale University Press.

Roper Poll. January 2003. "Child Tax Credit Survey."

Rosenthal, Robert, and Lenore Jacobson. 1968. *Pygmalion in the Classroom*. New York: Holt, Rinehart and Winston.

Schatz, Thomas. 1981. *Hollywood Genres: Formulas, Filmmaking, and the Studio System*. Boston: McGraw Hill.

Schlesinger, Arthur M., Jr. 1979. "Foreword." In *American History/American Film: Interpreting the Hollywood Image*. John E. O'Connor and Martin A. Jackson, editors. New York: Continuum.

Schneider, David M., and Raymond T. Smith. 1973. *Class Differences and Sex Roles in American Kinship and Family Structure*. Englewood Cliffs, NJ: Prentice Hall.

Schuman, Howard, Charlotte Steeh, Lawrence Bobo, and Maria Krysan. 1998. *Racial Attitudes in America: Trends and Interpretations*. Cambridge, MA: Harvard University Press.

Sewell, William H., Robert M. Hauser, and David L. Featherman, editors. 1976. *Schooling and Achievement in American Society*. New York: Academic Press.

Shary, Timothy. 2002. *Generation Multiplex: The Image of Youth in Contemporary American Cinema*. Austin: University of Texas Press.

Slater, Philip. 1976. *The Pursuit of Loneliness: American Culture at the Breaking Point*. Boston: Beacon Press.

Steele, Claude. M. 1997. "A Threat in the Air: How Stereotypes Shape the Intellectual Identities and Performance of Women and African Americans." *American Psychologist* 52: 613–629.

Swidler, Ann. 1986. "Culture in Action: Symbols and Strategies." *American Sociological Review* 51: 273–286.

Thomas, W. I. 1928. *The Child in America: Behavior Problems and Programs.* New York: Knopf.

Thomsen, Steven R. 1993. "A Worm in the Apple: Hollywood's Influence on the Public's Perception of Teachers." Paper presented at the Southern States Communication Association and Central States Communication Association joint annual meeting, Lexington, KY, April 15.

Thoreau, Henry David. 1960. *Walden.* New York: Signet.

Tocqueville, Alexis de. 1945. *Democracy in America.* Translated by Henry Reeve. New York: Vintage Books.

Trier, James D. 2001. "The Cinematic Representation of the Personal and Professional Lives of Teachers." *Teacher Education Quarterly* (summer): 127–142.

Tudor, Andrew. 1974. *Image and Influence: Studies in the Sociology of Film.* New York: St. Martin's Press.

Turner, Frederick Jackson. 1985. *The Frontier in American History.* Malabar, FL: Robert E. Krieger Publishing.

Turner, Ralph. 1960. "Sponsored and Contest Mobility and the School System." *American Sociological Review* 25: 855–867.

Varenne, Herve. 1977. *Americans Together: Structured Diversity in a Midwestern Town.* New York: Teachers College Press.

Vera, Hernan, and Andrew M. Gordon. 2003. *Screen Saviors: Hollywood Fictions of Whiteness.* Lanham, MD: Rowman and Littlefield.

Weber, Max. 1985. *The Protestant Ethic and the Spirit of Capitalism.* Translated by Talcott Parsons. London: Counterpoint.

Willis, Paul. 1981. *Learning to Labor.* New York: Columbia University Press.

Wilson, William J. 1987. *The Truly Disadvantaged: The Inner City, the Underclass, and Public Policy.* Chicago: University of Chicago Press.

Wilson, William Julius. 1996. *When Work Disappears.* New York: Knopf.

Wolfe, Alan. *One Nation, After All.* 1998. New York: Viking.

Wright, Will. 1975. *Sixguns and Society: A Structural Study of the Western.* Berkeley: University of California Press.

Zipes, Jack. 1993. *Fairy Tale as Myth: Myth as Fairy Tale.* Lexington: University of Kentucky Press.

Index

A Nos Amours, 161n5, 175
Academics
  merit in, 134–135
  in private school films, 10, 120–121,
    124–128, 130, 134–135, 143n9, 165
  race and, 58, 60
  in suburban school films, 20–21, 23, 47,
    81, 82, 83, 85–91, 97, 106, 115n3,
    116n6, 144n12, 164
  in urban school films, 10, 43, 47, 63–64,
    68, 74, 81, 85, 86, 106, 125, 126,
    127, 148, 164, 165
Achievement, ascription v., 141–142
Administration, school, 4, 46, 52–54, 97–99,
  105–106. *See also* Principals
Adolescence/adolescents, 9, 10, 19. *See also*
  Teenagers
  anxiety caused by, 36
  features of, 37
  as metaphor for future, 37
  as recognized stage, 34–36
  social class of, 33, 37
  sociologists on, 34, 37
Adulthood, transition to, 94, 99, 107–108,
  110, 111–113, 164
Adults, 4, 9, 10–11, 23, 34. *See also*
  Administration, school; Parents;
  Principals; Teachers
  as antagonists, 85, 93–97, 105–107, 164
  as fools, 97–99, 106
African Americans
  in private school films, 124–126
  in urban school films, 39n2, 46
  whites on, 50
All the Right Moves, 95, 152–153, 171
All Things Fair, 161n5, 176
American films. *See* Domestic films
  (American)
American Pie, 17, 108–109, 172
American studies, xvi
Angst, 10, 84, 85
Anomalies, in sample, 11, 63–66, 74, 78n47,
  135–139
Antagonists
  adults/teachers as, 85, 93–97, 105–107,
  164

football coaches as, 95–97, 116n11, 153
parents as, 99, 105
in suburban school films, 85, 93–97, 99,
  105–107, 164
wealthy, in private school films, 119,
  120, 128–130, 165
Athletics, 36
  football coaches in, 95–97, 116n11, 153
  jocks in, 105, 107, 111–113
  in private school films, 121–124
Au Revoir Les Enfants, 156, 161n9, 175
Audience
  age data, 42n45
  future research on, 168
  as middle class, 167
  middle-aged, 37, 42n45
  reaction, 7
Authority, 10
  defeating/challenging, 93, 97, 108–109,
  144n13
  obedience to, 85, 90

Balance. *See* Well roundedness
Banfield, Edward, 49
Battle Royale, 145, 146–148, 157, 161n5,
  161n11, 176
Beat, The, 52
Beauty standards, 107
Bell, Daniel, 13n7
Bellah, Robert, *Habits of the Heart* by, 19, 20,
  25, 32, 33, 73, 114, 159
Better Luck Tomorrow, 80, 173
Better Off Dead, 102, 171
Big Girls Don't Cry, 161nn6–7, 176
Bill and Ted's Excellent Adventure, 115n3, 172
Blackboard Jungle, xv, 18, 36, 173
  Dangerous Minds as, 45–46
  poverty and, 44–46, 47, 51, 53, 55–56,
    57, 60–61, 71–72, 75n6, 76n23
  Rebel Without a Cause v., 81
Boarding schools, 120, 121, 135
Box office results, 66
Boyz N the Hood, 39n2
The Breakfast Club, xv, 17, 86, 89, 105–107,
  109, 114, 171
Bring It On, 17, 172

Broderick, Matthew, 99
Bureaucrats. *See* Administration, school
"Burnouts," 111–113
Bush, George H.W., 79n51
Bush, George W., 50

Can't Buy Me Love, 78n47, 86, 172
Can't Hardly Wait, 17, 172
Capitalism, 25, 26–28, 35, 50, 131, 159
Catholic Church, 26, 28
Catholic school enrollment, 135
Catholic school films, 11, 39n1, 121,
    135–139
    middle class in, 135–139, 165
    social class in, 136–139
    suburban school films and, 136, 137,
        144nn12–13, 165
    urban school films and, 138–139, 165
Chambliss, William, 110–111
Cheaters, 63–64, 66, 74, 78n47, 174
The Chocolate War, 135, 174
Christian school films, 11, 135, 144n12, 165
A Cinderella Story, 86, 173
Clark, Joe, 79n51
Class Act, 78n47, 173
Class of 1984, 67, 68, 173
Class of Nuke 'Em High, 108, 172
Class, social. *See also* Lower classes/working
        class; Middle class; Poor/working-class
        students; Upper classes
    of adolescents, 33, 37
    in Catholic school films and, 136–139
    college and, 112
    in cultural power, 166–168
    fairy tales and, 167
    hierarchy, 10, 11
    inequality in, 139–142, 167–168
    in private school films, 119–121, 165
    race and, 46–47
    in suburban school films, 100–102,
        111–113, 168
Clueless, 86, 107, 109, 172
Cold War, 44, 45
Coleman, James, 36
Coleman Report, 59
College
    admission to, 121–123, 127
    social class and, 112
Community, 33, 40n18, 148
Conformity, 85
    individualism v., 113–115, 143n8
    middle class and, 10, 91–93
    in suburban school films, 85, 90, 91–93,
        164
Considine, David, 5

Contradictions, American cultural, 24–25,
    73–74, 113–115, 163–164, 168
Cookson, Peter, 120
Cooley High, 43, 78n47, 173
Cowboy, teacher as, 9, 43, 66–69, 74, 78n50
The Craft, 135, 174
Crane, Diana, 2
Crazy/Beautiful, 86, 172
Crime drama, 168
Cruel Intentions, 17, 174
Cry Baby, 86, 172
Cultural capital, 20, 39n4
Cultural power, 166–168
Culture
    film and, 2, 6–9, 13n3, 16, 162–169
    in genre films, 7
    significance of, 2
Culture, American, 2, 13n3, 33–37
    characteristics of, 23
    conformity in, 91–93
    contradictions in, 24–25, 73–74,
        113–115, 163–164, 168
    distinctiveness of, 148–149
    duality of, 121
    individualism and, 24–25, 73–74, 102,
        106
    inequality and, 138–142, 160, 164
    middle class and, 30–33
    myths of, 159–160
    optimism in, 159
    overview of, 9
Curriculum, 4, 10, 46

Dalton, Mary, 6, 84
The Dangerous Lives of Altar Boys, 135,
    136–137, 161n8, 175
Dangerous Minds, xv, 18, 173
    as *Blackboard Jungle,* 45–46
    box office results of, 66
    culture of poverty and, 19–20, 43, 45–46,
        47, 52, 53, 61, 62, 70–71, 72, 75n6
    real life v., 62, 78n45
Dazed and Confused, 95, 172
Dead Poet's Society, xv, 126–127, 128, 142n6,
    143n8, 174
Dean, James, 36
Delinquency, juvenile, 5, 35, 36, 44
Democracy, 25, 28–29, 40n18
Denby, David, 2
Depression, Great, 35
Detective film genre, 33
Detention, 67, 174
Deviance, perception of, 110–111, 117n19
The Disenchanted, 157–158, 161n5, 175
Disturbing Behavior, 87–89, 94, 105, 172

Doherty, Donald, 36
Domestic films (American). *See also* specific
    areas of interest
    cultural distinctiveness of, 148–149
    endings, foreign v., 11, 147, 148,
        149–158, 160n4, 161nn5–11,
        165–166
    foreign v., 4, 6, 11, 146–147, 149,
        152–153, 155, 156, 158–160
    individualism in, 11
Donnie Darko, 161n8, 175
*Don't Be a Menace to South Central When
    Drinking Your Juice in the Hood,* 39n2
Drugs, 51, 66, 67–68, 69, 70
    in suburban school films, 106, 108,
        109–111, 113
    use of, 4
Durkheim, Emile, 24–25

Eckert, Penelope, *Jocks and Burnouts* by,
    111–113
Educators. *See* Administration, school;
    Teachers
Ehrenreich, Barbara, 47, 92
Election, 99, 172
Elephant, 108, 173
Emerson, Ralph Waldo, 27, 80
The Emperor's Club, 128–130, 175
Endings
    in domestic v. foreign films, 11, 147,
        148, 149–158, 160n4, 161nn5–11,
        165–166
    in private school films, 165
    in urban high school films, 164
Erikson, Kai, 8, 114, 163
Expression, free, 7
Extracurricular activities, 4

The Faculty, 94, 172
Fairy tales. *See* Folktales (fairy tales)
Fame, 78n47, 173
Family, 4, 164. *See also* Parents
Fantasies
    film, as myth, 162–169
    Hollywood school, 56–63, 74, 150, 167
    middle-class, 9–10, 47, 49, 56–63,
        113–114, 127, 141–142
    of school destruction, 108
Farber, Paul, 5–6
Fast Times at Ridgemont High, xv, 17, 86,
    108, 109, 110, 171
Feminist scholars, 166
Ferris Bueller's Day Off, 17, 86, 98–99, 105,
    114, 171
The Fighting Elegy, 161n5, 161n11, 175

Film. *See also* specific areas of interest
    culture and, 2, 6–9, 13n3, 16, 162–169
    genre, 1–2, 5, 7, 33, 168
    production, 7
    sociology and, xv–xvi, 1–3, 8, 9, 13n3,
        13nn7–9, 50–51, 162–163
Film studies, xvi, 2, 3
Finding Forrester, 124–126, 128, 143n9, 174
The First American Teenager, 36
Flirting, 161n5, 175
Foley, Douglas, 116n11
Folktales (fairy tales), 8–9, 73–74, 162, 163,
    166, 167. *See also* Myths
Fools
    adults as, 97–99, 106
    wealthy as, 128–130
Football coaches, 95–97, 116n11, 153
Foreign school films. *See also* Subgenres,
        high school film
    characteristics of, 149–160
    domestic v., 4, 6, 11, 146–147, 149,
        152–153, 155, 156, 158–160
    endings in, 11, 147, 148, 149–158,
        160n4, 161nn5–11, 165–166
    future in, 152–155
    hero in, 149, 152, 156, 157–159, 166
    religious, 153–154
    running from society in, 157–158
    in sample, 4, 11, 14n10, 160nn1–2,
        175–176
    sex in, 150–151, 155–156, 158
    unresolved tension in, 149–152, 160n4,
        161n5
The 400 Blows, 145, 157, 158, 161n5, 175
Foxfire, 80, 172
Franklin, Benjamin, 27, 28, 47, 140
Frontier, American, 25, 29–30
Future
    adolescence as metaphor for, 37
    in foreign school films, 152–155

Gangs, 52, 66, 67–68, 69, 117n19
Genre films. *See also* Subgenres, high school
        film
    analysis of, 2, 168
    culture reflected in, 7
    detective, 33
    truths in, 1–2
    Western, 1–2, 33
    youth, 5
The Getting of Wisdom, 161n5, 161n11, 175
Ghost World, 160n4, 172
Girls Just Want to Have Fun, 135, 174
Giroux, Henry, 46
Gitlin, Todd, 76n22

Goodman, Madeline, 35
Graduate, The, 91
Grease, xv, 17, 171
Guns N' Roses, 51

Habits of the Heart (Bellah et al.), 19, 20, 25,
    32, 33, 73, 114, 159
Hall, G. Stanley, *Adolescence* by, 34–35
Halls of Anger, xv, 18, 173
Heathers, 103–105, 108, 114, 116n16, 172
Heaven Help Us, 135, 174
Heavenly Creatures, 161n9, 175
Heroes
    cowboy, 9, 43, 66–69, 74, 78n50
    in foreign school films, 149, 152, 156,
        157–159, 166
    individual, 11
    middle-class, 9, 10–11, 19, 22–23, 43–47,
        52, 54–56, 60–61, 62, 63–74, 78n50,
        93, 94, 120–121, 124–126, 127,
        130–135, 139, 141, 143n8, 158, 164,
        165, 168
    "normal," 166–167
    outsider, 9, 10–11, 33, 54–56, 143n9, 158
    principal, 54, 66–67, 68–69, 70, 72–73,
        124–126
    in private school films, 23, 120–121,
        124–126, 130–135, 141, 143n8, 148,
        165, 168
    society and, 158–160
    student, in suburban school films, 10–11,
        82–85, 89, 93, 97, 99–107, 115, 127,
        164, 168
    teacher/educator, 5–6, 9, 10–11, 15n26,
        19, 23, 43–47, 52, 54–56, 60–61, 62,
        63–74, 78n50, 93, 94, 127, 138–139
    in urban school films, 9, 19, 23, 43–47,
        52, 54–56, 60–61, 62, 63–74, 78n50,
        93, 94, 125, 126, 127, 158, 164, 168
High school
    Eckert, Penelope, on, 111–112
    enrollment, 135
    as new institution, 35
High school films. *See also* Foreign school
        films; Private school films; Subgenres,
        high school film; Suburban school
        films; Urban school films
    analyses of, 5–6
    patterns of, 16
    selecting sample of, 3–4
    spoof of, 17–18
    truths revealed in, 1–2
High School High, 18–19, 174
Hill, David, 6
Hollywood. *See also specific areas of interest*
    commercial interests of, 7

    marketing, 36
    pedagogy, 56, 62
    school fantasy of, 56–63, 74, 150, 167
    stories selected by, 79n51
Holm, Gunilla, 5–6
Homophobia, 105
hooks, bell, 1, 12n2
Horror, teen, 39n2
How to Deal, 110, 173
Hughes, John, 17, 105
Humanities, 3
Hurn, Christopher, 49

Identity, personal, 10, 81, 85, 88–89, 91,
    100, 105–108, 111–113
Ideology, hegemonic middle-class, 7–8,
    14n11, 33, 46, 49, 74, 167–168
Igby Goes Down, 130n7, 175
Immigrants, 35
Individualism, 7, 9
    American frontier and, 29–30
    capitalism and, 26–28
    conformity v., 113–115, 143n8
    contradictions in American, 24–25,
        73–74, 113–115, 163–164, 168
    democracy and, 28–29, 40n18
    in domestic v. foreign films, 11
    expressive, 20–23, 27–28, 37, 43, 81, 85,
        127, 128, 135, 140–141, 148, 168
    of heroes, 11
    lower classes and, 32–33
    middle class and, 30–33, 63
    private school films and, 22–23, 120,
        128, 135, 168
    rugged, 29–30, 159
    society and, 73–74, 102, 106, 120,
        158–160, 162–163
    upper classes and, 32–33
    utilitarian, 10, 19–20, 22–23, 27–28, 37,
        43, 47, 49–51, 59–63, 69, 72–74, 81,
        85, 127, 128, 140, 141, 148, 168
Industrialization, 34
Inequality
    American culture and, 138–142, 160, 164
    in schools, 140–142
    in social class, 139–142, 167–168
    socioeconomic, 11
Integrity, personal, 131–134
Internet Movie Data Base, 3

Janitors, school, 89–90
Jewish students, 122–123, 134
Jocks, 105, 107, 111–113
Johnson, LouAnne, 62
Juice, 39n2
July Rhapsody, 161n5, 176

Jungle metaphor, 51–52, 76n23
Junior high students, 14n10, 117n17,
   144n13

Kids, 3
Kozol, Jonathan, 58–59, 79n51

The Last American Virgin, 110, 171
Latino students, 46
Lean on Me, 18, 51, 53, 54, 60–61, 66, 68,
   71, 72, 79n51, 173
Levi-Strauss, Claude, 73, 163
Light It Up, 63, 64–65, 66, 74, 78n47, 95, 174
Lipsitz, George, 13n3
The Lonely Crowd, 91–93
Lost and Delirious, 156, 161n9, 176
Love Don't Cost a Thing, 78n47
Lower classes/working class. See also Class,
      social; Poor/working-class students
   individualism and, 32–33
   in private school films, 23, 119, 120, 127
   research on, 57–58
   in urban school films, 46, 48, 57, 63–65,
      74
Lucas, 17, 95, 172

MacLeod, Jay, Ain't No Makin' It by, 57–58
Maedchen in Uniform, 161n6, 175
Making the Grade, 22–23, 174
Marger, Martin, 31
Materialism, 43
McCarthy, Cameron, 48
Mean Girls, 116n16, 173
Menace II Society, 39n2
Merit, academic, 134–135
Middle class, 9. See also Class, social;
      Suburban school films
   American culture and, 30–33
   audience as, 167
   in Catholic school films, 135–139, 165
   conformity and, 10, 91–93
   curriculum, 10
   definition of, 31
   emphasis on, 10
   fantasies, 9–10, 47, 49, 56–63, 113–114,
      127, 141–142
   fears/anxiety of, 48–49, 74, 93
   in film sampling, 4, 14n11
   hegemonic ideology/values of, 7–8,
      14n11, 33, 46, 49, 74, 167–168
   heroes, 9, 10–11, 19, 22–23, 43–47, 52,
      54–56, 60–61, 62, 63–74, 78n50, 93,
      94, 120–121, 124–126, 127, 130–135,
      139, 141, 143n8, 158, 164, 165, 168
   individualism and, 30–33, 63
   industrialization/urbanization and, 34

"new"/ white-collar, 35–36, 91–93
   as outsiders, 22–23, 133
   in private school films, 23, 119, 120–121,
      124–126, 127, 130–135, 141, 142n6,
      143n8, 148, 165, 168
   privileging of, 8, 14n19, 23, 102
   sociologists on, 31
   status hierarchy and, 10
   in suburban school films, 23, 82–84, 88,
      91–95, 96, 97–100, 107–108,
      110–114, 116n16, 164
   upper, 20, 39n4
   in urban school films, 9–10, 19, 23,
      43–47, 49, 52, 54–74, 78n50, 93, 94,
      125, 126, 127, 158, 164, 168
   wealth and, 11
Middle-aged audience, 37, 42n45
Mills, C. Wright, 13n7, 32, 92–93, 119, 120,
   162
Mobster films, 1–2
Modell, James, 35
Moral bankruptcy, of wealthy, 119, 120,
   128–130
Motion Picture Association of America,
   42n45
Murmur of the Heart, 161n6, 175
Music of the Heart, 75n6
My Posse Don't Do Homework (Johnson), 62
Myths. See also Folktales (fairy tales)
   of American culture, 159–160
   film fantasies as, 162–169

Never Been Kissed, 17, 109, 172
The New Guy, 21–22, 173
"Normal," heroes as, 166–167
Not Another Teen Movie, 17–19, 89, 107, 172

Ogbu, John, 58
187, 67, 161n8, 174
Only the Strong, 67, 173
Optimism, 159
The Other Side of Sunday, 156, 161n6,
   161n11, 176
Outsiders, 83
   heroes as, 9, 10–11, 33, 54–56, 143n9,
      158
   middle-class, 22–23, 133
Over the Edge, 117n17, 144n13

Palladino, Grace, 36
Parents. See also Family
   as antagonists, 99, 105
   lying to, 99
   rebelling against/standing up to, 97, 105,
      164
   role of, 61, 89

Pedagogy, 4
    challenging, 84–85
    Hollywood, 56, 62
    unconventional, 10
    violence as, 66–67, 78n50
Peer relations, 4, 85, 106, 164
The Perfect Score, 116n6, 173
Persell, Caroline, 120
Picnic at Hanging Rock, 156, 161n9, 175
Pink Floyd, 94
Political messages, 69–72, 84, 167
Poor/working-class students, 9, 10, 19–20.
        See also Class, social; Lower
        classes/working class
    deviance of, 110–111, 117n19
    individualism, utilitarian, expected of,
        19, 23, 32–33, 37, 43, 47, 49–51,
        59–63, 69, 72–74, 81, 85, 148, 168
    as outside mainstream, 8
    in sample films, 4
Popularity
    concern with, 36
    stratified system of, 21–22
    in suburban school films, 87, 102–105,
        116n16, 164, 168
Porky's, xv, 17, 108–109, 175
Possibility, theme of, 37
Poverty
    Blackboard Jungle and, 44–46, 47, 51, 53,
        55–56, 57, 60–61, 71–72, 75n6,
        76n23
    Dangerous Minds and, 19–20, 43, 45–46,
        47, 52, 53, 61, 62, 70–71, 72, 75n6
    escaping, 19
    sociologists on, 49
    urban school films and, 43–79, 121, 127,
        168
Powder, 161n8, 172
Powers, Stanley, 13n7
Powers, Stephen, 13n7
Pregnancy, 110
Pretty in Pink, 17, 86, 171
The Principal, 18, 51, 52, 53, 54, 66–67, 173
Principals. *See also* Administration, school
    bad/evil, 61, 84
    as heroes, 54, 66–67, 68–69, 70, 72–73,
        124–126
    violence used by, 69
Private school enrollment, 135
Private school films, 10–11, 39n1, 119–144.
        See also Catholic school films;
        Christian school films; Religious
        school films; Subgenres, high school
        film
    academics in, 10, 120–121, 124–128, 130,
        134–135, 143n9, 165
    African American students in, 124–126

antagonists in, 119, 120, 128–130, 165
    athletics in, 121–124
    differences in, 4, 5–6
    endings in, 165
    heroes in, 23, 120–121, 124–126,
        130–135, 141, 143n8, 148, 165, 168
    individualism and, 22–23, 120, 128, 135,
        168
    integrity in, 131–134
    lower classes/working class in, 23, 119,
        120, 127
    middle class in, 23, 119, 120–121,
        124–126, 127, 130–135, 141, 142n6,
        143n8, 148, 165, 168
    in sample, 4, 174–175
    social class in, 119–121, 165
    suburban school films and, 121, 165
    triumph of merit in, 134–135
    upper class in, 119–121
    urban school films and, 121, 124, 125,
        126, 127, 143n8, 165
    wealthy in, 119, 120, 128–130, 165
    well roundedness in, 130–131, 143n8
Privileging
    of middle class, 8, 14n19, 23, 102
    of whites, 14n19
Production, film, 7
Proposition 21 (California), 117n19
Protagonists. *See* Heroes
Protestantism, 25, 26–27, 28, 50, 121–122
Psychologist, school, 88, 89
Puberty Blues, 161n6, 175
Public school films. *See* Schools; Suburban
        school films; Urban school films
Pump Up the Volume, 81, 82–85, 86, 105,
        114, 172
Putnam, Robert, 40n18

Race
    academics and, 58, 60
    racism and, 124–126, 128
    social class and, 46–47
    in suburban school films, 100–102
    in urban school films, 46–47
Reality
    in *Dangerous Minds,* 62, 78n45
    shaping/twisting of, 1–2, 62, 78n45, 80,
        163
Rebel Without a Cause, 36, 47, 81, 151–152,
        171
Reed, Joseph, 5
Reforms, educational, 60
Religious school films. *See also* Catholic
        school films; Christian school films
    foreign, 153–154
    suburban school films and, 136, 165
Remember the Titans, 100–102, 172

Research. *See also* Sample, research
  educational reform, 60
  future audience, 168
  on lower classes, 57–58
  social science, 59
Rich students. *See* Class, social; Upper
    classes; Wealth; Wealthy
Riesman, David, 32
Risky Business, xv, 3, 171
River's Edge, 144n13, 172
Rock and Roll High School, 86, 108, 171
Rock and Roll High School Forever, 108, 172
Rothman, David, 13n7
Rushmore, 119, 130–131, 174

Saint Clara, 161n6, 176
"Saints and the Roughnecks" (Chambliss),
    110–111
Sample, research. *See also* Research
  anomalies in, 11, 63–66, 74, 78n47,
    135–139
  assembling, 3–4
  films excluded from, 39n2
  foreign school films in, 4, 11, 14n10,
    160nn1–2, 175–176
  junior high students in, 14n10, 117n17,
    144n13
  listing of films in, 171–176
  middle-class students in, 4, 14n11
  poor/working-class students in, 4
  private schools in, 4, 174–175
  rich/upper-middle-class students in, 4,
    14n11
  suburban school films in, 4, 171–173
  urban school films in, 4, 173–174
Sarafina, 161n10, 175
Satire, 17–19, 39n2
Saved!, 135, 144n12, 175
Say Anything, 86, 172
Scary Movie, 39n2
Scent of a Woman, 132–134, 143n9, 174
Schatz, Thomas, 7
Schlesinger, Arthur M., Jr., 1
Schneider, David, 114
School Ties, 121–124, 127, 128, 134–135, 174
Schools. *See also* Catholic school films;
    Christian school films; Foreign school
    films; Private school films; Suburban
    school films; Urban school films
  fantasies, Hollywood, 56–63, 74
  fantasy of destroying, 108
  funding, 58–59
  grading of public, 54
  inequality and, 140–142
  resources of, 4
Schoolwork. *See* Academics; Curriculum
Science-fiction films, 168

Scream, 39n2
Sex
  in foreign school films, 150–151,
    155–156, 158
  sexuality and, 4
  in suburban school films, 108–111, 113
  virginity and, 108–109
Shakespeare, William, 62
Shary, Timothy, 2, 5, 39n2
She's All That, 17, 86–87, 107, 172
Sister Act 2, 135, 137–139, 174
16 Candles, 17, 171
Slasher films, teen, 39n2
Slater, Philip, 24
Small-town ideal, 115
Smith, Raymond, 114
Social class. *See* Class, social
Social sciences, 3, 13n7
Society
  Durkheim on, 24–25
  heroes and, 158–160
  individualism, 73–74, 102, 106, 120,
    158–160, 162–163
  making sense of, 1–15
  running away from, 157–158
Socioeconomic status, 6, 11, 50, 138
Sociological imagination, 162, 168
Sociology/sociologists
  on adolescence, 34, 37
  on ascription v. achievement, 141
  on culture, 2
  films and, xv–xvi, 1–3, 8, 9, 13n3,
    13nn7–9, 50–51, 162–163
  lens of, xiii
  on middle class, 31
  on poverty, 49
Some Kind of Wonderful, 17, 86, 172
Soundtracks, movie, 44, 45, 51, 94
South Central, 39n2
Spoofs, 17–19, 39n2
Sports. *See* Athletics
Stand and Deliver, xv, 18, 56, 61, 70, 173
Steele, Claude, 58
Straight Out of Brooklyn, 39n2
Students, 4. *See also* Middle class;
    Poor/working-class students; Upper
    classes
  African American, 124–126
  "at risk," 43, 62, 90–91
  complexity of, 47–48
  as heroes, in suburban school films,
    10–11, 82–85, 89, 93, 97, 99–107,
    115, 127, 164, 168
  Jewish, 122–123, 134
  junior high, 14n10, 117n17, 144n13
  peer relations of, 4
Studios, film, 7

Subgenres, high school film, 17–23, 18,
    39n2, 168. *See also* Foreign school
    films; Private school films; Suburban
    school films; Urban school films
Substitute, The, 18, 52, 53, 67–68, 174
Substitute 2, The, 53, 67, 78n50, 174
Suburban school films, 80–118. *See also*
    Middle class; Subgenres, high school
    film
    academics in, 20–21, 23, 47, 81, 82, 83,
        85–91, 97, 106, 115n3, 116n6,
        144n12, 164
    adulthood in, 94, 99, 107–108, 110,
        111–113, 164
    adults as fools in, 97–99, 106
    antagonists, 85, 93–97, 99, 105–107, 164
    Catholic school films and, 136, 137,
        144nn12–13, 165
    conformity in, 85, 90, 91–93, 164
    differences in, 4, 5–6, 10
    drug use in, 106, 108, 109–111, 113
    emphasis on, 10
    football coach in, 95–97, 116n11, 153
    individualism, expressive, in, 20–23, 81,
        85, 127, 148, 168
    middle class in, 23, 82–84, 88, 91–95, 96,
        97–100, 107–108, 110–114, 116n16,
        164
    personal identity in, 10, 81, 85, 88–89,
        91, 100, 105–108, 111–113
    political messages in, 84
    popularity, 87, 102–105, 116n16, 164,
        168
    private school films and, 121, 165
    race in, 100–102
    religious school films and, 136, 165
    in sample, 4, 173–174
    sex in, 108–111, 113
    social class in, 100–102, 111–113, 168
    student heroes in, 10–11, 82–85, 89, 93,
        97, 99–107, 115, 127, 164, 168
    teachers in, 88, 89, 98
    themes, 85
    triumph of youth in, 105–107
    urban school films v., 4, 5–6, 10, 43–44,
        80–81, 85, 86, 90–91, 93, 94, 106,
        110–114, 164
Success, types of, 121, 130, 130n7, 141
Suicide, 103–104, 106, 126–127, 128, 133
Sweet Sixteen, 161n5, 161n11, 176

The Taming of the Shrew (Shakespeare), 62
Teachers
    as antagonists, 85, 93–97, 99, 105–107,
        164
    cowboy, 9, 43, 66–69, 74, 78n50

    films focusing on, 5, 6
    impact of, 60
    incompetent, 52–54, 61
    negative image of, 5
    role of, 4
    in suburban school films, 88, 89, 98
    as "teacher-hero," 5–6, 9, 10–11, 15n26,
        19, 23, 43–47, 52, 54–56, 60–61, 62,
        63–74, 78n50, 93, 94, 127, 138–139
    in urban school films, 9, 19, 23, 43–47,
        52, 54–56, 60–61, 62, 63–74, 78n50,
        93, 94, 125, 126, 127, 158, 164, 168
    violence used by, 69
Teachers, 18, 51, 52, 53, 71, 72, 173
Teaching Mrs. Tingle, 94–95, 105, 108, 114,
    172
Teenagers. *See also* Adolescence/adolescents
    American culture and, 33–37
    marketing aimed at, 36
10 Things I Hate About You, 17, 86, 87, 172
Tension, unresolved, 149–152, 160n4, 161n5
Thirteen, 160n4
Thomas, W. I., 30
Thoreau, Henry David, 27–28, 80
To Play or to Die, 155–156, 161n9, 175
To Sir, With Love, xv, 175
Tocqueville, Alexis de, 28–29, 33–34, 40n18,
    114
Torment, 153–154, 157, 161n11, 175
The Trouble with Angels, 135, 174
Truths, revealing of, 1–2
Tudor, Andrew, 8
Tuff Turf, 108, 171
Turner, Frederick Jackson, 30

United States. *See also* Culture, American;
        Domestic Films (American)
    dominant ideology in, 7
    inequality in, 138–142
Up the Down Staircase, xv, 18, 53, 71, 173
Upper classes, 9–10. See also Class, social;
        Middle class; Wealthy
    in film samples, 4, 14n11
    individualism and, 32–33
    as morally bankrupt, 119, 120, 128–130
    as outside mainstream, 8
    in private school films, 119–121
    upper-middle class in, 20, 39n4
Urban school films, 9, 10. *See also* Subgenres,
        high school film
    academics in, 10, 23, 43, 47, 63–64, 68,
        74, 85, 86, 106, 148, 164, 165
    African Americans in, 39n2, 46
    anomalies in, 63–66, 74, 78n47
    Catholic school films and, 138–139, 165
    conclusions on, 164

differences in, 4, 5–6, 10
endings, 164
individualism, expressive in, 43
individualism, utilitarian in, 19, 23, 37,
    43, 47, 49–51, 59–63, 69, 72–74, 81,
    85, 148, 168
jungle metaphor in, 51–52, 76n23
lower classes in, 46, 48, 57, 63–65, 74
political messages of, 69–72
poverty and, 43–79, 121, 127, 168
private school films and, 121, 124, 125,
    126, 127, 143n8, 165
race in, 46–47
in sample, 4, 173–174
satirizing of, 19, 39n2
subgenre of, 18, 39n2
suburban school films v., 4, 5–6, 10,
    43–44, 80–81, 85, 86, 90–91, 93, 94,
    106, 110–114, 164
teacher as cowboy in, 9, 43, 66–69, 74,
    78n50
teacher-heroes/middle-class heroes in,
    9–10, 19, 23, 43–47, 49, 52, 54–74,
    78n50, 93, 94, 125, 126, 127, 158,
    164, 168
teachers/administrators as incompetent
    in, 52–54, 61
Urban teen genre, 39n2
Urbanization, 34

Varsity Blues, 17, 95–97, 105, 114, 116n11,
    172
Violence, 52, 70
    as pedagogy, 66–67, 78n50
    prevalence of, 4
    teacher/principal use of, 69
Virginity, losing, 108–109

War movies, 168
Wealth
    in America, 139–142
    middle class and, 11
Wealthy. See also Upper classes
    as antagonists, 119, 120, 128–130, 165
    as fools, 128–130
Weber, Max, 13n7, 27
Weird Science, 17
Well roundedness, 130–131, 143n8
Western genre, 1–2, 33
Westerns, 168
Whites
    on African Americans, 50
    archetypes representing, 46
    privileging of, 14n19
The Wild One, 47
Wild Reeds, 150–151, 175
Wilson, William Julius, 49–50
Wolfe, Alan, 50
Work ethic, 7, 19, 43, 167
Working class. See Class, social; Lower
    classes/working class; Poor/working-
    class students
World War II, 36, 159
Wright, Will, 12, 13n8, 15n30, 79n55,
    169n4

The Year My Voice Broke, 161n5, 161n11, 175
Youth
    film genre, 5
    triumph of, 105–107

Zanuck, Darryl F., 44
Zebrahead, 78n47, 173
Zero de Conduite, 161n10, 175
Zipes, Jack, 8–9, 167